中文社会科学引文索引（CSSCI）收录集刊

# 清华西方哲学研究

第七卷 第二期（二零二一年冬季卷）

# Tsinghua Studies in Western Philosophy

Vol.7, No.2 (Winter 2021)

中国社会科学出版社

**图书在版编目(CIP)数据**

清华西方哲学研究．第七卷．第二期：2021 年．冬季卷／
蒋运鹏主编．—北京：中国社会科学出版社，2022.3
ISBN 978－7－5203－9562－5

Ⅰ．①清…　Ⅱ．①蒋…　Ⅲ．①西方哲学—文集
Ⅳ．①B5－53

中国版本图书馆 CIP 数据核字（2022）第 007194 号

出 版 人　赵剑英
责任编辑　刘亚楠
责任校对　张爱华
责任印制　张雪娇

出　　版　中国社会科学出版社
社　　址　北京鼓楼西大街甲 158 号
邮　　编　100720
网　　址　http://www.csspw.cn
发 行 部　010－84083685
门 市 部　010－84029450
经　　销　新华书店及其他书店

印　　刷　北京君升印刷有限公司
装　　订　廊坊市广阳区广增装订厂
版　　次　2022 年 3 月第 1 版
印　　次　2022 年 3 月第 1 次印刷

开　　本　710×1000　1/16
印　　张　16
插　　页　2
字　　数　244 千字
定　　价　98.00 元

## Editorial Board (编辑委员会)

FANG Xianghong（方向红） *Sun Yat-sen University, China*

FU Youde（傅有德） *Shandong University, China*

FU Yongjun（傅永军） *Shandong University, China*

GUO Dawei（郭大为） *Party School of the Central Committee of C. P. C, China*

HAN Lixin（韩立新） *Tsinghua University, China*

HAN Shuifa（韩水法） *Peking University, China*

HAN Donghui（韩东晖） *China Executive Leadership Academy, Yanan, China*

HUANG Yusheng（黄裕生） *Tsinghua University, China*

JIANG Yi（江怡） *Beijing Normal University, China*

LI Daqiang（李大强） *Jilin University, China*

LI He（李河） *Chinese Academy of Social Sciences, China*

LI Meng（李猛） *Peking University, China*

LI Wentang（李文堂） *Party School of the Central Committee of C. P. C, China*

LIU Fenrong（刘奋荣） *Tsinghua University, China*

LIU Zhe（刘哲） *Peking University, China*

MA Yinmao（马寅卯） *Chinese Academy of Social Sciences, China*

MO Weimin（莫伟民） *Fudan University, China*

NIE Minli（聂敏里） *Renmin University of China, China*

PENG Gang（彭刚） *Tsinghua University, China*

SHANG Jie（尚杰） *Chinese Academy of Social Sciences, China*

SHANG Xinjian（尚新建） *Peking University, China*

SONG Jijie（宋继杰） *Tsinghua University, China*

SUN Xiangchen（孙向晨） *Fudan University, China*

TANG Hao（唐浩） *Tsinghua University, China*

TIAN Wei（田薇） *Tsinghua University, China*

WANG Heng（王恒） *Nanjing University, China*

WANG Qi（王齐） *Chinese Academy of Social Sciences, China*

WU Guosheng（吴国盛） *Tsinghua University, China*

WU Tianyue（吴天岳） *Peking University, China*

XIA Ying（夏莹） *Tsinghua University, China*

XIE Wenyu（谢文郁） *Shandong University, China*

XU Xiangdong（徐向东） *Zhejiang University, China*

**【联系方式/Contact Information】**

清华大学哲学系《清华西方哲学研究》编辑部
联系人：蒋运鹏（主编）
地址：北京市海淀区清华园1号清华大学蒙民伟人文楼208室，邮编100084
E-mail：tsinghuawp@ sina. com

## TSWP Editorial Office

Asher Jiang　Editor-in-Chief
Tsinghua Studies in Western Philosophy
Department of Philosophy
Tsinghua University
Room 208, Meng Minwei Building, Qinghuayuan Nr. 1
Haidian District, Beijing, P. R. China, 100084
Email：tsinghuawp@ sina. com

# 目　　录

## 新书研讨专栏

# Contents

## Theoritical Philosophy



## Practical Philosophy

**New Monography Symposium**

# 理论哲学
# Theoritical Philosophy

# 亚里士多德哲学的科学秩序*

贺博特·博德（Heribert Boeder）**
戴晖（DAI Hui）/译（trans.）
黄水石（HUANG Shuishi）/
校对和注释（Proofreading & Commentary）***

**摘要：** 历史地看，哲学思想的样态影响了“亚里士多德全集”的编纂方式。将诗学附属于修辞学，而修辞学则紧随逻辑学，甚至被视作逻辑学的部分，这实际上接受了希腊晚期的哲学划分。这种划分经由拜占庭的中介重现于阿拉伯的亚里士多德翻译和注疏传统。目前学界通用的贝克版全集则是19世纪古典学的产物，接受了近代哲学的分类方式。相对于贝克版已成标准的习惯性理解，博德从根本上重构了亚里士多德哲学整体的秩序。他不仅将修辞学与诗学作为创制的科学放在实践的科学和理论的科学之前，而且特别重视创制的科学。他采用的从政治学到伦理学的顺序与通常做法完全相反（早年曾接受过从伦理学到政治学的顺序）。要明白博德对亚里士多德哲学科学顺序所做的调整，必须由理性关系建筑学所洞见到的亚里士多德哲学使命本身来考察他哲学思想的整体。博德的判断是亚里士多德哲学本质上只与逻各斯打交道，而不是研究经验或者现象。科学整体从一开始就是关于逻各斯的。由此科学顺序首先是作为证明科学的逻辑

* 2019年国家社科基金西部项目专项经费资助（批准号19XZX018）。
** 贺伯特·博德（1928—2013），德国当代哲学家。
*** 戴晖，陕西师范大学哲学系教授；黄水石，中央美术学院人文学院讲师。

学（即“工具论”），但鉴于人的“自然”的区分，落实到事的科学划分为创制的、实践的和理论的。创制的科学就是创制的诗艺学。在先的修辞学服务于具有证明力量的说服，但不再停留为技艺层面的东西，而是已经从技艺提升到科学；进而尽管具有逻辑证明的外观，重心却转移到逻各斯的制作了。

**关键词**：理性关系建筑学；亚里士多德；荷马；逻各斯；哲学；智慧

# The Scientific Order of Aristotle's Philosophy

**Abstract**: Historically the configurations of philosophy have shaped the different compilations of *Corpus Aristotelicum*. To subordinate *Poetics* to *Rhetoric*, which is following immediately the logic science and even treated as its essential part, this received in fact the conception of philosophy during the Hellenistic period, which recurred through the Byzantium influence in the Arabic tradition of translations and commentaries concerning Aristotle. The Bekker edition in academic use was an outcome of the nineteenth century classical philology especially prosperous in Germany and demonstrated the philosophical understanding of the modern age until Hegel. Comparing with the standard understanding according to Bekker edition, Boeder has essentially reconstructed the order of the totality of Aristotle's philosophy. He not only puts *Rhetoric* and *Poetics*, as poetic sciences, before the practical and theoretical sciences, but particularly highlights the significance of the poetic sciences within the whole *cosmos* of sciences. The scientific order from *Politics* to *Ethics* is precisely contrary to the common opinion he himself once employed, i. e. the order should be from *Ethics* to *Politics*. To appreciate such a rebuilding of the order of Aristotelian sciences, it is necessary to investigate the totality of his philosophy in light of the philosophical mission undertaken by Aristotle himself, with which the logotectonic thinking is specifically concerned. Now that Boeder's decisive insight is that Aristotle's philosophy deals in essence with *logos*, and by no means with the study of experiences, the scientific totality focuses exclusively on the *logos* from beginning to end. Thus the science in the first place is the *Logic* in the sense of science of proof, while in terms of the distinction of man's *physis*, it then realizes its division according to the topic (Sache) in the sciences distinguished as the poetical, the practical and the theoretical. The poetical science in its true sense is the productive *Poetics*, which itself is essentially accompanied in advance by *Rhetoric*. Although Rhetoric serves especially to persuade with demonstrative force, it cannot be understood only through the perspective of *techne*, because it is entirely raised up to be poetic science, which owns still the appearance of proof, but whose concern is actually transferred from persuasion to the production of *logos* as a composed unity that would be treated as the main subject in the *Poetics*.

**Key words**: Logotectonic, Aristotle, Homer, logos, Philosophia, Sophia.

## 一　亚里士多德逻各斯科学的和谐秩序

我们研讨课的题目叫“亚里士多德与荷马”。为什么不是“荷马与亚里士多德”？按照时间叙述的顺序人们会期待后者。不仅如此，有必要提及克塞诺芬尼（Xenophanes）关于荷马所说的话：“我们所有人都向荷马学习过。”① 这句话对亚里士多德也有效。荷马与亚里士多德，两人并不按照时间叙述的顺序进入我们的视线。

我首先想起的是，他们两人就“坐”在我从前的大学，也就是弗莱堡大学的古老大门前。“亚里士多德与荷马”，为什么是这两位？对此，铭刻在雕像基座上的引文有所指示。首先荷马的引文是：“**αἰὲν ἀριστεύειν καὶ ὑπείροχον ἔμμεναι ἄλλων**。”翻译过来是说：“永远要成为最好的并且超越其他。”这句话引自《伊利亚特》第 6 卷第 208 行。这让人想起希腊从政者的“此在”的好斗性格；但凡棋逢对手，他们理应

① “ἐξ ἀρχῆς καθ’Ὅμηρον ἐπεὶ μεμαθήκασι πάντες...”（*Xenophanes*, 1951, B. 10）.

证明自己是优胜的；这里的每一个人都应该证明他的ἀρετή（才能的卓越）。根据构词法，ἀρετή来自ἀρείων / ἄρειον，意即“更好”。

至于亚里士多德，那里引述的是他《形而上学》开篇的话：“πάντες ἄνθρωποι τοῦ εἰδέναι ὀρέγονται φύσει（求知是所有人的本性）。”① 一个大胆的断言。可是他视线里的“人”与今天的“人”不是同一个本质类型。今天的“人”把 animal rationale（有理性的生灵）这个古老的规定销蚀殆尽了。

在今天，这两个引文不如说似乎是有问题的，也就是说是不值得相信的，因为它们称谓的“人”是地地道道的历史鉴定。我可以肯定，无论是荷马还是亚里士多德，乃至这些“言辞”（Worte），人们今天都不会再将其放到大学的入口处。特别是也刻在这所大学的古老建筑上的另一些言辞：“真理将使你们自由”。这句话引自《约翰福音》（8，32）。在建造这些建筑的时代，也就是在现代（Moderne），这句话就已经从狄尔泰的解释学，而不是根据基督的启示性的知来获取自己的意思。“真理将使你们自由。”一句伟大的话，难得听见。虽然不像高高悬挂的题词“永恒的德意志文化”那样难以听见。② 这句话的位置也在“现代”（Moderne），但却是这么一个“现代”，与前述两个引文不同，它属于与这二者的决裂；现代事实上并不归属于思想的“历史”（Geschichte）。人们也为今天的人把字母上的镀金层刮掉了。是的，这些话在我们的世界无一不是静默无声的。对于这个世界，即便不是令人反感的“当下”，它们也终究已成“往事”。——荷马的“言辞”并没有成为过去；亚里士多德的“言辞”以另一种方式也没有成为过去。③ 它们至多遭受毁灭；在德国本土，人们尤其操心怎么彻底地毁掉它们。但严格说来，这做得并不彻底。

---

① *Arist. Metaph.* 980a21. 中译引自亚里士多德（1993）。

② 译按：第二次世界大战结束之后，人们对这句纳粹时代的题词持激进的否定态度。因为争议巨大，题词仅仅是作为纪念碑才被保留下来。但正如下文所言，人们特意把题词的镀金层刮掉了。即便如此，争议至今未息。

③ 译按：这里荷马与亚里士多德“方式”的不同涉及博德关于哲学与智慧相区分的洞见。一言以蔽之，荷马的“言辞”作为智慧，而亚里士多德的“言辞”则是哲学，二者都并不在时间历史的意义上消逝，因而并不成其为过去。根据上下文语境和通常的理解，这里 Worte 当然可以译为“文字”，但为了避免与亚现代例如德里达等人混淆，我们仍然将之译为“言辞”。在此，博德所意指的智慧的“言辞”乃至哲学的“言辞”与当前流行的“语言”乃至“言语”具有根本区别。

“亚里士多德与荷马”。请诸位回想一下早期近代。那时伦勃朗（Rembrandt van Rijn，1606－1669）有一幅画，受西西里伯爵之托而创作，如今收藏于大都会博物馆。亚里士多德站立在荷马的半身塑像前，沉思地凝视着他；甚至将手放到荷马的头上。[①] 在古人的评价里，曾是如此。可是亚里士多德在伦勃朗的时代已经受到指责。拉斐尔（Raffaello Santi，1483－1520）的“雅典学派”[②] 不再闪耀光辉。近代人不仅不再能够凭借亚里士多德来造就开端，亚里士多德对于他们甚至成了敌人，他们必须从敌人那里解放出来。但这是怎样意义上的敌人呢？作为一种占据统治地位的学派现象，在大学课堂上对亚里士多德学派进行冲击，反对经院哲学，这在当时是必要的，为的是解放“现代人”，使近代人获得自身，获得近代人的知。这项任务十分艰巨，没有一所大学完成了它。直到康德时期，大学一直为这样一种思想方式所占据。有理由称之为“经院哲学”的思想。无论是新教的还是天主教的大学，一概如此。将思想向新时代的知推进的人们并不在大学里，他们拒绝了大学的职位。必须抛弃亚里士多德，这些新知的先驱者们，布鲁诺、培根、伽利略，他们统统猛烈地反对亚里士多德。近代哲学的真正开端也是如此。近代哲学的真正开端是“新科学”，也就是在笛卡尔和霍布斯意义上的作为方法的科学。

他们对亚里士多德的攻击是如此之不留余地，以致从 17 世纪中叶直到 19 世纪初，都没有出版过“亚里士多德全集”。仅有不属于亚里士多德哲学核心的单本著作问世，也就是《伦理学》和《诗学》；至于《物理学》，甚至“第一哲学”，即所谓的《形而上学》，也就是亚里士多德称之为 Theologik 的神学科学，则一无所有。注意：按照亚里士多德的称谓，不是神学（Theologie），而是神学科学（Theologik）。神学科学的最后一个独立版本于 1577 年出版，而下一个则出版于 1823 年。在亚里士多德的知的

① 伦勃朗，《亚里士多德凝视荷马半身像》，布面油画，143.5 X 136.5 cm，1653 年，纽约大都会艺术博物馆藏。

② 译按：《雅典学派》，拉斐尔的代表作，装饰在梵蒂冈教宗居室的大型壁画。拉斐尔将柏拉图和亚里士多德、将基督教和异教统统融合到一起，创造出和谐的场面。这里博德的引述，并非意指拉斐尔的绘画，而是指绘画主题所涉及的希腊哲学，尤其是雅典时期的柏拉图和亚里士多德的哲学。

中断背后是什么？

我们再一次追随这种历史学的考察。具有标志性的是，18 世纪末人们才开始做新的亚里士多德版本，这个版本却在市场上失败了。它半途搁置了下来，也就是说没有人感兴趣。转折点在哪里呢？在出版方面，1830 年我们才看到这个转折点。对此，普鲁士科学院是有功绩的。那是在怎样的关联中呢？伴随着怎样的转折？转折在于对亚里士多德的地地道道的历史学兴趣。但是黑格尔为这次转折从哲学上做了重要准备，并且是他才做了这样的准备。在前人当中，莱布尼兹算是唯一推崇亚里士多德的一位，可是他 1686 年的著作 *Discours de Métaphysique*（《形而上学谈话》）［当时］并没有发表。只是到了 19 世纪，亚里士多德才找到反响，而这也并非因为莱布尼兹的哲学。

哲学是怎么又关心起亚里士多德的？我们这里提一下康德的评价和推崇。他说：在两千年之后，亚里士多德的逻辑一定仍然总是作为完满的学科而发挥作用。只不过［对他的逻辑的］变更着的解释性补充一向就有。康德视亚里士多德的逻辑为完满的。① 他自己的后继者才开始反对这个观点，他们给予逻辑科学以新的转折。特别是黑格尔，他促进了这个转折。

黑格尔很早就已经和亚里士多德打交道，并且持之以恒。黑格尔知道自己在说什么。黑格尔在他的《哲学史讲演录》中说道："亚里士多德是曾经出现过的最广博且最深刻的科学天才之一。一个在任何时代都无与伦比的名字。"② 如前所述，黑格尔确切地知道自己所说的个中滋味。他自己就转化了亚里士多德的逻辑。他的意图在于改变第一哲学，亦即改变形而上学。他说：这在本质上是思辨哲学的整全性（Totaliät）。他再度树立了第一哲学作为如此之第一哲学的整全性，具体说来就在他的科学体系之中。黑格尔的思想，伴随着他的思辨科学却相当快地告终了——不是像人们以为的那样，因为他的"知"（Wissen）变得"不值得相信"了，而是因为他的"知"完成了它的使命，正是因此开放了向现代的征程。当时这是第一哲学理念的遗产在现代条件下的破晓（Aufbruch）——并非启程走

① 可参见康德（2010：19 A18）。

② 可参见黑格尔（1999：269）。

向弗雷格的科学哲学，并非通向马克思的“非—哲学”（Nicht-Philosophie），而是迈入解释学，成为历史理解的理论，就像它甚至也促成了前面所提及的“亚里士多德全集”的新版本。“历史理解”，这却在其科学形制上没有给亚里士多德特殊的价值。在狄尔泰的哲学史考察进程中，他将亚里士多德视作众多其他人中的一个，并没有加以突出的表彰。

与历史解释学相分离，与讲究博学的研究分开，以哲学方式与亚里士多德打交道的第一人是海德格尔。从早年开始，一直持续不断，这一定有其特殊原因。亚里士多德是他最优秀的对手，这是因为他的对手是整个形而上学传统，他相信在这儿能够刨根问底，以“什么是形而上学?”的追问使之真相大白。他的答案是：形而上学是本体—神学。对于海德格尔来说，整个形而上学显现在这种两面性中。因为持这种观点，他分明对亚里士多德置若罔闻；显然本体论对于亚里士多德根本没有用，唯一重要的是作为第一科学的“神学科学”。

由此至少已经表明了整个的张力。我们是在海德格尔之后，并且在与海德格尔相分离的张力中，在哲学的“当下”中与亚里士多德和荷马相遇。这同时意味着我们并非出于历史叙述的兴趣而与亚里士多德和荷马相遇；是出于我们当下自身所提出的任务而与之相遇。

但是我们要再次简短回顾亚里士多德哲学的命运，更确切地说是回顾亚里士多德哲学对诗学的探讨。现在我们只谈他的《诗学》。《诗学》首先出现在阿杜斯（Aldus）1536 年版《亚里士多德著作全集》的附录之中。之后，[《诗学》的出版] 在 18 世纪中叶得到了全新的激励。对《诗学》的兴趣以前所未有的方式被激活了。这也包括感官方面的兴趣。因此 18 世纪末出版了亚里士多德《诗学》的豪华精装本。该豪华精装本在英国出版并非偶然之事，因为英国人自为地具有这样一种表示尊敬的方式，不仅限于一般而言的编辑文字，而且在于赋予文字美的外观。这就是 1794 年的牛津版。

还要补充对《诗学》翻译的回顾。这些细节绝非无关紧要，它们表明具有决定性的兴趣及其方向。第一个是 1549 年的意大利语译本，第二个是 1626 年西班牙语译本，接着是法语译本于 1671 年出版。与贺拉斯的

《诗艺》和布瓦洛的《诗的艺术》一道，这个法语译本在 17 世纪的精神史中具有十分重要的意义。1692 年，达西尔（Dacier，1651 - 1722）① 出版了权威的法译本。达西尔的译本也为 1705 年的英译本奠定了基础。但在此之前，英国于 1674 已有过一个译本。在此，我们必须问：德语译本在哪里？只是在其他这些民族都关心过《诗学》之后，1753 年才出版了第一个德译本。这与德国文学古典时期的开始阶段同步。那时亚里士多德及其《诗学》如此令人感兴趣，以至人们不仅想用法语来阅读他［当时流行这样］，而且尝试自己用德语翻译。对《诗学》效应的一瞥就这么多。

而荷马呢？荷马的情形如何？可以说，在西方，荷马一直保持为当下的并且受到尊敬；虽然高低不一，但却是一贯的；较大的裂缝出现在“居中时代”②。希腊人自己那里情况如何？我们还要再看看荷马在现代获得的评价。就像以前对他的无数庆祝和加冕一样，荷马保住了“诗人之王”的头衔。这里要提起艾兹拉·庞德（Ezra Pound，1885 - 1972），提到他始终值得阅读的《阅读 ABC》。直到“一切皆无所谓”的年代，荷马都保住了他的地位。而这个“一切皆无所谓”的年代就是我们的年代，也就是“后现代”（Postmoderne），或者像我说的“亚现代”（Submoderne）。只要学习古典语文学，就面临这种无所谓，或者染上它：“一切皆无所谓。”它是所有尊敬的真正死亡，对作为如此之成就的完满的推崇和评价死了。

在希腊人那里从来就不可能对荷马无所谓。为什么不能呢？因为他是规范性的σοφός（有智慧的人），这意味着他精通希腊人的所有教养。在希腊人的教育中，荷马自始至终都起着主导作用，也就是直到我们在亚里士多德这里所认出的终点，荷马始终居于主导地位。［荷马始终在希腊人当

---

① 达西尔（André Dacier）1651 年 4 月 6 日生于法国塔恩省卡斯特尔镇新教律师家庭。1722 年 9 月 18 日于巴黎逝世。法国语文学家和王室图书馆管理员。翻译过贺拉斯、柏拉图、亚里士多德和普鲁塔克等古典思想家与作家的作品。

② 译按：“居中时代”是博德对中世纪的称呼。按照理性关系建筑学，西方哲学的历史是在时代精神的原则危机中自我更新的历史，每一个时代皆具备自身的全新的原则，因此哲学历史不是同一个主题不断变化抑或进步的历史，而是由三个原则上不同的历史时代构成的多元而稳健的历史。通常所称的古希腊罗马时代、中世纪和文艺复兴所开启的近代，在理性关系建筑学中被称作第一时代、第二时代和第三时代，其中第二时代也叫“居中时代”。

中占据主导地位］这也由于因他而起的争执；争论不是因为他作为诗人。请诸位想一想：荷马在5世纪才作为“诗人”（ποιητής）受到尊敬，也就是到了品达（Pindar，前522/518－前442/438）的年代。在此之前，人们并没有把荷马称作“诗人”，而是视之为σοφός，这已然不同寻常。正因如此，哲学家有可能望其项背，成为荷马的对手，当然不是哲人作为诗人的对手，显然在诗人份上他没有什么可被撼动。但在荷马的知上，在他的教诲上，在所有年轻的希腊人都随之而成长的教说上，哲学家要对他有所撼动。在哲学内部，特别是克塞诺芬尼作为第一个荷马的批评者而亮相；接下来再一次且更为有效的［批评者］是柏拉图。柏拉图在荷马这位“老师”身上，而不是在“诗人”身上认识到一种危险。哪一方面的危险呢？即对于青少年的道德教化。柏拉图的攻击在亚里士多德那里完全平息下来。这种平息表现在，对于涉及荷马的事情，亚里士多德有理由心平气和。他如何能够获得这样一种平和？唯一的途径是在他的科学架构里承认和赞同荷马。

亚里士多德详细地研习荷马。他甚至是一位荷马爱好者，具体说来，就像古代留下的记载所说，他把荷马放在自己的枕头下面。在一部关于诗人的著作里，他证明了对这位诗人的爱，可惜这部著作已经遗失，就是他的*Περὶ Ποιητῶν*（《论诗人》）。后来在《诗学》里，即在关于诗艺（创制）的科学中，他表明自己对荷马的尊敬。在那儿他谈到荷马，没有任何人像荷马一样懂得诗的关键是什么。在其他特点之外，为此作证的尤其是，荷马从来不谈论自己，而是完全投身于他的使命，眼中只有这项使命，他的使命！究竟什么样的使命呢？亚里士多德视之为μίμησις（摹仿），如真呈现，这是他研习荷马的基本词。我们还必须追问什么是呈现。

在《诗学》之外，亚里士多德在其他著述中用古典的方式向荷马致敬，也就是用引证荷马的方式致敬荷马。他在一个极为显耀的位置上引用荷马，即在第一科学，也就是在神学科学的结束之处。要懂得这个位置，我们现在必须把目光投向亚里士多德的科学的总体结构，看科学的和谐整体秩序（κόσμος）。这不仅仅是秩序，而且是美的建造活动。

亚里士多德的知的和谐秩序，同时启示知的完整性，其梗概展示如下：

亚里士多德著作的和谐秩序是诸科学的和谐秩序。亚里士多德促进了基于经验的诸多科学，这方面无人可与他相比。在希腊语中什么叫经验？ἱστορία（历史叙述），也就是来源于观察的知。亚里士多德作为观察者是无与伦比的，甚至在不是由λόγος（逻各斯）标识的生命领域，也就是动物领域，也是如此。基于对动物所做的观察，他写就了 *Περὶ Ζώων Ἱστορίας*（《论动物》）。[①] 这是一部庞大的著作。他的学生泰奥弗拉斯托斯通过对其他生命，也就是对植物的观察使之得到补充。一直到岩石矿物为止，他对自然整体中可观察的整个界域都考察了个遍，对此所作的研究也到了尽头。[②]

回到亚里士多德的科学秩序。它不仅具有观察探究的特征，而且它是对伴随理性（μετὰ λόγου），亦即对伴随着 *ratio* 而出现的事物的观察。我已经用康德的引文说过，亚里士多德被视为逻辑的创立人。在亚里士多德的意义上，逻辑当然是一门技术，不是科学。人们往往没有注意到，是随着斯多葛学派的逻辑，情况才有所改变。也就是在第一个时代结束之后，在居中时代的开启阶段，情况才有所改变。这时逻辑成为科学。为什么？现在不予解释。

总之，逻辑是一门技术。亚里士多德从λογίζεσθαι（逻各斯的作为/推论）来理解它。这个λόγος到底是什么？我们要渐渐地加以澄清。λογίζεσθαι是动词，表明一种活动，也就是让逻各斯有所作为的活动。这种逻各斯的最高形式是συλλογισμός（三段论法），我们称之为推理（Schluss）。亚里士多德是第一位发展了推理过程和方法的人，推理的技术服务于科学，作为科学的准备，这也是从前把学习逻辑作为科学的入门原因。在《浮士德》里还能听到这个道理。然而逻各斯的独到之处在哪儿？就此我们已经更接近它了。亚里士多德说：δηλοῦν，意思是澄清，使之变

① 译按：这里单就意思没问题，可能有口误或临时做了转换性表述，严格说来，根据亚里士多德著作（贝克版全集）应该是指 *Περὶ τὰ ζῷα Ἱστορίων*（《动物志》）。

② 译按：泰奥弗拉斯托斯（Theophrastus，前 372 – 前 287 年），亚里士多德的学生。这里指他的《植物志》《矿物学》以及关于地水火风的考察与研究。这些著作基本都佚失了。

得清楚。谈论具有规定性的开端和结束，于此获得清晰性。这样的清晰性是在推理意义上的逻各斯的第一个收获。这是指弄清楚什么为知奠基，在知的基础上得出的结论是什么。但这样的整体、这样的整个技术服务于亚里士多德称为ἀπόδειξις（证明）的东西，希罗多德在他之前就已经如此称谓，也就是指清楚地呈现和展示（aufzeigen），展示使之得以看见（herzeigen）。

展示使之得以看见，不仅以三段论推理（συλλόγιστικ）的方式呈现诸逻辑形式，而且与事情本身打交道，亦即与现成在此者（Vorliegenden）打交道，就像亚里士多德称之为“ὑποκείμενον”那样。“ὑποκείμενον”，是指来到眼睛底下的东西，在观察者面前，现成在此的东西。后来翻译为substantia（实质，实体）。但是我们不愿受之误导，而是宁可守在希腊语这儿。[①] 那么，亚里士多德在何处把“逻辑之物”纳入具体之中？这个具体意味着，“逻辑之物”作为现成在此者，用它来有所作为。用现成在此者做某事。这个“做”是怎样一种方式？亚里士多德将它与科学联系起来，因而这是某种为了自己本身而做的活动。在这里亚里士多德做出区分。这是在此要考虑的第一门科学。因为这门科学有自己的“现成在此者”，并且不仅是像人们所说的“形式上的现成在此者”，而是拥有某种“质料之物”。就如所有科学实际上都是“逻各斯的科学”，是“*ratio* 的科学”一样，与这个“现成在此者”相应的第一门科学是“逻各斯的科学”。而 *ratio*，和希腊语的意思一样，指的是“关系”（Verhältnis）。科学考察的是关系，绝不是单纯地考察某些事物，而是考察事物之间的关系。这是科学在最宽泛的意义上所涉及的东西。

如此之关系首先在进行仔细探讨的能力上可以看到，一场交谈（Gespräch），并且带有明确的目的。如果人们今天频繁地谈论对话（Dia-

---

① 译按：这里ὑποκείμενον，意即“躺在底下的东西”或者“在下的支撑者”，但这是就其自身所是而现身于逻各斯的“在下的支撑者”，即作为逻各斯的事情本身而在逻各斯的作为中得以澄清显明。作为逻各斯的科学，亚里士多德的哲学只与这样的当下现前者打交道。只是在逻各斯的作为中成为其事情，这“在下的支撑者”才成为来到眼前、进入观察之中的“现成在此者”（das Vorliegende）。这个词几乎无法翻译，这里仅就上下文略作说明。

log)，那么这种对话明显地成为废话。这根本不是对话的艺术，不是辩证法。辩证法是带着目标进行的相互交谈，恰好不是对话，不是交换意见。这种意见交换也污染了我们的大学体制，特别是在哲学系里。具体说来就是这儿并没有“交谈”。交谈要借助技艺导向事先确定的目标。毋宁说是交换意见，因为这显得“民主”。辩证法与之截然不同。辩证法，亦即创造一场有导引的交谈的艺术，它的对照面是修辞学。正如亚里士多德所说，辩证法和修辞学以对照的方式相互归属。修辞学的艺术究竟与什么打交道呢？与辩护和控告。它与法庭相关，却不与法本身相关，也就是说，什么是正义，这一定已经是知道的了，它关系到使人信服或者否定在各自案件中什么是公正的，这是指在法庭辩论中有待判决的案件。在首要的意义上，修辞学与文辞优美无关，而是与导致某一决定的论证相关。这是逻各斯作为如此之逻各斯的第一个形式，辩证法和修辞学这两个方面，后者是说服的艺术。这里诉讼活动是第一，鉴于什么应该是公正的，在意见辩论中使人信服。

逻各斯的第二个领域同样是艺术，但这种艺术不由外在于艺术的目标所推动。无论是通过论辩的方式还是用修辞的方式令人信服，外在于艺术的目标旨在引导做出判断。它是一种言谈（Reden），为了自身而呈现出来，这是诗学的对象。诗学的主题是什么？这不是像在法庭上那样对有争议的事情展开辩论，而是在史诗和戏剧（悲剧和喜剧）中呈现有争议的东西。因此，对于亚里士多德的诗学来说，人们通常所习见并且不自问为什么这样来领会的东西，就已经被取消了。——请读一读现代诗学，我会说施塔格尔（Staiger）① 以解释学为基础的诗学。那里绝没有明显地限制在史诗和戏剧，而是首先谈论人们称作抒情诗的东西。对于亚里士多德的诗学，抒情诗不在考察范围之内。为什么不呢？抒情诗里对争执的当下不置一词，而是特别为已经决出胜负的斗争献上赞歌。请诸位想想品达——已经了结的斗争，已经决定了的争辩。κέκριται是完成时，是胜负已定。参赛

① 施塔格尔（Emil Staiger，1908－1987）是瑞士苏黎世大学德国语言文学教授。其著名的论著有《时间作为诗人的想象力》（*Grundbegriffe der Poetik*，1946），《阐释艺术》（*Die Kunst der Interpretation*，1955）以及三卷本对歌德的研究（1952—1959 年）。

者的奔跑胜负已定，摔跤比赛胜负已定，诸如此类各位在品达的赞歌里找得到，更不用说其他抒情诗，例如阿尔基库罗斯①和萨福②。

上述亚里士多德视为主题的诗艺，涉及史诗和戏剧。两者呈现“曾经之所是”（das Gewesene），它是值得思考的，就像在荷马那里，“曾经之所是”就在缪斯的记忆之中。而至于《伊利亚特》，“曾经之所是”是阿基琉斯的怨恨（Grimm）。顺便要说明的是，这并非愤怒（Zorn）。因为愤怒会烟消云散，怨恨却持久。这种怨恨的独特之处是它导致毁灭（Verderben）。这对于史诗在悲剧中的延续是重要的。毁灭成了主题。荷马一开始就这样说。《伊利亚特》开头的诗行这样说道：“ἐξ οὗ δὴ τὰ πρῶτα διαστήτην ἐρίσαντε.”“他们最初在争吵中陷入分裂。”在阿伽门农和阿基琉斯的争执中陷入分裂。也因此，《伊利亚特》开始于阿基琉斯的怨恨。

在《奥德赛》中不一样。它是怎么开始的？

[学生：ἄνδρα μοι ἔννεπε, Μοῦσα, πολύτροπον, ὅς μάλα πολλὰ / πλάχθη……告诉我，缪斯，精明睿智的男子，他浪迹天涯……

老师：您知道，这非常好。您做得很好。]

也就是这位四处流浪的人，他精通人的心思，知道什么样的情思引导着人。而这里继续唱道：伙伴们被从他身边夺走了，他们因为自己的过错而陷入毁灭。这里《奥德赛》又树立了人之为人的对照：首先是“这一个人”，他以其谨慎而获救（σωζόμενος），从毁灭中拯救了自己，而其余所有人沉沦于毁灭之中；他们由于狂妄鲁莽的行为而毁坏了回家的归途。“这一个人”与“其余的人”。这些其余的人，他们毁灭了自己。希腊语ὄλοντο即毁灭，即死亡。在《伊利亚特》开始的诗行里，这叫作οὐλομένην（被诅咒的，不幸的，致命的）。又是这个共同的主题：ὄλεθρος（毁灭，

---

① 阿尔基库罗斯（Archilochos），来自帕雷斯岛（Paros），盛年约在公元前650年，古希腊最早的抒情诗人。抑扬格讽刺诗的代表，善用动物寓言。残存的诗约有500行，没有完整的诗篇留存于后世。他与荷马、赫西俄德的区别十分清楚，是富有个人色彩的抒情诗的创立者，其辛辣刻薄与他的身世密切相关。

② 萨福（Sappho），来自累斯博斯岛（Lesbos），盛年约在公元前600年，是古希腊最重要的抒情诗人，她的诗具有古典文学的典范性，柏拉图称其为第十位缪斯。

死亡）。ὄλεθρος区分为英雄的死和不谨慎者的死。死亡在两者情形下具有截然不同的质。

现在来看亚里士多德的科学的第三大领域。是什么？我们首先辨别了：辩证法、修辞学和诗学。这些是呈现的艺术。一种情况是在法庭上作展现和阐述，另一种情况是在诗中进行呈现和展示。显然，实践的、行动的科学与这些呈现的艺术不同。按照其渊源，第一个行动是在共同体内，即在πόλις（城邦）内的行动。

什么是πόλις？它是一个共同体，这个共同体的主旨是“善（好）”，共同体所有人都应该为之操劳。因为这种共同的善（好），就有了组织，许多人在一个共同体中组合起来（σύνθεσις）。亚里士多德说：συνεστηκυῖα κοινωνία πολιτική（政治共同体）①。在这个共同体中，不是按照量来做判断，即不是按照人数多少来做判断。这里只以合目的性为标准，而合目的性把希腊的共同体限制在多个小单位上，这与罗马人的帝国不同。这些单位，首先按照男女区别建立起来。为什么？为了人类的自我保存。这里亚里士多德解释说：男性和女性的区分，这在野蛮人那里同时是主人和奴隶的区分，也就是说女人成为奴隶。不仅是女人，所有人都在一个统治者之下成为奴隶。造成野蛮的就是这一点。

于是这是正当的：βαρβάρων δ᾽ ἕλληνας ἄχειν εἰκός②，于是这是恰当的：希腊人，也就是海伦人［希腊人］统治野蛮人。一个奇怪的论断。显然希腊人从来没有要统治野蛮人。这是因为他们就像我刚才说的那样，涉及政治体制，他们坚持狭窄而清楚的界限，留守在各自本有的πόλις中。不存在共同的城邦。那么亚里士多德的视线中有什么？当然是我们今人翻译错了。这句话今天引用得相当多，用来揭露海伦人［希腊人］的狂妄自负，尤其是他们的哲学家。但是［引述的这句话］说了些什么？“ἄρχειν”，这叫作位置上处于第一。确实他们在政治上曾经是第一。就何而言呢？他

① 译按：这实际上应该是博德组合过的短语。συνεστηκυῖα κοινωνία（共享家灶的、共同居住的共同体）首先是家，然后是聚落或村落，最后是城邦。

② 参见 *Arist. Polit.* 1252b8 = *Eur. Iph. Aul.* 1400，亚里士多德《政治学》引欧里庇得斯悲剧《伊非格尼亚在奥利斯》语。βάρβαρος，即非希腊人的，说希腊语以外的语言的；“野蛮的”为引申义。

们是第一等人，是因为他们作为第一等人实现了自由，实现了政治的自由。——不再承认古人在我们历史的诸时代中完满实现了的东西，这是亚现代的情形。

希腊人掌握住自身。“统治自身”（Selbstbeherrschung）曾是他们城邦政治的充分实现。这种政治在αὐτάρκεια（自足）的意义上划定城邦的界线：就像城邦自给自足所需要的一样多，属于城邦的东西一定正好是这么多。城邦必须能够自足。下次我会进一步解释这件事。现在我要简明地说明亚里士多德科学的更进一步的建筑构造。

首先肯定是神学科学。但这个“第一”并不是指在我们的学习中排在第一位。排在逻辑技艺之后，① 作为位于第一的科学，这里出现的是辩证法，更确切地说是修辞学。作为另一种创制的科学，作为关于诗艺的科学，诗学与修辞学结伴现身。在第二个层次上，从根据奠基来说是在更高的层次上，实践科学走到前台。这首先是政治学，其次是伦理学。为什么恰好在这样一个秩序中？这还得说明。

进而也是最后出现的是理论科学。这是第一流的科学。这里首先是物理学。物理现象具有醒目的标志，它们在自身中具备自身运动的根据。这是某种自由类型，即在物理现象自身中具备自身运动的根据，直至诸天的自身运动都具备自身运动的根据。诸天的自身运动区别于以产生和消灭为特征的地上的运动。从这种理论科学上升到最高的科学就是神学科学。神学科学和什么打交道？不被推动者；甚至不可动者。为什么不可动？因为神没有理由以任何一种方式出离自身，他无欲。正是如此，他是主宰者［统治者］。他仅要自身，这是因为他是“善（好）”，是完美。只有理性（νοῦς）能显示这种完美。理性在自身的现实性活动中是作为νόησις（所思）的理性。除了理性自身的现实性，这种现实性活动根本没有任何别的对象，因此这是“νόησις νοήσεως”，即“思想的思想”。这是最令人欢乐的思想！

① 译按：“逻辑技艺”指的是单纯在形式上达致科学的三段论逻辑。但相对于亚里士多德真正关心的事情的“科学”，逻辑还只是先行的，尚未真正达到科学，因此仍从技艺方面来理解。

还需要指出亚里士多德本人给予我们的一个提示。他的神学科学最后一句说道："τὰ δὲ ὄντα οὐ βούλεται πολιτεύεσθαι κακῶς. ‘οὐκ ἀγαθὸν πολυκοιρανίη· εἷς κοίρανος.’"① 意即"诸存在者，存在者的多样性宁可接受不坏的统治"。最后是荷马的引文："王者众多并非善。只应有一个统治者。"（《形而上学》，XII. 1076a3）。这适用于如此之世界秩序（Kosmos）。因此，这对于这位主宰者是适用的，因为作为"第一"，他是自己主宰的世界秩序的根据。与诸城邦的统治者们不同，这位主宰者为城邦的政治思想提供根据。具体说来，城邦的政治思想就是对"什么是最好？"的思想。正是因为这样的主宰者，荷马能如此思想："εἷς κοίρανος ἔστω."（"只应有一个统治者"）（《伊利亚特》，II. 204）。

## 二 哲学的经典定义及其主导思想

亚里士多德的科学的建筑学以此为基础得到安排：每一次就我们来说，什么是先行的，这区别于按照事情来说是先行的东西。亚里士多德的科学必须如此。因为科学开始于落入感性经验的东西。这是与我们相关的"第一"；与此相对的另一个也许是概念，纯粹概念。这里更切近的是纯粹概念。亚里士多德说过，科学就以对于我们是在先的东西为基础做出安排。"我们"？我们是谁？他的回答：ζῷον λόγον ἐχῶν，即 animal rationale 或者具有逻各斯的生灵。

这个逻各斯究竟是什么呢？它造成人在所有生命体中的唯一性。亚里士多德在《政治学》中这样说："λόγον δὲ μόνον ἄνθρωπος ἔχει τῶν ζῴων."② 就是说："在生灵中只有人具有逻各斯。"就此亚里士多德首先解释道：逻各斯不只是欢悦或者痛苦的感受的表达。同一个地方他接着说道："ὁ δὲ λόγος ἐπὶ τῷ δηλοῦν ἐστι τὸ συμφέρον καὶ τὸ βλαβερόν, ὥστε καὶ τὸ δίκαιον καὶ τὸ ἄδικον." 就是说："逻各斯的任务是弄清楚，即弄清楚损益、正义与不正义。"这是逻各斯的任务。首要的是根据任务，而非通过名词释义来

① *Arist. Metaph.* XII. 1076a3f.

② *Arist. Polit.* 1253a10.

解释说明逻各斯是什么。逻各斯的任务指的是逻各斯要实现和完成的任务。这显然是一个慎思明辨、做出区分的任务，即辨别损益，区分正义与不正义。这里，在我们在政治方面的唯一对象这儿。关于政治可以这么说，只在人这里有政治。与其他生命体相比较，正是这一点是人本具的东西。只有人有好和坏的感受，正义与不正义的感受以及属于这些的东西。亚里士多德结束了这个解释。这里诸位可以看到，“λόγον ἔχειν”（具有逻各斯）是多么的根本。可我们还无法翻译它。合理性（Rationalität）对于政治是多么的根本！亚里士多德结束（这一段）时说：政治的共同体由家和城邦构成；后者是人的共同生活的两种形式。必须以逻各斯为出发点。值得注意的是，逻各斯首先在政治体中得到实现。从这个逻各斯出发。

[——提问：家也属于政治体吗？

——回答：确实如此。家所缔造的共同生活是政治体的第一个要素。]

按照这个对逻各斯的先行说明，对于亚里士多德而言，逻各斯显然具有根本性的意义。逻各斯对于“人之为人”（Mensch-sein）是奠基性的；只有人拥有逻各斯。众神没有逻各斯吗？没有。他们不需要逻各斯。这一点不同寻常。

今天仍在谈论的逻各斯（logos），它是语言（Sprache）。人们把它和“语言”放到一起。人有语言。然而，亚里士多德的逻各斯，一般而言的希腊人的逻各斯，进而一般而言的 *ratio*，一如 *ratio* 在“现代”之前于哲学中所表达的那样，绝不会与语言相等同。用“语言”来翻译和校量逻各斯，这已经是哲学没落的后果，是哲学的历史、哲学的科学分崩离析的后果。科学，更准确地说今天在运作的各种科学，只在名相上与从亚里士多德到黑格尔的哲学所说的科学是同一个“科学”。人们以名词使用的连续性来抹掉区分。于此什么也思想不到。为什么坚持这个区分？如我所说：这个区分对于科学是奠基性的。

亚里士多德谈到这些科学，它们都与对某物进行透彻思想（διανοείσθαι）的能力有关。διανοητική（透彻思想的技艺），意即对某物就其自身而言进行透彻思想的艺术。相互间就某物进行透彻交谈正是依据这种透彻的思想。这种言说的语言当然并非哲学传统中的“第一”，毋宁说驻留于自身的透彻思想是“第一”。这里遭遇的是哲学的少数几个词语之一，对这些词诸位最好熟记成诵，以便深入内心来学习它们。

在《后分析篇》的开篇之处，这是与科学概念相关的卓越位置，亚里士多德说道：“πᾶσα διδασκαλία καὶ πᾶσα μάθησις διανοηστικὴ ἐκ προϋπαρχούσης γίνεται γνώσεως.”① 就是说：透彻思想的每一种教和每一种学。或者就像在我们的日常语言中说的那样，理智的每一种教和学。令人惊奇的是教在先。每一种以理智发生的教和学都源自预先给定的知识。

这让我们想到缪斯的知的意义。正是鉴于荷马的知由缪斯先行赠予这一点，才能理解为什么亚里士多德把“教”安排在“学”之前。因为一个人只能够教他已经知道的东西。在我们理智的基本状况中，处于第一位的正是这种 προϋπαρχούση γνώσις（先行给定的知）。科学，理智的活动每一次都要从前定的知识出发。先行给定的知识是第一位的。然而这里可能要问：是一直如此吗？难道所有知识不都是我们提供的吗？因而首先是学习所有知识，其次才是教授知识？然而在希腊人这里不是这样，在亚里士多德这里尤其不是如此。之所以不是如此，这是因为亚里士多德与荷马有共同之处，也就是说他们两人回溯到先行给定的知识。总是已经在缪斯的记忆之中先行给定，从记忆中宣布出来。（科学从）前定的知识（开始）；否则的话，知识的论证就会回溯至无穷（ad infinitum）。寻找根据直至无穷（ad infinitum）的论证，从来不会抵达某种根据，而是停留于持续运作的前进或回溯的过程。无穷前进或者回溯的进程兴许只能每次都建立起根据，但却不会接受这一根据。

如前所述，在我们今天的思想中，人们为了“语言”而排斥逻各斯之所曾是。似乎以不言而喻的权利。在向亚现代的推进中这有不可抵抗的强力。在当今哲学中，“语言”可算是所有思想的真正视野。再来一遍：在亚现代中如是，并非在现代就已经这样。亚现代（Submoderne）在特质上与现代（Moderne）相区别。就如今天人们称之为艺术的东西情形一样，诸位尤其能够在艺术上看到这种区别。对于每一个还没有见出这一点的人

① *Arist.*, *An. Post.* 71a1f. Verstand（知性或者理智）也是德语翻译διανοητική的通常选项。

而言，现时代的艺术掺和了与艺术之"所曾是"的决裂，更准确地说，是掺和了与现代的艺术之"所曾是"的决裂。而现代的艺术之"所曾是"曾经是现代对历史的伟大否定。其伟大之处在于不懈地去除。去除什么？正如亚里士多德所知，正如我们的整个历史直至20世纪中叶所知，这个"什么"一定关系着"美"，关系着美的概念的实现。"美"对于许多人是暗淡的言谈，对于许多人只还是混杂的思想，里面杂乱无章，一片混乱。

亚现代弥漫开来。这里只是提起这一点，好让诸位离开亚里士多德也学会看我们的当下。这是绝对有必要的，由此诸位不将哲学当作过去的各种意见的垃圾来对待，而是要如同哲学始终当下地驻留于自身的诸多危机之中那样、在διανοητική（透彻思想的艺术）的诸危机之中那样来对待哲学。διανοητική是对已完成的所思（Gedachtes）进行透彻思想的艺术；已完成的所思总是一再树立起思想的使命。

在亚现代，也就是在今天，与我们遭遇的首先是无序的思想。我已经提到过，无序的思想笼罩在当今之人的种种现象之上。（首先）是"无—序"（an – archische）的思想！在第二个层次上是结构主义的思想。基于对现代解释学中作为体验基础而有效的东西的告别，结构主义的思想得到确认。体验基础（Erlebnisboden）保藏过思想的不可思议的源泉；诸位也可以称之为"原始的无意识之物"。第三，语言分析的思想，它从功能性的、科学的理论思想的支配中解脱出来。这个解脱过程也是整整一代人以来支配哲学、掌控语言分析前沿的进程。

但是让我们回到当今思想最为纠缠的现象，也就是回到其无序的基本特征。这意味着什么？诸位将会看到，我并非离题太远，而是回到我们的亚里士多德。"无—序"（an – archisch），是从字面上来听。在怎样的字面上呢？脱离了思想在第一义上对诸原则（prinzipien）的关注。但是按照亚里士多德在《形而上学》第一卷里所给的定义，哲学是关于诸第一根据、第一原则和起因的理论。"无—序"指的就是哲学的原则的消失。与原则思想的决裂在现代就已经露出端倪；在亚现代却更进一步，而这是什么？也就是不只排斥扎根于哲学的principia（原则），而且也排斥关于princeps的思想；因为众所周知亚现代思想的冲击瞄准任何一种统治的形式。对每一种统治形式的冲击和瓦解是现时代思想的关切，尤其是针对“逻各斯中心主义”统治的冲击和瓦解。“逻各斯中心主义”是由哲学巩固下来形成统治的。取消这种哲学的逻各斯中心的统治，这一点诸位可以在无序思想的最重要的现时代现象上看见，也就是在德里达那里可以看到。我们当下的无序思想［所论及的］亚里士多德的思想已经被剥除了根基，这是从亚里士多德思想的第一开端处着手，也就是从其第一根据和原因当中的“第一开端”处着手的根基剥除。我们一定会看到，从中可以救出什么，或者不如说，假如局面仍还具有逼迫性的话，我们如何从这个局面中救出自身。

亚里士多德给出的哲学的经典定义是：“哲学是关于诸第一根据和原因的理论科学。”（《形而上学》，982b9）这个哲学的定义仍然是规范性的。值得注意的是，此处亚里士多德进一步展开阐述，并且用了“因为”（由此可见随后的思想的重要性）。“因为善（好）与为何是起因之一”，也就是从某物是“好的”（Gutsein）来进行论证。我想为诸位朗读，好让大家听得进去：“δεῖ γὰρ ταὐτὴν（也就是哲学）τῶν πρώτων ἀρχῶν καὶ αἰτιῶν εἶναι θεωρητικήν· καὶ γὰρ τἀγαθὸν καὶ τὸ οὗ ἕνεκα ἓν τῶν αἰτίων ἐστίν.”[①] 为了让诸位再次意识到，就关涉亚里士多德而言，现代所出现的情况，我要提醒大家注意，海德格尔在他的文章《这是什么——哲学?》[②] 中正引用了亚里士多德的那个定义，但是去掉了关于“善（好）”的补充说明。海德格尔是一位出色的读书人，他肯定没有忽略“善（好）”所涉及的这一点。在亚里士多德这里叫作“因为”，这提供一个论证，这个论证返照其哲学的整个定义。取消这个论证，一定是有意为之。“善（好）”去掉了。我将于适当的机会回到这一点；显然人们也会在其他关联上辨认出同样的做法。

为什么提起这一点？是为了批评海德格尔吗？尽管今天反对他以谋取利益仍然是一种习惯，可没有什么比这离我更遥远的了。冲着他是唯一彻

① 译按：“它应该是对最初本原和原因思辨的科学，因为善以及何所为或目的是原因的一种。”（《形而上学》，982b9－10）参见亚里士多德（1993）。

② Heidegger（*Gesamtausgabe*，Bd. 11，Klostermann，2006：S. 16）.

底思考了思想的历史性的人，他思考形而上学的整个历史，尤其是其第一个开端。在现代产生并且必然产生的省思之内，他绝无仅有地穿透了思想的历史性。针对科学的整个历史他提出“不”，而科学就是亚里士多德这里所界定的。“不!”他说了并且做了论证。他指出与历史相分离的必要性。但是海德格尔，乃至一般而言整个现代所看到的必要的分离，其实是鉴于历史的诸项使命的圆满完成而能够认识到的过程，而这一历史是亚里士多德标识为第一科学的知的历史。许多人依附于所谓的形而上学批判，但是单纯就对形而上学的了解而言，没有人可以与海德格尔平分秋色。所有那些赞成或者反对他的关于形而上学的命题的人并非偶然。海德格尔追问过“什么是形而上学?”，而他们在理解这个历史整体上是些蹩脚汉。我知道，我在说什么。因为他们的学识即使在广博之处——这在今天已经稀有——也没有达到海德格尔提问的水平。通过这个提问，才提及“一切/万物”（Alles）；“一切”不容许或多或少的“大概”。

“一切”（πάντα）：这总是哲学的事，从开端以来就已经如是。πάντα：哲学的主题是一个 *totum*（整体）。因此，作为全整性的思想，哲学和哲学的传统变得声名狼藉，而这种对哲学的谴责在今天的人当中，在亚现代，是不可能停止和消失的。如前所述，πάντα即“一切/万物”，在最初的哲学家们那里就能够找到这个哲学真正之事的名字。“一切”，具体说是这个在比例关系中的“一切”，按照赫拉克利特所说，这是在λόγος（比例关系）中的“一切”，并且是在与“一”的比例关系中的“一切”。因此，哲学所说的第一个逻各斯，用赫拉克利特的话说就是“ἓν-πάντα”（“一”—“一切”）。这是与哲学相关的第一个逻各斯，第一个比例关系。哲学在其总是从新造就开端（Anfang）的自由中与之相关。恰恰不是通过所谓哲学问题的继续滚动，（而是通过哲学的新的）开端。哲学一再［从新］造就开端。并且在首要的意义上，哲学是这样来造就开端的，即哲学思想的时代按照自身思想的使命区分开来。思想的诸使命由思想自身所造成，从而我们可以在思想的使命中辨识出不同的原则；这些以划时代的方式区分开来的原则，对于希腊人［的时代］首先出现巴门尼德这里，对于中间时代首先出现在普洛丁这里，对于最后的时代则首先出现在康德这里。

今天与科学打交道的情形表明，科学是多么彻底地与科学之“所曾是”相分离。我仅向诸位指出一个标志性的征兆：古代史研究建立了题为“古代的贪污腐败”的研究领域。诸位请看，古代人认得腐败。在某种程度上说，腐败从属于生命。尽管如此，他们绝不会动心思做这么一个研究。之所以如此，因为历史学的任务，乃至政治史学的任务，都是在完全不同的意义上来领会的，也就是从历史中已经具备的卓越者（Vortreffliches）那里来理解历史的使命。因此历史是出类拔萃的事件的历史。无论是在好的方面还是在坏的方面出类拔萃。绝无平庸之事，绝无日常之事。但诸位可以看到，这里有一个与当今通行理解完全不同的判断。贪腐研究完全而彻底地丧失了直到 19 世纪科学都处于其支配之下的标准。我已经说过，要看到科学中造就了区分的“善（好）”的准则。“善（好）”构成亚里士多德哲学定义的根据。哲学的科学要关注“善（好）”。这是一桩承认（Anerkennen）的事，具体说是在古人完满实现了的东西之中的事情。因此，要强调和突出的是：什么是承认的根据？什么具备完满的特性？在亚现代的批判膨胀中，在批判理论的扩散中，承认和赞同的思想被排斥到一边去了。

承认和赞同的思想。我们如何从亚里士多德和荷马那里学习它？在荷马这里，这种思想具有根本的意义。具体说一个人以他所完成的功业而获得承认和赞同；用希腊人的话说，即证明了他的ἀρετή（卓越）而获得承认和赞同。对此，我们的当下因失明目盲而丧失辨别力了吗？如果是这样，就要问：是什么样的失明目盲？因为我们知道有两种意义上的失明目盲。[一是] 生理的失明目盲，这是一种病。另一种是什么？是命中注定的失明目盲。希腊人在他们的歌者，在他们的荷马的失明目盲上看到这种命定。他们在先知泰瑞西亚斯（Teiressias）的失明目盲上看到这种命定。因此，失明目盲是要加以区分和辨认的。

此外还有一个出自早期希腊哲学的例子。赫拉克利特拾起一则古老轶事：有人说，荷马是因为一个谜语而死。小孩们向他提出谜语，他却因为眼睛看不见而不能够解谜。这是赫拉克利特的讲述和解释：“关系到显现于眼前的事物，人们几乎和荷马一样弄错；在希腊人中，他比所有人都σοφώτερος（更智慧/更有本领）。”[①]从荷马这儿，诸位获得了我们的关键词“σοφία”（智慧）。哲学看σοφία却是另一种评价。在赫拉克利特的讽刺中，我们就已经发觉这一点了。他继续说道：“掐虱子的小孩欺骗荷马。他们说：‘就我们所见所抓住的，我们将之甩到后面。我们看不见和抓不住的，我们就带着。’”——他们总还是满身虱子。赫拉克利特要说什么呢？荷马在智慧上优胜于所有人，却因为失明而不能够看穿简单易懂的事情。他看不到小孩子们在做什么，所以他不懂他们在说什么，所以这话对于他一直是谜。甚至他也是通常观点的牺牲品。只有当这些观点挠他痒痒而他捉住它们，他才摆脱这些观点；此外他处处担负着它们。我们暂时不去管赫拉克利特的相关自我评价。

这桩轶事背景所涉及的，还有源自另一种态度的相关趣闻值得一提。猜谜上的失败成为诗人荷马为自己写墓志铭的缘起。为自己刻下这样的墓志铭，这在古代并不罕见；在近代也仍然有。据说荷马草拟如下：“这里泥土遮盖神圣的头颅，神性的荷马，κοσμήτωρ（建立秩序者）[②]，英雄男子的修饰者。”[③] 是的，荷马说到自己是神性的，因为他是安排秩序者。兴许诸位记得，我从亚里士多德神学科学的结束处引用的话。那里说的是：位于第一的神是κοσμήτωρ（组织秩序并发号施令者），他是至上而唯一的主人。“εἷς κοίρανος ἔστω”，即“当以一人为君”。因为这位主人所本具的事，即为“善（好）”操劳，照管“一切”。

我们回到亚里士多德，回到他经典的哲学定义：“哲学是第一科学，因为它询问一切的第一根据和原因。”并且这是组织成完整和谐的秩序体

---

① 赫拉克利特残篇 B56，参见 Diels，Kranz（1951）。

② 译按：κοσμήτωρ，一般含义即列阵司令官，指挥官，将领。但从词根上涉及的是κόσμος（秩序），因此这里译作安排秩序者，组织秩序并发号施令者。

③ 译按：就此博德补充说：“参看瓦尔策（Walzer）版关于赫拉克利特的证言；就证言方面而言，瓦尔策版仍是最好的版本。”译校者手头没有瓦尔策的版本，无法查证其具体关联。所引荷马墓志铭铭文出自托名希罗多德的《荷马传记》（*Vita Herodotea*）。《荷马传记》同样讲述了荷马死前遭到一群年轻人考问的情节。不过《传记》作者显然有为荷马辩护的意思，而且似乎正是针对赫拉克利特所散布的意见，认为荷马死于生病而不是因为猜不出谜语。段首博德所谓轶事的“另一种态度”，应当就是指《传记》所述而言的。可参见：Allen（1912：215－216）。

（Kosmos）的“一切”。因此，亚里士多德的神的作用是组织作用，不是因为他自己插手，而是因为他如如，如其是，也就是如其是最高的“善”和欢乐。之所以这样，是因为他就是“如此”，其余的（一切）处于对他的ἔρως（欲求）关系之中。用“爱”（Liebe）来翻译ἔρως是不幸的。ἔρως是欲求。具体说这里欲求指的是，像“第一”那样而“是其所是”，也就是成为完美的所是。

至于神，在哲学中向来都如此。这里我引用黑格尔《逻辑学》第一卷“存在”部分的话。具体地就是这个问题：“必须用什么作哲学的开端?”[①]开端必定由什么造就？这个问题与亚里士多德面对面。在 1832 年的《逻辑学》第二版中，也就是在快要逝世之前，黑格尔对原先的文字做了补充。在补充的位置他说道：“神会具有最无可争辩的权利，以神造就开端。”[②] 神“会”具有最无可争辩的权利，以自身为开始。值得注意的是，“具有”（hätte）用了虚拟式，这当然完全可以从黑格尔科学的原则来解释。不过这里不是解释的地方。无论如何黑格尔的科学与亚里士多德的第一科学仍是如此靠近，以至于黑格尔用很长一段关于神圣理性的希腊语引文来结束他的哲学全书，这段引文正出自亚里士多德的θεολογική（神学科学）。于此诸位可以看到，这个主题曾有多么巨大的凝聚力。

在现代则不是如此。决绝的“不”。必须一再弄清楚这个“不”，并且问：与如此之哲学的决裂是怎么来的？一种决裂，它对于现代是基本构成性的。就此而言，海德格尔与亚里士多德的形而上学打交道，对我们是很有启发的。这里要强调的是不显眼的一点，也就是涉及亚里士多德“科学”的这一点。我已经从论文《这是什么——哲学?》引证过。我们已经看到，这里略过了某些东西，具体说忽略了在关于“第一”的规定中“善（好）”的主导思想。那么我们怎么办呢？那就再来一遍：我们把目光投向亚里士多德的知的建筑学，并且由这一知来开阐荷马思想的建筑学。

诸科学全都是逻各斯的科学。逻各斯之“所是”，如前所述，并不表

① 译按：博德直接说“哲学”（Philosophie），黑格尔原文则是“科学”（Wissenschaft）。这并非口误，因为对于黑格尔，哲学与科学在其完满的意义上是同一的。

② 参见 Hegel（1984：S.65，Z.12）。

现在单一的名词释义中，也就是说逻各斯是这是那。这些诸位能够在词典里查阅；而我们必须追究：逻各斯做什么？亚里士多德回答：δηλοῦν（使成为可见的/显而易见）。澄清是逻各斯的任务，并且总是鉴于某物，在与某物的关联中。

前面出自《逻辑学》的引文清楚表明：如果我们愿意从亚里士多德思想的开端来理解其思想，那么我们必须回溯到διανοητική（透彻思想的技艺），回到透彻思考某物的能力。διανοητική联结所有的科学；它也做出决定。正是这种透彻思想的能力［对此］做出决定：在亚里士多德的科学中必须以什么为开端。我已经说过，亚里士多德自己提供了导线。他区分创制的、实践的和理论的科学；而且这个顺序从创制的科学开始，而不是相反。涉及他的建筑，亦即思想的建筑学，亚里士多德总是十分准确。他知道：从逻各斯自身开始，而不是像人们也许以为的那样从经验开始。从经验开始，这是通常习惯的答案。如果您问，亚里士多德哲学的特征是什么？一般可以听到的是这样：他的哲学从经验中获取出发点。这里什么是经验就已经很不清楚。现在让我们抛开这个，忘却这种愚笨的谈论。亚里士多德坚定地从逻各斯出发。对亚里士多德的科学的建筑学没有后来学院传统为了物理学及其适合感性的经验而带上的偏见。我已说过，在我们对逻各斯的展开中，处于第一位的科学是具备双重性的科学，亦即创制的科学（Poietik）。它首先问：我们用逻各斯做什么？逻各斯创造什么？这一方面显示在修辞学中，并且出现在直接的目标上，法庭制度和法庭演说将这些目标推向前台。其次，在诗艺意义上的创制的科学，也就是说并非在其直接动机上来理解的创制，毋宁说是这样，言辞（Rede）在此也变得举足轻重，只不过这是被看作所曾是（gewesene）的言辞，即史诗（叙事）。希腊人也讨论过通往完满呈现的道路，具体说即戏剧（Drama），一种“对话剧”（Sprechdrama）。对第一科学的回忆或者宁可说最亲近逻各斯的科学的回忆就到此。［这里］逻各斯指的是：言辞，在戏剧中的言辞，在此之前则是法庭上的言辞。

与此明显不同的是诸实践的科学。如前所述，实践的科学首先是政治学。政治学在本质上建立在对共同体目标的认识的基础之上。共同体的目标并非生活下来，即并不是创造生活条件，而是在一种本质上得到引导的生活中“好好生活”。这里“好”却并非意味着享受和如意，而是有根据的“好”；我已经说到了这个根据。“好好生活”，政治学以之为主题。与政治学相对的另一门科学是伦理学。它以特别的方式与“善（好）”相关，不是与城邦的“善（好）”相关，而是关涉到对于人来说普遍适用的“善（好）”，也就是与ἀνθρώπινον ἀγαθόν（属人的善好）相关。而这是什么？希腊人用一个诸位肯定已经知道的名字来称呼它。就像希腊人所理解的那样，这是“最好的”［“善（好）”］。我们说：“幸福”（Glück）；希腊人不这么称呼它。

［——您知道这个希腊名字吗？

——回答：εὐδαιμόνια。

——完全正确。］

这究竟是什么意思？［“εὐδαιμόνια”指的是，］拥有好的δαίμων（神灵/精灵），就像在我们的古德语中也说的那样，“为一种好的精神（Geist）所指引”。“εὐδαιμόνια”谈到在一种精神、在一种好的精神引导下的生活方式，希腊人称这种好的精神为δαίμων（神灵/精灵）。这个δαίμων不是和神（Gott）一样的东西。那么δαίμων的特性是什么呢？

［——您知道吗？柏拉图说过的。

——回答：是居间者①。

——完全正确。］

δαίμων处于人和众神之间的中间位置。而这个中间位置清楚地表现在，δαίμονες（诸神灵/精灵）从最优秀的人当中集聚而来；这是些最优秀的人的精神。这些人因为其得到证明的贤明而注定获得极乐。就此而言，δαίμων以及εὐδαιμόνια（幸福）的名称的意义也就彰明较著了。也就是说，亚里士多德伦理学的主题最终是解释这样一种生活的条件——而这些条件在哪里呢？在ἀρετή（德性/卓越），在人的优越品质。第一个ἀρετή是公正。再问：为了εὐδαιμόνια（幸福）必须满足什么条件？个人的卓越德性；显

① 译按：出自柏拉图《会饮篇》。苏格拉底转述迪奥提玛的教诲，称爱神［Eros］为“居间者”。参见Plat. Symp. 201e－202e。

示其公正［德性］的标志，必须由个人加以完成和实现。

就像我们的康德哲学所称的“幸福”，这里幸福是什么样的状态？“εὐδαιμόνια”（为一个好的精神所指引的状态）。另外，亚里士多德的回答是富有建筑性的，建筑起生活形式的基本类型。第一，ἀπόλαυσις即享受，生活的目标在于享受；ἀπολαυστική（享受的/为了享乐的）指的是具有享受的能力。第二，以τιμή（荣誉）为准则的生活。诸位很容易可以注意到，这里一种等级区分在起作用。第三，什么样的βίος（生活）？θεωρητικὸς βίος（沉思或理论的生活方式），献身于“善/好”的知的生活。并非一般的知，而是关于“善（好）”的知。这是亚里士多德的“理论”（Theorie）的含义。而这种含义完满实现在亚里士多德的神的现实性之中。在理论中的生活，这是实践的最高形式。这儿您也看到（科学的）联结和亚里士多德的建筑：科学的下一个阶次是理论科学。

理论科学首先是自然的科学（die physische Wissenschft）。自然的科学以什么为内容？首先是标识出自然诸现象的特性的东西，这是依据亚里士多德从物理学的证明［来标识出的特性］。

［——什么造成自然的自然性（das Physische der Natur）？

——回答：运动。

——是的，并且是自身运动。］

自身运动，即不为他者所冲击，而是为自身推动。亚里士多德物理学（自然学）也将目光投向“好的”东西，投向自身完满实现的东西。亚里士多德的物理学首先就与此打交道：在显现者当中的“什么”是什么？具有怎样的运动？请诸位回想一下［显现者的］等级秩序，这个等级秩序必须成为可见的。在下的层级由在自然中产生和消逝的东西占据着。与之有别的是在自然中永恒运动的东西，亦即天空。天空处于永恒运动之中，它自身运动。然而这里有效的是：天空为第一推动者所推动，第一推动者本身是不动的。如此，天体也仍然是不生灭的永恒的欲求。亚里士多德的科学自身完满实现于此，也就是实现在对那个本质所本具的现身性（Anwesenheit）的思想中。在对神的思想中。更确切地说，是对这位神的思想，他区别于自然，区别于自然整体。之所以如此，因为他是理性的纯粹活动，黑格尔在《哲学全书》结束处甚至也引用同样的话。就此我们结束我们遍历亚里士多德的科学建筑结构的暂时行程，从现在起转向这一建筑结构的单个部分，然而总是以荷马为前瞻。

## 参考文献

Allen, T. W., 1912, *Homeri Opera* V, Oxford.

Burnet, I., 1901, *Platonis Opera*, II, Oxford Clarendon.

Diels, H., Kranz, W., Die Fragmente der Vorsokratiker, 1951, Bd. 1, 6Aufl., Weidmannsche Verlagsbuchhandlung.

Hegel, 1984, *Gesammelte Werke*, Bd. 21, hrsg. F. Hogemann, W. Jaeschke, Felix Meiner Verlag.

Heidegger, 2006, *Gesamtausgabe*, Bd. 11, Vittorio Klostermann.

黑格尔，1999，《哲学史讲演录》第 2 卷，贺麟、王太庆译，商务印书馆。

康德，2010，《逻辑学讲义》，许景行译，杨一之校，商务印书馆。

亚里士多德，1993，《形而上学》，《亚里士多德全集》第 7 卷，苗力田译，中国人民大学出版社。

# A Conceptualist Reading of Kant's Aesthetic Judgment of Beauty

Jiyao TANG *

**Abstract**: This essay offers a conceptualist reading of Kant to address two central issues in *Critique of Judgment*: what is the nature of the judgment of beauty, and how it bears on the a priori principle of judgment. Challenging the popular subjectivist approach which conceives Kant's judgment of beauty as a non-conceptual mental state, I argue that the judgment of beauty in Kant is a full-fledged judgment whose conceptual contents are aesthetic appreciation and criticism, and that the principle of subjective purposiveness in judgment refers to a generic concept instead of a mental episode. My view has the advantage over the subjectivism of both preserving the intuitive idea that aesthetic judgments have rich conceptual contents, and of avoiding the theoretical difficulties which subjectivism suffers. To sharpen my focus, I will present a sophisticated subjectivist reading of Kant's aesthetics given by Hannah Ginsborg in section 2, and in section 3 give my criticism of Ginsborg's theory, which also reveals a fundamental limit of the subjectivist approach in general. Finally, in section 4 I give my own conceptualist reading of Kant's aesthetics and respond to potential challenges from the subjectivist camp.

**Key words**: Kant, aesthetics, the judgment of beauty, free play, conceptual content, appreciation and criticism

* Jiyao Tang, University of Chicago.

# 1 Introduction

In *Critique of Judgment*[①], Kant begins the first part on aesthetics with an observation of a paradox distinctive of the judgment of beauty. On the one hand, the judgment of beauty is essentially one's subjective feeling of pleasure. Beauty is not a matter of proof, and everyone must feel and judge for herself (5: 231, 285 – 6). On the other hand, reason balks at the idea that an aesthetic judgment merely appeals to a private and arbitrary preference. As Kant observes, when one makes a sincere judgment of beauty, she genuinely thinks and feels that there is something universal in her judgment, which should be recognized by any of her fellow with equally well-cultivated aesthetic taste (5: 282). [②] The first task of Kant's aesthetics is thus to give a consistent account of this universal pleasure of beauty. Further, Kant claims, through the notion of subjective purposiveness, investigations of aesthetic judgments would reveal the a priori principle of the power of judgment. Yet exactly how Kant argues for this position has been a rather controversial issue. In this essay, my primary goal is to provide a consistent account of Kant's aesthetic judgment, and explain its relation to the a priori principle of judgment. This will hopefully shed further light on topics of beauty, aesthetic judgment and pleasure in general.

In contemporary Anglophone literature, it has been often argued that, to answer the two questions above, Kant (1) denies that judgments of beauty having conceptual content, yet (2) carves out and reserves for judgments of beauty a special mental state of "free-play between imagination and understanding" in his

① In this paper I use Werner Pluhar's translation of the Kant's *Critique of Judgment*. References to Kant's works are in parenthesis, with pagination following the standard Kant *Schriften*.

② For some discussions on the nature of "disagreement" and "demand" of the judgment of beauty, see: Crawford (1970), Cavell (1976: 73 – 96), and Guyer (1997: esp 129 – 130).

transcendental psychology, which also explains the a priori principle of judgment. Consequently, recent debates have been centered around making sense of this pleasant yet universal mental state. Since this strand of thought identifies the content of judgment of beauty with a subjective mental state, I'll call it "subjectivist" approach. ①

At first glance, Kant appears to be an apparent subjectivist:

> "*In order to consider something good, I must always know what sort of thing the object is meant to be i. e. , I must have a determinate concept of it. But I do not need this in order to find beauty in something. Flowers, free designs, lines aimlessly intertwined and called foliage: these have no significance, depend on no determinate concept, and yet we like them*" (*5: 207*).

Kant seems to reiterate this idea that judgments of beauty have no concept throughout his aesthetics (e. g. , 5: 220, 5: 228, 5: 287). For Kant, a concept of the object determines what the object is or should be. So, to apply an empirical concept is to predicate the object as actually exhibiting (in the theoretical case), or should exhibit (in the practical case), certain general features that the concept contains (5: 280). But in the case of beauty, to have such a concept would mean finding determinate rules which can prove whether the object is beautiful (5: 231, 5: 286). This suggestion is absurd. A judgment of beauty is a judgment of "taste", which must be based on the subjective feeling of pleasure (5: 285).

---

① Paul Guyer's two-act subjectivist view of beauty (1997: esp133 – 136), which adds a further "assertion" of the universal validity of free-play, has been widely accepted as the standard approach to Kant's aesthetics-see discussion later. For those who follow Guyer, for example: Wenzel (2005, esp 46 – 52), Janaway (1997: 67 – 87). For those who disagree with Guyer but still take a subjectivist stance: Bell (1987: esp 241), Longuenesse (2006: 203 – 208), and Ginsborg (2015).

Regarding beauty's universal validity, Kant's passages seem again consistent with the subjectivist reading. Kant writes, free-play is a "universal referential point", which we become conscious of its "universal validity". (5: 217) And this gives rise to the widely-accepted interpretation that takes our "liking" or "pleasure" as a causal and salient mental state, upon which we further reflect and judge it to be universally valid. ① Further, the free-play thus construed seems the most suitable candidate for "the underlying principle of judgment", which *Critique of Judgment* claims to lay bare. According to the subjectivist, free-play differs from the full-blown cognitive judgment as free-play "has no concept of object" yet; but since it is the "harmonious" mental-state "suitable for cognition in general", it is the grounding foundation for cognition, whose presence is necessary for judgments of all kind (5: 218, 5: 290). ②

Despite various textual evidence, this non-conceptual subjectivism appears perplexing as it so stands. ③ While judging a work of art to be beautiful relies on aesthetic feeling instead of rules, it is quite another thing to insist that we cannot employ any concept in judging beauty. Rather, when one judge something as beautiful, one often does articulate some of its aesthetic features that intrigue her, in virtue of which she thereby holds that it should aesthetically attract her cultivated fellows in the same way. Moreover, the clarity and acuteness of such articulations seems to be what we mainly rely on to distinguish a genuine, rich, and "disinterested" aesthetic appreciation from confused exclamation, the "interested" liking of the sensible and from many things else, or from anything else. If the judgment of beauty is a non-conceptual mental state, it seems mysterious for Kant to insist it must be "universally communicable", and unclear on what ground we can claim for its universal validity.

---

① Guyer (1997: esp133 – 136).

② Ginsborg (2015), Bell (1987)

③ For complains like that of this paragraph, see Ameriks (2003) and Makkai (2009: esp 388)

Further, if free-play is identified with the "condition of power of judgment" for cognition in general, then the subjectivist approach is faced with a surprising conclusion that, in effect, Kant is claiming that free-play is pervasive in every empirical judgment, therefore every object of cognition is also beautiful. In fact, this "pervasive pleasure challenge" has been one of the most serious challenges to Paul Guyer's classical subjectivist reading. According to Guyer's "two-act-view", free-play is a "raw and unintentional harmonious mental state", and a full judgment of beauty requires a second additional "reflective judgment" to assert this non-conceptual state to be universal. ① Yet, if this free-play also lays the a priori ground for all empirical judgments, many criticizers rightly point out, it would be present in every cognitive judgment, and Guyer must admit that every cognition will produce aesthetic pleasure. ②

In this paper, I will develop my criticisms of the subjectivist approach along these two ideas above, and argue for an alternative conceptualist reading of Kant's judgment of beauty. According to my view, the judgment of beauty or free-play requires an aesthetic mode of conceptualization consisting in appreciation and criticism. And the a priori principle of subjective purposiveness is a generic concept. Neither free-play nor subjective purposiveness refers to a causal mental state. To sharpen my focus, in section 2 I present a sophisticated version of the subjectivist reading offered by Hannah Ginsborg. In section 3 I criticize Ginsborg's theory in the same spirit of the pervasive pleasure challenge, which also reveals a fundamental limit of the subjectivist approach in general. Finally, in section 4 I offer my own conceptualist reading of Kant's aesthetics, and respond to potential challenges from the subjectivist camp.

---

① Guyer (1997: 110 - 119, 133 - 136, 151 - 160).

② The pervasive pleasure challenge to subjectivism has been a topic for on-going debates, for example, see Allison (2001: 184 - 192), and Ginsborg (1991).

## 2 Ginsborg's Subjectivism: Theory of Primitive Normativity

To make my criticisms concrete, I will focus on Ginsborg's interpretation of Kant's *Critique of Judgment*, which presents a sophisticated version of the subjectivist reading. Then I'll explain how my criticism could also generalize to other subjectivist views.

In a series of collected papers, Ginsborg has developed her theory of primitive normativity to account for Kant's conception of judgment of beauty. As Ginsborg sees the problem, the only feasible solution to Kant's paradox of beauty is to conceive the judgment of beauty, argued to beidentical with free-play, as a "purely self-referential" singular act of judging (Ginsborg, 1991: 46). This self-referential act of judging employs no concept, and its only content is a transcendentally normative "disposition" that claims "the object ought to be perceived this way" *simpliciter*. Ginsborg then explain, this disposition is universal since it will demand "everyone ought to judge the object as I do"; and it is non-conceptual since it does not further determine "how the object ought to be" but only to be as such *simpliciter* (1991: 47; 1997: 88; 2006: 149, 160). Meanwhile, Ginsborg emphasizes this self-referential act "must be a feeling of pleasure", since it asserts nothing but "I ought to be in that very state of mind", and thus meets Kant's characterization of pleasure as "a state of mind in which a representation harmonizes with itself, as a ground··· merely for maintaining this very state of mind". (1997: 89) Therefore, Ginsborg claims her self-referential view manages to reconcile the non-conceptual pleasure and transcendental universality of beauty into one singular act.

Despite holding on to Kant's two requirements of beauty, Ginsborg's proposed self-referential act is hardly a self-intelligible idea in itself. And it is unclear why we should find so attractive this forceful reduction of beauty to such a thin normative disposition. To understand Ginsborg's view, we need now to turn to her detailed arguments.

Ginsborg's account of beauty is part of her general theory of original concept-acquisition. According to her, when perceiving an object, even before we grasp relevant empirical concepts of that object, we have a "primitively normative" disposition to perceive or react to the object as such *simpliciter*, built into our "transcendental psychology" (1991: 48). To unpack this theory, she gives an example of children's initial concept-acquisition, in which a child playing the game of "sorting the blocks of various different shapes, putting the cubes in one pile, the pyramids in another, and so on" (2001: 185). Ginsborg holds, even before the child has grasped empirical concepts of "cube" and "pyramid", already "[this] child can be aware of herself as responding to the blocks appropriately, or as she ought" (ibid: 185). And this child perceives and sorts the blocks based on his "feeling that this is where the block belongs" (ibid: 189). Ginsborg calls such feelings the "primitive appropriateness" and argues it to be transcendental, instead of empirical, in the sense that these basic psychological facts of the child constitute "the condition of possibility of empirical concepts" (1997: 83-4). In other words, it is only because the child reacts naturally in a certain way towards the blocks, that it becomes possible for the child to learn these corresponding geometric concepts (2001: 188-190).

Next, as the topic of concept-acquisition indicates, this primitive feeling of appropriateness is often "suitable for" further developing into conceptual analysis. In case of cognition, the "primitive appropriateness" gives rise to the judger's "disposition" to further conceptualize the objects. And once the so-called primitive judger acquires the relevant concepts in this case, "cube" and "pyramid", the normativity of his further judgments of the objects will be a "derivative normativity", that is, derived from the determinate concepts, instead of a self-referential normativity appealing to the harmony between cognitive powers themselves

(2001: 189). In the derivative mode, judging something as appropriate requires the antecedent conception of what the object ought to be. The validity of such a judgment would then lie in the harmony, i. e., correspondence, between the object and the concept (1997: 80).

Appealing to Kant's distinction between determinate and reflective judgments, Ginsborg then explains how her theory bears on the nature of beauty as well as the "subjective purposiveness" principle of judgment in Kant. For Kant, a judgment is "determinate" if it judges the object by subsuming it under the empirical concept, which he also calls the "purpose" of that object. The object so judged is then "purposive" in the "objective" sense (5: 180). Its normativity is in Ginsborg's terms "derivative", since it is derived from the accordance of its empirical object with the "concept". By contrast, the normativity of Kant's reflective judgment, as Ginsborg conceives, is "primitive". For Kant, "reflective judgments" are those in which concepts are lacking and to be found. Ginsborg argues, reflective judgment includes not only judgments of beauty and discovery of new laws of nature, but moreover initial concept acquisition, since, in all three, only "the particular is given, and judgment has to find the universal for it" (5: 179). If reflective judgment is possible at all, Kant argues, there must be an underlying principle that assumes "the presented objects [in nature] are actually suitable and possible for conceptual cognition" (5: 180), without of which "the understanding would be lost in [the manifold] of nature" (5: 193). The object under reflective judgment is thus "purposive" only in the subjective sense: it is only assumed to be purposive by the judging subject, without any determinate concept that objectively justifies it is so, since that is precisely what is to be found (ibid.). Kant explains that this subjective purposiveness is revealed in the paradigmatic reflective judgment-the judgment of beauty (5: 191): in free-play our cognitive powers undergoes a special "harmony" that attains merely "the principle of subsumption", without specifying "any concepts subsumed". (5: 286 - 7) Here Ginsborg concludes, her account of primitive normativity as a non-conceptual yet universal disposition refers precisely to this Kantian subjectively purposive harmony, which not only explains the peculiar nature of the judgment of beauty, but also reveals the a priori principle of judgment that grounds empirical judgments in general (1997: 88). In this way, her theory gives a unifying account of the subjective purposiveness in Kant's discussion of both the judgment of beauty and the principle of judgments in general (1997: 88).

Ginsborg's discussion so far still leaves a crucial question unresolved: is the primitive normativity in concept-acquisition identical with the judgment of beauty? Or are they two species of the same genus? This lingering question can be clarified from her response to the pervasive pleasure challenge.

To demonstrate that her theory does not fall into the "pervasive pleasure challenge", Ginsborg emphasizes her view of primitive normativity focuses on concept-acquisition, instead of empirical cognitions in general. She replies, although the primitive appropriateness is the "pure principle" of all judgments, in empirical cognitions it remains "hidden", and "we are unaware of it" (1997: 88; 2004: 200). Only in acquiring empirical concepts, she argues, do we have the primitive appropriateness; and when it is analyzed and articulated into the derivative mode, the judgments, even including the prior primitive judging itself, will then become governed by determinate concepts (1997: 87). Although cognitive achievements might bring the judger intellectual pleasure, that pleasure is determinate, thus no longer free. Even if primitive appropriateness refers to "the condition required for cognition in general", it is only in the experience of beauty that we can feel this salient pleasure (ibid).

Therefore, Ginsborg does identify the primitive appropriateness in free-play with that in concept-acquisition. And to the pervasive pleasure challenge, her strategy is to argue that, during the process of original concept-acquisition, there occurs a transition from "free-play" to "determinate cognition", therefore no empirical cognition will produce aesthetic pleasure. Although the resulting account of beauty is impossibly thin and reductivist, Ginsborg insists, since Kant explicitly identifies the experience of beauty with the a priori principle of reflective judgment, therefore a non-conceptual harmony of mind, "he [Kant] leaves us no choice but to conclude that judgment of taste has a self-referential structure" (1991: 52).

## 3 Objection to the Ginsborg's Theory and Subjectivism in general

Bracketing her view of concept-acquisition,① I argue in this section that Ginsborg's theory is still flawed and fails to address a modified version of the pervasive pleasure challenge. My criticism of Ginsborg also exposes a fundamental limit of the general subjectivist approach.

As we saw, according to Ginsborg, the judgment of beauty is a "self-referential judging" that the object "ought to be as such*simpliciter*", and it is identical with the first of the two steps of empirical concept-acquisition. Consequently, in Ginsborg's theory, the judgment of beauty is conceived as the sheer primitive normativity in the absence of a further derivative conceptualization. And we can no longer distinguish the primitive appropriateness in concept-acquisition from that in the judgment of beauty.② Since central to Ginsborg's argument is the view that primitive appropriateness in beauty is also constitutive of concept-acquisition, further distinguishing "aesthetic" and "cognitive" primitive appropriateness will

① For the sake of my argument, I will bracket the issue of concept-acquisition. Though I think Ginsborg's theory of concept-acquisition still falls into a Sellarsian myth of the Given (1997), a full criticism of her theory deserves the length of another paper. Just to notice, Sellars' distinction between the child who is acquiring concepts and we as rational adults (1997: sec 30, 64 – 65) can be seen as a direction objection to Ginsborg's theory.

② Richard Moran (2016) makes a similar criticism complaining Ginsborg's equivocation. But Moran's concern differs from mine, as he goes on: "she fails to mark the difference between taking my own response to be 'as it should be' and approving of, praising the object I am responding to." (Moran: 399) defeat her purpose.

But this equivocation brings a serious challenge to the cogency of Ginsborg's view. Ginsborg claims that the judgment of beauty is a paradigm of primitive appropriateness, but also insists that in the appropriate experience of beauty we must not have any disposition to go on for further derivative conceptual analysis. "Rather than becoming aware of specific features of... how the object ought to be perceived," Ginsborg writes, "I take the activity to be an exemplary *simpliciter* of how the object ought to be perceived. [and] I do not specify that standard in terms of determinate rules … I take the object... ought to be [perceived] this way". (1997: 88) Yet this mere assertion is unwarranted. If the same primitive appropriateness underlies both the judgment of beauty and empirical cognition, Ginsborg then owes us a story of what unique feature prevents the primitive appropriateness in free-play from producing the same disposition for further conceptual analysis. Modifying the "pervasive pleasure challenge", we now have a "pervasive cognition challenge". It is not enough for Ginsborg to claim the aesthetic appropriateness is judging it ought to be as such *simpliciter*. Rather, she has to explain why it can be so. Otherwise, the purported pleasure of beauty becomes internally unstable: as if we must try hard to stay at this level of "primitive appropriateness", and resist the illusory disposition to articulate and cognize free-play. This mental state then seems to be not free, but an arduous refusal to the temptation for further conceptual analysis of the beautiful object perceived, in favor of an empty normativity. It is not clear then in what sense we can legitimately call this mental state a pleasure at all. Ginsborg's aesthetic theory fails to give a plausible view of the aesthetic pleasure itself.

This difficulty of Ginsborg's theory also exposes a fundamental limit of the subjectivist approach in general. The subjectivism proceeds with the basic premise that (1) free-play is a special kind of non-conceptual and causal mental state, to further argue for two theses: (2) such mental state is identical with, or at least essentially constitutive of, the judgment of beauty; and (3) free-play, as the "harmonious state suitable for cognition in general", is identified with the "subjective purposiveness" that conditions judgments in general. Now we saw, for both Ginsborg and Guyer, this double role assigned to free-play inevitably equivocates its status and blurs the distinction between judgment of beauty and cognitive judgment. While Ginsborg claims her sophisticated view has the advantage over Guyer's of savingevery cognition from being aesthetically pleasant, her account fails to, from the opposite direction distinguish aesthetic pleasure form cognition.

## 4 A Conceptualism Reading of Kant's Aesthetics-Appreciation and Criticism

I take this fundamental limit of the subjectivist, alongside its counterintuitive reductive account of aesthetic judgments, to be good reasons for us to seek an alternative reading of Kant's aesthetics. In the rest of the essay, I give my conceptualist reading of Kant. Rejecting all three subjectivist theses summarized above, I argue instead that (1) the "subjective purposiveness" is a generic concept which contains at least two species. (2) The aesthetic judgment of beauty, identical with free-play, is a full-fledged judgment with conceptual contents, instead of a non-conceptual primitive stage of cognition. Therefore, (3) neither subjective purposiveness nor the judgment of beauty refers to a single episodic mental state. Since thesis (3) naturally follows if both (1) and (2) are justified, I shall first defend my thesis (1).

Central to my thesis (1) is a further distinction between free-play and the subjective purposiveness. According to the subjectivist, the subjectively purposive harmony and free-play are one single mental state. I propose a different reading of Kant, under which the subjectively purposive harmony refers to a genus which contains (at least) two species of relation of cognitive powers: one suitable for theoretical cognition, and another for free-play, i. e., the judgment of beauty.

That the two kinds of judgment do not share a same subjectively purposive harmony as a common factor is made explicit by Kant:

> "*this attunement* [*i. e.*, *harmony*] *of the cognitive powersvaries in its proportion*, *depending on what difference there is among the objects that are given*" (*5*: *238*).

Though harmonious relation between cognitive powers is essential for both cognition and judgment of beauty, Kant tells us, the actual harmony attainednevertheless "varies in its proportion", with regard to the kind of "objects given". Kant continues, "there must be one attunement in which this inner relation is most conducive to the (mutual) quickening of the two mental powers… and the only way this attunement can be determined is by [aesthetic] feeling" (5: 238 – 9). And another harmony, differently proportioned, would be suitable for "turning a presentation into [theoretical] cognition" (ibid). Based on this passage, We can now see that Kant, I further differentiates two kinds of "subjective purposiveness" to draw the boundary between empirical and aesthetic judgments.

One might object to my sophisticated anatomy on the ground that Kant states in the introduction that, a critique of judgment will not seek a "domain", but only a "principle, which would lack a realm of objects as its own domain" (5: 177). So, the subjective purposiveness does not determinte its proper objects. My response is that by "principle" here Kant refers to the principle of subjective purposiveness as a generic concept. As a genus, subjective purposiveness does govern all kinds of judgments. But each species further specifies the kind of judgment it governs, as well as the proper objects judged, for example, the beautiful or the cognized.

Still, my interpretation is at least an unusual one, and Kant seems to make explicit my proposed distinction only once, in the passage cited. But all I want to argue for now is that my account is not incompatible with Kant, and the impression that Kant identifies the subjective purposiveness solely with free-play is unnecessary. The merit of my reading will be shown by the further elucidation on where exactly the distinction of these two species of harmony lies.

Under my account, what distinguishes the harmony suitable for beauty, i.e., free-play, from that for cognition is that, only in the cognitive mode does the judger try to find a determinate concept for the object judged. In the judgment of beauty, aesthetic conceptualization appreciates and criticizes the "singular empirical object", instead of trying to find a determinate concept of beauty. Hence my elucidation of thesis (1) is internally connected to the justification of thesis (2): the judgment of beauty has conceptual contents like appreciation and criticism. To justify thesis (2), I first explain what aesthetic appreciation and criticism consist in, meanwhile I will reconcile my view with the prevalent opinion that Kant claims aesthetic judgment must be non-conceptual. Finally, I deal with another apparent difficulty that Kant explicitly states that reflective judgment in general "has to find the universal for it [i.e., the object given]" (5: 179).

To start, let's look at the passage where Kant seems to deny that judgment of beauty can have concept or conceptual content:

> "*To find beauty in something*… [*does*] *not depend on any determinate concept*... [*but*] *a liking for the beautiful must depend upon reflection, regarding an object, that leads to some concept or other* (*but it is indeterminate which concept this is*)" (*5: 207*).

In fact, whenever Kant criticizes the idea that judgments of beauty can have concept, he always means only the determinate concept for cognition (e.g., 5: 207, 5: 220, 5: 222, 5: 229, 5: 282 5: 287). As Kant reiterates, a determinate concept is what the object is meant to be, and therefore an antecedent rule that determines the relevant features that the object is supposed to "exhibit" (5: 192, 5: 343). But Kant also writes, "the liking of beauty must depend on reflection of the object" which "leads to some concepts or other, only indeterminate" (5: 207). I think Kant is not denying that the judgment of beauty has conceptual content, but instead argues that it has conceptual content different in kind from cognitions.

First of all, that the judgment of beauty requires conceptual understanding is made clear by Kant when he states that judgments of beauty are "sharpened by practice" and by "learning" of classical models (5: 282 – 3). Kant points out, aesthetic cultivation is essential to "common sense of taste", since cultivation initiates us into "a new way of thinking", and "broadens" our judgments (5: 295). Thus the judgment of beauty is an acquired intellectual capacity, not a causal "stimulus-reaction" mechanism, nor is it marked by a certain expression of admiration or mental episode. An empty exclamation of "Beautiful!" alone cannot suffice an aesthetic judgment. If a Russian does not understand English but tells us he finds a piece of English sonnet marvelous, we would not count him as making any judgment at all①. Kant also holds that conceptual understanding enhances one's taste of natural beauty, which according to him is "freer" than dependent artistic beauty (5: 229). Since natural beauty symbolizes morality, Kant argues, the deeper one's moral understanding is, the better one will appreciate the beauty of nature (5: 353). And "no matter how free", our judgment of taste "would fail… if each subject had to start from nothing but the crude predisposition given him by nature" (5: 283).

Further, even a sincere and meaningful exclamation will not suffice a pure judgment of beauty, since Kant also differentiates the interested liking of the sensible and the disinterested liking of the beauty (5: 203 – 4). I argue that an essential mark of the disinterested judgment of beauty is the judger's capacity of properly appreciating and criticizing the singular aesthetic object. Unlike the interested liking, appreciation and criticism do not merely express one's arbitrary and

① This example is given by Wittgenstein, in his *Lecture on Aesthetics* (1967: I. 17).

private preference, but also guides others with common sense to judge and appreciate the object in the same way. And this "guiding" or "letting others see" is where the universal validity or communicability of aesthetic judgments come from. Kant points out, the task of art critics is precisely to "correct and broaden our judgments of taste… through examples" (5: 286). When an art critic composes an essay on a certain artwork, the quality of his aesthetic appreciation depends on his capacity of pointing out the work's aesthetic aspects in virtue of which the object is to be judged beautiful, and of guiding his readers to see the beauty themselves①. Similarly, an aesthetic "criticism" in the narrow sense "corrects" our erroneous judgments, as well as gives instructive advice to the artist for how to improve his works. For greater art critics, like Gombrich or John Berger, they not only guide the audiences to see the beauty or defect of one single aesthetic object, but also "broadens" their "ways of thinking" and "ways of seeing" in general, i. e., they cultivate our aesthetic "common sense".

In analyzing the specific aesthetic qualities, however, a judgment of beauty does not derive its normativity from the authority of any objective rule of beauty, but only from the "example", i. e., the aesthetic object. Certainly, in most cases the art critic knows relevant rules, which Kant also regards necessary for properly judging artworks as well as for the genius to create any great work (5: 318). But learning those rules are only one among many necessary steps towards cultivating proper aesthetic ways of thinking and seeing. For an aesthetic judgment, what is at stake is to point out the harmonious composition, or the lack of it, of this singular aesthetic object. If a composer comments on a piece to "lower the piano, then the concerto is perfect", then the lowering of the piano is the end of that criticism, not a means for any further end. In Kant's words, "we linger in our contemplation of the beautiful", and become fully "occupied" by the

① Katalin Makkai's view seems close to mine when she writes, "critical description [in aesthetics], unlike ordinary communication, does not designate the quality it communicates… its point, rather, is to get us to see-to give us *directions* for perceiving-*a* quality" (Makkai, 2009: 394).

object, "without further aim" except our aesthetic "reflection" itself (5: 222).

Finally, the aesthetic judgment of beauty thus understood is a "free-play". In aesthetic discourses, there can be no single correct answer to the evaluation of an artwork like a mathematical proof. On the contrary, as I already suggested above, the greatest art critics are just those who can "broaden" our ways of thinking and seeing. Thus understood, aesthetic criticism is precisely a pleasant "free game [*Spiel*]": it contains inexhaustive possibilities, though at the same time is normatively constrained. Good art criticisms let us see things in an artwork that we didn't see before, but in an important sense we feel these same things have always already been there.

I've explained that the aesthetic mode of conceptualization in judgments of beauty consists inappreciation and criticism. Now a last problem remains. Kant explicitly states that, "reflective judgments [in general] try to find universal concept in the particular object" (5: 179), thus apparently contradicting my thesis (1) on judgments of beauty. My final task is to show how Kant's notion of reflective judgments can be compatible with my proposed reading.

A short answer to why Kant does not view aesthetic conceptualization as attempting to grasp the determinate concept of beauty is that the context where hemakes the claim about reflective judgment is only a discussion of theoretical cognition of laws of nature, and aesthetic judgment of beauty has not yet been introduced in section 4 of the introduction (5: 179 – 181).

The longer path will find recourse to Kant's discussion of "ideas" in *Critique of Pure Reason*, in relation to "aesthetic ideas of the supersensible", which is another name Kant gives for the determinate concepts of beauty (5: 314, 343). In *First Critique*, Kant introduces the "dialectical inferences of reason", which refer to reason's illegitimate attempts to grasp "rational ideas" i.e., soul, world, and God. Kant argues, since in intuition "we can have no acquaintance with an object that corresponds to an [rational] idea", dialectical inferences of reason do not contribute anything positive about human understanding, but reveal only "unavoidable illusions" generated when we transgress the legitimate boundary of human reason (B396 – 8). Therefore, these inferences about the supersensible are not proper parts of empirical cognition, but exemplify pathological symptoms of reason and need a cure.

Now I suggest that we understand Kant's aesthetic ideas analogous to his discussion of rational ideas. While rational ideas are concepts that lie beyond adequate intuition, the aesthetic ideas are, by contrast, supersensible ideas which "human understanding with its concepts never reaches" (5: 342 – 3). Therefore, any attempt to grasp a determinate aesthetic idea and attain the objective rule of beauty is "a fruitless endeavor", not because our aesthetic conceptualization is always in adequate; but because, analogous to inferences of the supersensible, the attempt for the rule of beauty also lies beyond the legitimate scope of aesthetic judgment proper.① We could try in vain to reach aesthetic ideas and strive for a principle of beauty. But then we transgress the legitimate scope of aesthetic judgments and venture for "something that is impossible and intrinsically contradictory" (5: 231).②

① Thus my conceptualist view differs from what I would call the quasi-conceptualist view, represented by Henry Allison. The quasi-subjectivist rightly rejects the subjectivist, but wrongly argues the aesthetic conceptualization is an attempt to grasp the aesthetic ideas. As Allison writes, "[in free-play,] understanding is 'energized' to *grasp the rule that seems to underlie* this apprehended content." But there are "an indeterminate number of possible conceptualizations…, *none of which is fully adequate*, thereby occasioning further reflection" (Allison, 2001: 51). Ginsborg rightly points out, "what Kant describes as our lingering in our contemplation of the beautiful [should] be the result of our continually renewed efforts… which are *fully adequate*" (Ginsborg, 2003: 98) Therefore, Allison's quasi-conceptualist is faced with Ginsborg's "displeasure challenge: since such "trying to find aesthetic ideas" is necessarily "a failure of our cognitive faculties to arrive at an adequate conceptualization," it will produce displeasure instead of pleasure (Ginsborg, 2003: 98 – 101).

② In Wittgenstein's word, this "trying" violates the very grammar of beauty, thereby is logically senseless.

## Concluding Remarks

To conclude, in this essay, based on my criticism of the subjectivist reading, I offered my alternative conceptualist account of Kant's aesthetics. I argued that the judgment of beauty is a full-fledged conceptual judgment which consists of appreciation and criticism, and that a priori principle of "subjective purposiveness" refers to a generic concept which contains at least two species-neither is identical with a salient mental state. My account thus has two advantages over the subjectivist reading of Kant's aesthetics. First, my account of aesthetic judgments is more plausible on its own term, since it does not reduce the experience of beauty to a contentless mental state, and makes room for rich conceptual contents in aesthetic discourse. Further, my account avoids the internal instability of the subjectivist view, which obscures the status of free-play in Kant's holistic conception of judgment.

But my subjectivist opponent can object that an important issue remains unsolved, namely, how can my account reconcile with Kant's explicit claim that aesthetic pleasure is a subjective feeling (5: 206 – 7), or "must rest on a mere sensation" (5: 286)? To reply, I think this essay must postpone this difficult question regarding the relation between sensation and aesthetic pleasure, for two reasons. (1) Exegetically, Kant's own attitude towards this question is itself controversial. Just to give a few examples, in the same place Kant claims that aesthetic pleasure is a subjective feeling, he also explicitly states that "liking of beauty must depend on reflection of the object, and differentiates itself from the agreeableness which rests entirely on sensation" (5: 207). Again, in the famous section 9, Kant is even more ambivalent in exclusively identifying aesthetic pleasure with either sensation or judgment. ① Therefore, I suggest, instead of taking for granted that pleasure and conceptual content are mutually exclusive, we should rather pose the exegetic question whether the older Kantian conception of pleasure still holds onto *Third Critique* at all. Accordingly, (2) by showing the exegetic and philosophical difficulties of reducing Kant's aesthetic pleasure to mere feeling, this essay serves as a necessary theoretical preparation for further discussion of the relation between pleasure and sensation in general. ②

Therefore, if the arguments presented here do hold, this essay on Kantian aesthetic judgment then gestures towards the further investigation of the nature of pleasure in general, the proper analysis of which requires not only interpretive cogency internal to Kant's system, but also sound philosophical understanding in its own term. This work remains to be done.

**References**

Allison, Henry, 2001, *Kant's Theory of Taste*, Cambridge University Press.

Ameriks, Karl, 2003, "How to Save Kant's Deduction of Taste as Objective", *Interpreting Kant's Critiques*, Oxford: Clarendon Press, 285 - 306.

Bell, David, 1987, "The Art of Judgment", *Mind*, New Series, Vol. 96, No. 382, April 1987, 221 - 244.

Cavell, Stanley, 1976, "Aesthetic Problems in Modern Philosophy", *Must We Mean What We Say?*, Cambridge University Press, 73 - 96.

Crawford, Donald, 1970, "Reason-Giving in Kant's Aesthetics" in *The Journal of Aesthetics and Art Criticism*, Vol. 28, No. 4, 505 - 510

Ginsborg, Hannah, 1991, "On the Key to Kant's Critique of Taste", *Ginsborg* (2015), 32 - 52.

——, 1997, "Lawfulness Without a Law: Kant on the Free Play of Imagination and Understanding", *Ginsborg* (2015), 53 - 93.

——, 2003, "Aesthetic Judging and the Intentionality of Pleasure", *Ginsborg* (2015), 94 - 110.

① The interpretation of section 9 has undergone extensive debates, see note 3 above.

② On this topic, Alexandra Newton (2017) gives an insightful discussion on "Kant on Animal and Human Pleasure" which distinguishes animal pleasure determined by instinct and human being's self-determined rational pleasure.

——, 2006, "Thinking the Particular as Contained Under the Universal", *Ginsborg* (2015), 148 - 169.

——, 2004, "Aesthetic Judgment and Perceptual Normativity", *Ginsborg* (2015), 170 - 201.

——, 2015, *The Normativity of Nature*, Harvard University Press.

Guyer, Paul, 1997, *Kant and the Claims of Taste*, Cambridge, Mass. : Harvard University Press.

Janaway, Christopher, 1997, "Kant's Aesthetics and the Empty Cognitive Stock", *Kant's Critique of the Power of Judgment*, Paul Guyer, ed. , Roman & Littlefield, 67 - 87.

Kant, Immanuel, 1987, *Critique of Judgement*, Trans. , Werner Pluhar, Hackett Publishing Company.

——, 1999, *Critique of Pure Reason*, Trans. , Paul, Guyer, Cambridge: Cambridge University Press.

Longuenesse, Béatrice, 2006, "Kant's Leading Thread in the Analytic of the Beautiful", *Aesthetics and Cognition in Kant's Critical Philosophy*, ed. , by Rebecca Kukla, Cambridge: Cambridge University Press.

Makkai, Katalin, 2009, "Kant on Recognizing Beauty", *European Journal of Philosophy* 18 (3), 385 - 413.

Moran, Richard, 2016, "The Topic of the Judgement of Beauty", *British Journal of Aesthetics*, Vol. 56, Number (4), 397 - 400.

Newton, Alexandra, 2017, "Kant on Human and Animal Pleasure", *Canadian Journal of Philosophy*, 47 (4), 518 - 540.

Sellars, Wilfrid, 1997, *Empiricism and the Philosophy of Mind*, Harvard University Press.

Wenzel, Christian Helmut, 2005, *An Introduction to Kant's Aesthetics: Core Concepts and Problems*, Wiley-Blackwell.

Wittgenstein, Ludwig, 1967, *Lectures and Conversations on Aesthetics, Psychology and Religious Belief*, Notes taken by Yorick Smythies, Rush Rhees and James Taylor, Edit, Cyril Barrett. University of California Press.

# Kant's Argument for Freedom in the *Groundwork*: A Response to Ameriks's Critique

Yang CHEN [*]

**Abstract**: In this paper, I intend to reconstruct Kant's argument for freedom in the *Groundwork* in light of Ameriks's challenge. Ameriks worries that the freedom justified in the Groundwork is merely phenomenological (Ameriks, 2003: 233). To defend Kant's argument against Ameriks's critique, I first specify phenomenological freedom into three kinds: (1) freedom is merely an illusion; (2) "free" actions are "internally" determined by sensible impulses; (3) freedom is necessitated by reason. I then argue that Kant successfully excludes the possibility of the second kind of phenomenological freedom and proves that the third kind does not undermine the concept of freedom. As for the first kind, I suggest that Kant cannot fully repudiate it. However, Kant offers enough reason to convince us of the opposite, viz., reason has actual causal efficacy, can be rationally (coherently) presupposed.

**Key words**: Freedom, Reason, Morality, Ameriks, *Groundwork*

## Introduction

Kant applies different approaches to justify human freedom in his different

* * Chen Yang, PhD candidate, Purdue University.

works. Normally Kant uses a transcendental argument: if morality is possible for human beings, the condition of morality, viz., freedom, should be possible for human beings as well. Nevertheless, such a transcendental argument is undermined by moral skepticism, according to which no moral facts can be taken for granted.[①] Thus, the argument in the *Groundwork* is of special significance because here Kant tries to justify human freedom almost *a priori*, without resorting to any facts of morality. A brief comparison with the first critique and the second critique can illustrate this point clearly.[②] In this first critique, Kant argues "that our reason has causality, or that we at least represent it to ourselves as having causality, is evident from the *imperatives* which in all matters of conduct we impose as rules upon our active powers" (KrV A547/B575)[③]. Similarly, in the second critique, Kant claims that "freedom is real, for this idea reveals itself through the moral law" (KpV 5, 4). Briefly speaking, Kant applies a similar transcendental argument in both critiques: since certain moral laws or imperatives are self-evident, the freedom, is thus justified.[④] Despite that this argument can be convincing for people with a strong moral sense, it does not work for any moral skeptics because there are no self-evident moral laws or imperatives for them. In the *Groundwork*, Kant's argument for freedom[⑤] is entirely

① Unsurprisingly, as any claims about Kant, this one is not uncontroversial. Nevertheless, scholars more or less agree that it is necessary to take moral skepticism into consideration if one wants to fully understand Kant's moral philosophy. For detailed discussion about the relationship between moral skepticism and Kant's moral philosophy, see (Stern, 2011) and (Ware, 2016b).

② For a detailed articulation of the development of Kant's concept of freedom see (Alison, 2020).

③ In this paper, all citations of Kant's work are in German pagination.

④ This argument parallels Kant's argument in the *Prolegomena*, where Kant argues that mathematics has already offered us paradigms of synthetic a priori judgments and then we only need to figure out how such judgments are possible.

⑤ Strictly speaking, Kant never directly argues for freedom in the *Groundwork*. He only argues that it is a necessary presupposition. Nevertheless, for the convenience of expression, I will use terms like "arguments for freedom".

different. [①] Not only does Kant not base the argument for freedom upon "self-evident" moral laws or imperatives, but he also resorts to the concept of freedom to justify *a priori* that "there really is such an imperative, that there is a practical law, which commands absolutely of itself and without any incentives" (G4, 425). Therefore, in the *Groundwork*, Kant should never refer to any moral facts to argue for freedom, otherwise his argument will be circular. In this sense, the *Groundwork* requires a different argument for freedom, which further addresses the concern of moral skepticism. Scholars have noticed the uniqueness of the argument in the *Groundwork*, though most of them believe that Kant later abandons this project in the *Groundwork*. Among them, Ameriks offers an interesting argument: in the *Groundwork*, Kant only justifies a phenomenological freedom, whereas only the absolute freedom can further guarantee autonomy and moral laws. *Pace* Ameriks, in this paper, I argue that the freedom justified in the *Groundwork* is far from merely phenomenological. Instead, Kant successfully shows that we can consistently presuppose the absolute freedom, which then guarantees moral laws. In light of this aim, I first analyze the structure and aim of Kant's argument for freedom in the *Groundwork*. Section 2 examines Kant's argument for the necessity of presupposing the idea of freedom for any practical rational beings. Third, I consider how Kant justifies human freedom. Finally, I investigate how Kant reconciles the potential contradiction between freedom and the law of nature[②].

---

① Scholars have noticed the uniqueness of the argument in the Groundwork since Henrich's and Beck's work, see (Henrich, 1960) and (Beck, 1960), though they believe that Kant abandons the deduction of freedom because he realized the problem of the *Groundwork*. Such interpretations are usually labelled as the Reversal reading. My anonymous reviewer kindly points out that there are indeed different interpretations of the argument in the *Groundwork*, some of which argue that the argument in the *Groundwork* also relies on moral facts, though in a different format, see (Ware, 2016A). I will explain in detail why I insist that the argument in the *Groundwork* differs from that in the critiques in section 1.

② By the law of nature, I mean the statement that every empirical event is fully determined by preceding events. In this sense, I use it interchangeably with empirical/sensible causations/determinations.

# 1 The Structure and Aim of Kant's Argument for Freedom in the*Groundwork*

Though this paper focuses on Kant's argument for freedom, it is necessary to briefly review the general structure of his argument in the third section of the-*Groundwork*. In the first two sections, Kant clarifies that human morality needs to be grounded by the categorical imperative. However, he has not yet justified the categorical imperative. In other words, Kant needs to show that the categorical imperative and morality are not merely "chimerical ideas without any truth" (G4, 445).① For this aim, Kant first introduces a new concept, viz., freedom, and then tries to derive the categorical imperative from it through the mediation of autonomy. However, even if we grant the validity of this deduction, a more fundamental problem remains: Kant has never demonstrated that freedom is possible for human beings. Indeed, according to the third antinomy in the first critique, such a demonstration is impossible. Therefore, Kant spends much effort in *Groundwork* III addressing two issues. First, Kant argues that freedom is a necessary presupposition for rational beings, and thus human beings to some extent. Second, he further tries to show that this presupposition of freedom does not transcend the limitations of human cognition and thereby can be reconciled with the law of nature.

With this framework in mind, we can now delve into several details. First, in Kant's argument, the subject of freedom switches back and forth between rational beings and human beings. On the one hand, Kant requires that freedom needs to

① I am indebted to my anonymous reviewer for the following clarification. Though the *Groundwork* starts with moral facts, the argument for freedom does not rely on those facts, because the structure of the *Groundwork* is indeed regressive. Kant starts with moral facts in common sense, and then seek to ground them upon the categorical imperative. Then in section 3, Kant needs to find a proper foundation for the categorical imperative. Ware makes a similar point: "Kant's argument in *Groundwork* III rests on a moral conception of the intelligible world" (Ware, 2016a: 116). I will address Ware's critique in section 3.

be shown as a property of all rational beings rather than just human beings. On the other hand, the morality eventually justified by freedom is in the form of categorical imperative, which applies only to human beings, who can be affected by sensible desires as well. In this sense, merely showing that rational beings are capable of free actions is not enough. Kant needs to show that freedom applies to human beings. ① Someone might use a simple syllogism to resolve this problem:

> Major Premise: All rational beings are free.
>
> Minor Premise: Human beings are rational.
>
> Conclusion: Human beings are free.

However, this argument is invalid because human beings are not fully rational, insofar as they are also determinable by sensible desires. Therefore, unless Kant successfully reconciles the potential contradiction between freedom and sensible determinations concerning human beings, the argument for freedom should not be regarded as valid.

Second, as was noted, the concept of freedom functions to justify morality through the mediation of autonomy. This indeed leads us into a further question: what kind of freedom can justify autonomy. The crucial distinction here is not that between transcendental freedom and practical freedom that Kant puts forward in the first critique. ② On the contrary, it is the distinction between absolute freedom and phenomenological freedom that matters here. Phenomenological freedom, as suggested by Ameriks, seriously challenges Kant's argument for freedom seriously. Briefly speaking, it refers to illusionary freedom. In other words, Ameriks worries that human beings believe that they are free, but they are in fact completely determined by something beyond their consciousness. Indeed, Ameriks's use of this term is ambiguous and there can be at least three different kinds of phe-

---

① In this paper, I will not consider how the categorical imperative can be deduced from human freedom. For this topic, see Schönecker (2012: 229).

② Indeed, since transcendental freedom is the foundation of practical freedom (KrV, A533/B561), Kant's argument for freedom in the *Groundwork* involves both.

nomenological freedom. First, freedom can be phenomenological insofar as its causal efficacy is illusionary (Ameriks, 2003: 236, PF1 hereafter). For example, I believe that I freely drink a cup of whereas that I drink a cup of water does not happen at all. Moreover, freedom can be phenomenological insofar as the subject is further determined by external causes. This can further diverge into two different kinds. Second, our free actions are further determined by sensible impulses (Ameriks, 2003: 243, PF2 hereafter). For example, I think I freely drink a cup of water while in fact I am driven by the impulse of thirst. Third, the subject is further determined by reason in the intelligible world. In this case, it can be fully rational while unfree (Ameriks, 2003: 233, PF3 hereafter). For example, I think I freely accepted a friend's suggestion to do more sport while in fact I was convinced or even forced by reason to accept such a suggestion. Ameriks believes that none of these three kinds of phenomenological freedom can justify autonomy.

However, according to Kant, autonomy is "a possible giving of universal law through its maxims" (G4, 439). First, Kant does not regard autonomy as an arbitrary process of legislation. On the contrary, the law given by autonomy should be examined by reason so that it can be a universal law. Therefore, the autonomous agent is indeed guided by its reason. Moreover, Kant stresses that this process of legislation involved in autonomy is a possible process rather than an actual one. In other words, as long as the agent takes a law which can be regarded as if given by himself/herself, the agent is autonomous. In this sense, the autonomous agent can take suggestions or guidance from others as long as they are examined and then approved by his/her own reason.① As a result, a free subject can be guided by other rational beings, as long as such guidance is examined and

① Kain suggests that we should pay attention to the distinction between an author and a legislator of a law (Kain, 2004: 260). This leads us to notice that Kant never claims that an autonomous agent should be the author of any law. Indeed, autonomous agents are self-legislative insofar as they can examine and then approve or deny a law as if this law is given by themselves.

then approved or denied by his/her own reason. Therefore, PF3 can justify autonomy. In other words, Kant only needs to show that freedom for which he argues in the *Groundwork* is neither PF1 nor PF2.

Based on the above analysis, first, Kant's argument for freedom needs to reconcile itself with sensible determinations. Moreover, Kant needs to show that freedom justified in the *Groundwork* is either PF1 or PF2.

## 2 Freedom as Necessary Presupposition for All Rational Beings

Clarifying the structure of Kant's argument, in this section, I examine how Kant argues for the freedom of rational beings per se.

As was noted, since Kant believes that morality in his discussion is not just for human beings but for all rational beings, the foundation of morality, viz., freedom, should also be freedom for all rational beings. As Kant puts it, "since morality serves as a law for us only as rational beings … freedom must also be proved as a property for all rational beings" (G4, 447). In other words, any argument for freedom that relies on human nature or experience is not enough for Kant. Therefore, Kant's argument for the freedom commences analyzing rational beings per se. Scholars have realized this characteristic of Kant's argument. However, they either stick to the moral argument① or believe the argument in this subsection is incomplete②. However, we should notice that the moral argument does not work in the *Groundwork* because here morality needs to be justified by freedom. Moreover, in this subsection, Kant does try to argue for the necessity of

① For example, Timmermann (2007) claims that "for practical-i. e. moral-purposes we must conceive of ourselves and all other rational beings as free" (127).

② For example, Sedgwick (2008) claims that "he does not suggest that we yet have any warrant for supposing that there are beings that 'cannot act otherwise than under the idea of freedom'" (179).

presupposing the idea of freedom rather than just take freedom as a bare presupposition:

> *Now I assert that to every rational being we must necessarily lend the idea of freedom also, under which alone he acts. For in such a being we think of a reason that is practical, that is, has causality with respect to its objects. Now, one cannot possibly think of a reason that would consciously receive direction from any other quarter with respect to its judgments, since the subject would then attribute the determination of his subject not to his reason but to an impulse* (G4, 448).

Kant's argument is rather straightforward. As a rational being, ideally①, any determination of his/her subject should be from reason rather than anywhere else. According to Kant, judgments are nothing more than the subsuming of particular representations or actions② under general rules. Since a rational being should not be determined by anything except its③ own reason, concerning judgments it allows no guidance except that from its reason. Therefore, general rules, under which particular representations/actions are subsumed, are from reason and nothing else. Then if any rational being is practical, all its actions should be directed by reason alone. According to Kant's definition of negative freedom: "freedom would be that property of such causality that it can be efficient independently of alien

① Post-modern philosophers tend to disagree with Kant insofar as they believe that such reason does not exist. However, this does not influence Kant's argument here. Kant's argument does not rely on the actual existence of any rational being. Rather, he is only analyzing the concept of a rational being as such.

② Alison (2020) believes that this argument concerning judgments only justifies logical freedom while leaves either practical freedom or transcendental freedom unsettled (320). However, judgments are not necessarily about logic. As Kant later suggests, a judgment can be "upon actions as being such that they *ought to have been done even though they were not done*" (G4, 445). Therefore, freedom justified here is not limited to logical freedom.

③ I will use it or the corresponding possessive pronoun to refer to a particular rational being.

causes determining it" (G4, 446). In this sense, the practical rational being[①], whose action is determined by its own reason alone, is practically free. Moreover, if a rational being can be practical, it will start a causal series independent of sensible determinations. In this sense, rational being is not merely practically free but also transcendentally free (A533/B561).

We should notice that this argument is conditional or hypothetical.[②] Kant has not demonstrated that rational beings are practical, viz., "having causality with respect to its object" (G4, 448). He only shows that if rational beings are practical, it will be free. In other words, Kant demonstrates that any rational will is necessarily free while he does not argue that there exist such rational wills. In Kant's review of this subsection, he summarizes that "we saw only that we must presuppose it [freedom] if we want to think of a being as rational and endowed with consciousness of his causality with respect to actions" (G4, 449). Here we encounter the challenge of PF1: if there is no rational will at all, the idea of freedom will be an illusion. However, we should notice that it is not the idea of freedom but the existence of any rational will that is called into doubt in this challenge. In other words, it is a challenge with extreme prejudices against any rationalism rather than just the idea of freedom. In the *Groundwork*, as I will show later, Kant does try to address this challenge though he does not completely resolve it.[③]

## 3 The Freedom for Human Beings

Though Kant has shown that the idea of freedom is necessarily presupposed

---

① For Kant, practical reason, reason with causal efficacy, or rational will can be used interchangeably.

② Ameriks also holds that the argument about rational beings is hypothetical, see (Ameriks, 1981: 62).

③ Even if Kant fails to fully justify the existence of any rational will, it is not a problem specific to the concept of freedom. This challenge indeed undermines the foundation of rationalism, viz., the possibility of a practical reason, and influences any arguments built upon it.

for any rational beings who are practical, he has not shown human beings can be free. As was noted, it cannot be proved by a simple syllogism because human beings are usually driven by sensible impulses and thereby, they are not fully rational if not completely irrational. Therefore, Kant needs to prove that: first, human beings can be rational despite the hindrance of sensible impulses; second, the freedom for human beings does not contradict the law of nature. I will explicate how Kant addresses the first problem in this section and leave the second for section 4.

To argue that such freedom is possible for human beings, Kant first tries to show that human beings can be free in some sense. Kant reminds us of human's cognitive process in the first critique. ① To cognize any objects, humans need to be affected by objects first. If something never has any causal interaction with us, humans will never be able to cognize it. Moreover, merely being affected by the object is not enough for us to have any cognition of it. Indeed, humans need to actively produce certain necessary concepts so that they can synthesize the manifolds of our being affected. Though this is just a rough summary of the cognitive process of humans, it is already clear that certain spontaneity of human beings, viz., the active production of concepts by understanding, is necessary for human cognition. As a result, Kant makes a distinction between the world of sense (sensible world) and the world of understanding (intelligible world) (*Groundwork*, 4, 451). In the world of sense, humans are affected by external causes while in the world of understanding they actively produce concepts.

However, the spontaneity of understanding is not purely active. As Kant frequently suggests in the first critique, the application of concepts should be limited to possible experience. In other words, "it [understanding] can produce from its activity no other concepts than those which serve merely *to bring sensible representations under rules* and thereby to unite them in one consciousness" (*Groundw-*

---

① For an insightful work on the similarity between the freedom in cognition and the practical freedom, see (Kohl, 2015).

ork, 4, 452, original emphasis). Therefore, the spontaneity of understanding is mixed with the receptivity of the sensibility. Kant argues that humans are capable of a far purer activity, viz., reason. Different from understanding, reason does not limit its own creation, viz., the idea, to the sphere of possible experience and thereby it does not mingle its pure self-activity with the receptivity of the sensibility. In Kant's words, "reason... shows in what we call 'ideas' a spontaneity so pure that it thereby goes beyond anything that sensibility can ever afford it, and proves its highest occupation in distinguishing the world of sense and the world of understanding from each other and thereby marking out limits for the understanding itself" (*Groundwork*, 4, 452). As a result, by creating ideas, which do not blend with any possible experience, reason indeed completely elevates humans into the world of understanding, in which they are completely active.

Here I can exclude the possibility of PF2 from Kant's argument for freedom. Since the freedom of human beings is in the intelligible world, which cannot be influenced by anything in the sensible world, we do not need to worry that our freedom is indeed driven by hidden impulses.

However, here we still encounter a serious problem. Kant argues that reason's capacity of creating ideas elevates us to the world of understanding, where we are purely active.① However, according to this argument, we are active only insofar as our reason can create ideas. In this sense, this spontaneity of reason is far from either transcendental freedom, which is the capacity of initiating a series of causal relations, or negative practical freedom, which refers to the property of will's independence of external determinations, not to mention the positive practical freedom. As a result, there is a gap between the theoretical

① Ware argues that the intelligible world is indeed a moral concept (Ware, 2016: 122). However, as I have shown, the intelligible world is "derived" from the spontaneity of cognitive reason, which is independent of any moral facts. Ware is fully aware of this interpretation (Ware, 2016: 130), because it pushes Kant to transcend the cognitive limitation set up in the first critique. Different from Ware, I argue that Kant can consistently presuppose a non-moral concept of intelligible world, without transcending the cognitive limitation.

spontaneity of reason and freedom. Indeed, this gap can hardly be bridged in Kant's philosophical system. This problem indeed parallels the challenge of PF1. Kant has shown that human beings can be active and spontaneous in the intelligible world, but he does not show that such activity and spontaneity can be practical, viz., having causal influences upon objects. This problem is quite pressing. If human beings are active only in the world of intelligence, how can they have any causal influence upon their objects, some of which are supposed to belong to the world of sense? Both problems push us to reconcile the tension between freedom and laws of nature. In the next section, I will discuss Kant's resolution to this tension, which entails at least a partial solution to both problems here.

## 4 Two Kinds of Causality

As was noted, Kant argues that freedom is possible for human beings because they can be elevated into the intelligible world, where they are independent of any external determinations. However, a crucial problem remains unresolved. Both transcendental freedom and practical freedom requires that human beings should be capable of influencing the sensible world. Nevertheless, according to Kant, it seems that there cannot be any causal relationship between the intelligible world and the sensible world.

To address this problem, Kant distinguishes two kinds of causality (KrV A538/B566; KpV 5, 98; G4, 457). The first kind dwells in the sensible world and thereby is under the temporal order. For any event, it will be determined or caused by other events antecedent to it. Since these past events were not under the control of human beings, there can be no freedom in this temporal order. In other words, human beings cannot be free in the sensible world because there were always past events that escape the control of human beings. Besides the temporal causation in the sensible world, Kant reminds us of the causation in the intelligible world: "the human being, who this way regards himself as an intelligence, thereby puts himself in a different order of things and in a relation to determining grounds of an altogether different kind when he thinks of himself as intelligence endowed with a will, and consequently with causality" (G4, 457). However, the problem of how we should make sense of the causality in the intelligible world remains. Kant gives us several hints. First, since this causality belongs to the intelligible world, we can have little theoretical cognition of it, otherwise, we will transcend the limitation of our cognition. Despite the limitation of our cognition, we can still know something analytic about the intelligible causality. Primarily, in the intelligible world, "pure reason independent of sensibility, gives the law" (G4, 457). In other words, it is reason itself that initiates a causal series in the intelligible world. Moreover, the causal relationship in the intelligible world is not subsumed to the temporal order. In this sense, there is no need to worry about being determined by past events.

Given these facts, it is natural to infer that the intelligible causality differs completely from the sensible one. However, Kant claims that these two kinds of causality interact with each other. In the first critique, Kant illustrates this point clearly by an example (KrV A554/B582). Kant suggests that we think about a voluntary action of any human being, e. g., a malicious lie. We can find many empirical factors that may lead to this action, like defective education, bad company, viciousness of a natural disposition, levity and thoughtlessness, etc. All these factors seem to completely determine the action of the human being. However, Kant does not think these empirical factors can function as the sufficient condition of any voluntary action. Rather, Kant insists that the human being, as an agent, can "begin in this action an entirely new series of consequence" despite all preceding conditions (KrV A555/B583). According to this example, Kant believes that reason alone is the sufficient cause of any voluntary action of the human being. [1] Although many human actions seem to be predetermined by preceding empirical facts, Kant insists that reason has causal efficacy upon empirical events insofar as it is always able to begin a new series of consequences independent of any preceding facts. As Kant puts it, "reason as a cause that irrespective of all the above-mentioned empirical conditions could have determined, and ought to have determined, the agent to act otherwise" (KrV A555/B583).

Now that Kant holds that the human being can always originate a new series of events independent of any preceding empirical facts (KrV A553/B581), it is natural to infer that Kant indeed suggests that reason as a causality not only interacts with empirical causations but also interrupts the latter. However, Kant believes that any single action, "with all the past which determines it, belongs to a single phenomenon of his character, which he gives to himself and in accordance with which he imputes to himself, as a cause independent of all sensibility, the cause of those appearances" (KpV 5, 98). In this sense, reason as a cause of appearances does not jump into the empirical causal series. On the contrary, reason originates a new series of empirical events by giving the agent a new character, which includes a new series of events. Moreover, we should notice that reason as a causality of human actions or empirical events, is outside the temporal order. In Kant's words, "in respect of the intelligible character, of which the empirical character is the sensible schema, there can be no *before* and *after*; every action, irrespective of its relation in time to other appearances, is the immediate effect of the intelligible character of pure reason" (KrV A553/B581). In other words, reason as a cause does not interrupt the empirical causations. On the contrary, the intelligible causality of reason, which is outside the temporal order, grounds the empirical causations, which is under the temporal order. Every action of human beings can be an immediate effect of pure reason. Such intelligible cau-

---

① Here I do not assume that humans are capable of voluntary actions. I refer to Kant's example of voluntary actions to illustrate that he thinks that the intelligible causality has empirical results. Later, I will show how Kant defends this claim in the framework of the *Groundwork*.

sation expresses itself in the sensible world through empirical causations. In this sense, reason's capacity of originating a new series of events refers to nothing more than its causal relationship to a new character, which will be expressed in a different series of empirical events. To conclude, reason does have causal efficacy to appearances insofar as it can always originate a new series of empirical events.① Nevertheless, it does not interrupt the empirical causations because it dwells in a completely different order.

The final question for Kant is how he knows the existence of causality in the intelligible world if we cannot have theoretical cognition of it. Put differently, how can Kant exclude the possibility that intelligible causality is just an illusion? In both the first critique and the second critique, Kant responds that intelligible causality is necessary because it is the only way to make sense of moral obligations (KrV A555/B583; KpV 5, 99). Nevertheless, as was noted, in the *Groundwork*, Kant cannot resort to any moral facts, like moral obligations, to argue for freedom. Therefore, Kant admits that it is a presupposition that reason has causality upon empirical events. Indeed, Kant even claims that "reason would overstep all its bounds if it took upon itself to *explain how* pure reason can be practical" (G4, 459). In this sense, Kant never tries to argue that pure reason can be practical in the *Groundwork*. This might not be a satisfactory answer to the problems, viz., why reason has causal efficacy; or why Kant claims transcendental and practical freedom for human beings whereas only justifies theoretical spontaneity, puzzling us throughout this paper. Nevertheless, Kant at least offers a defense to this presupposition. Presupposing that empirical causations are indeed sensible schema of the intelligible causation of reason, Kant at least reconciles the potential contradiction between freedom and empirical causations. In other words, though Kant cannot demonstrate that practical will has causal efficacy, he does

---

① One way to clarify this kind of causality is put forward by Watkins, who hold that such causality is not temporal but substantial, see (Watkins, 2005). For the application of the substantial causality in Kant's moral philosophy, see (Ameriks, 1992: 224).

demonstrate that there is one consistent way to presuppose that practical will has causal efficacy. ① As a result, the presupposition of the causal efficacy of reason is at least a reasonable presupposition.

## Conclusion

In the *Groundwork*, Kant tries to argue for freedom so that he can lay a solid foundation for morality. First, by analyzing the concept of rational beings, Kant argues that any practical rational being is free. Second, he argues that human beings can be free insofar as they can be elevated to the intelligible world by reason. Both arguments confront a serious problem: why do we presuppose that pure reason is practical? Kant partly addresses this problem by discussing the relationship between intelligible causality and sensible causality. Despite occupying different "worlds" and thereby obtaining different orders, they can interact with each other insofar as the intelligible causality can always start a new series of sensible causations. Nevertheless, since we cannot have theoretical cognition of the intelligible world, this claim is nothing more than a reasonable presupposition. In this sense, Kant does offer a defense of the possibility that pure reason can be practical. However, he can never demonstrate it because such a demonstration transcends the limitation of human cognition.

In the *Groundwork*, Kant applies a different approach toward freedom from both the first and the second critique. In the first critique and the second critique, Kant resorts to certain moral facts, like moral obligations or the "ought to" to ar-

① One might question the meaning of this paper: why we bother changing the presupposition of moral facts to the presupposition of the causal efficacy of reason, now that neither can help Kant escape the challenge of skepticism. Part of the answer is that this, from my perspective, is Kant's actual project in the *Groundwork*. Moreover, to question moral facts, one only need to be a moral skeptic. However, to question the causal efficacy of practical reason, one needs to question reason in general. In this sense, Kant does find a solider foundation for morality in the *Groundwork*.

gue for freedom. Nevertheless, this argument is not strong enough for moral skeptics, who do not believe these moral facts. Therefore, in the *Groundwork*, Kant tries to justify freedom from reason alone. Despite his brilliant argument, Kant must *presuppose* that pure reason is practical. Upon such a presupposition, Kant successfully argues that human beings, insofar as they belong to the intelligible world, are free. This approach toward freedom addresses certain worries of moral skepticism and the PF challenge. As was noted, there are three different senses of phenomenological freedom. PF3 does not influence Kant's argument in the *Groundwork*. His argument successfully excludes PF2. As for PF1, Kant does not argue against such a possibility, viz., the causal efficacy of reason is indeed an illusion. He only defends that the opposite possibility, viz., pure reason is practical, is a reasonable presupposition insofar as it is self-consistent and does not contradict the law of nature. This is not a fully satisfactory answer. However, it is not a problem specific to Kant's argument for freedom in the *Groundwork*. More or less, this problem challenges all theories of rational morality, if not all theories of rationalism.

## References

**Kant's work:**

Kant, I., & Wood, A., 1996, *Practical Philosophy* (The Cambridge Edition of the Works of Immanuel Kant), ed., by M. Gregor, Cambridge: Cambridge University Press.

Kant, I., & Smith, N. K., 1929, *Critique of Pure Reason*. London: The Macmillan Press.

**Other works:**

Alison, H., 2020, *Kant's Conception of Freedom: A Developmental and Critical Analysis*, Cambridge: Cambridge University Press.

Ameriks, K., 2003, *Interpreting Kant's Critiques*, Oxford: Oxford University Press.

Kain, P., 2004, "Self-Legislation in Kant's Moral Philosophy", *Archiv für Geschichte der Philosophie*, 86 (3), 257 – 306.

Schönecker, D., 2012, "A free will and a will under moral laws are the same", Kant's concept of autonomy and his thesis of analyticity in Groundwork III, *Kant on Moral Autonomy*, ed., by Sensen, O., Cambridge: Cambridge University Press, 2012.

Sedgwick, S. , 2008, *Kant's Groundwork of the Metaphysics of Morals: An Introduction* (Cambridge Introductions to Key Philosophical Texts), Cambridge: Cambridge University Press.

Timmermann, J. , 2007, *Kant's Groundwork of the Metaphysics of Morals: A Commentary*, Cambridge: Cambridge University Press.

# 胡塞尔现象学中的时间客观性问题

郭世恒（KWOK Sai Hang）*

**摘要：**学界一般认为胡塞尔的时间意识现象学旨在探讨意识的超越论建构。这个解读经常导致一种误解，即胡塞尔的现象学排除了日常意义下独立于意识之外的客观时间，乃至无法谈论一个不被经验的时间，比如远古时期等。这个解读导致胡塞尔现象学在法国当代哲学传统中多被诟病。本文试图证明，通过对客观时间的还原，胡塞尔的现象学并没有排除客观时间，而是企图获得时间客观性的根基。这个问题意识可以追溯至奥古斯丁的时间问题，即时间三相（过去、现在、将来）引致的悖论。在这个问题意识下，自然态度下把时间理解为一个客观的流淌过程恰好是可疑的。相反，胡塞尔的现象学能给予一个可理解（comprehensible）的回应：根据胡塞尔于《贝尔瑙手稿》的研究，时间的客观性来自于不同的刚性时间形式（Zeitform）或时间秩序（Zeitordnung）。时间三相只是对象被给予的时间模态（Zeitmodalitäten）。笔者认为这个通过现象学方法获得的客观时间理论，才更符合我们真正在日常生活乃至自然科学中使用的时间观。

**关键词：**胡塞尔；现象学；时间；意识；客观性；观念

* 郭世恒，澳门大学哲学与宗教学部。

# Problem of the Objectivity of Time in Husserl's Phenomenology

**Abstract**: It is believed that Husserl's phenomenology of time consciousness aims at discovering the transcendental constitution of consciousness. This interpretation usually leads to the misunderstanding that Husserl's phenomenology has entirely refuted any possibility of conceiving time as external to our subjective experience, such as the objective time under the natural attitude or the ancient antiquity. This misunderstanding has led to many criticisms of Husserl, especially in contemporary French philosophy. In this paper, I aim to show that the phenomenological reduction of objective time does not entail the refutation of it; instead, it is a method towards reconstruction of the objectivity of time. This project refers back to Augustine's question of time which uncovers the paradoxical nature of the three time-phases—past, present, and future. Under this premise, time conceived under the natural attitude as an objective flow is indeed problematic. Husserl's phenomenology can be regarded as a comprehensible response to this puzzle. According to Husserl's *Bernau Manuscripts*, objectivity of time is rendered by rigid temporal forms (*Zeitform*) and temporal orders (*Zeitordnung*). The three time-phases are only time-modalities through which an object is given. I argue that this phenomenological analysis of the objectivity of time is coherent with how time is actually understood in daily life as well as in natural sciences.

**Keywords**: Husserl; Phenomenology; Time; Consciousness; Objectivity; Idea

学界一般认为胡塞尔的时间意识现象学旨在探讨意识的超越论建构，对时间意识的探讨因此预设了对客观时间的排除。这种流行的看法很可能来自于胡塞尔（1996：203）在《纯粹现象学通论》中对时间意识的阐述：

> 意识由于现象学还原不仅失去了与物质现实及其（尽管是间接的）空间体现的统觉“联系”（这当然是一个隐喻），而且也失去了它在宇宙时间秩序中的地位。那样一种本质上属于体验本身的时间，以及它的现在、在前和在后的、通过它们具有确定样式的同时性和相续性等等的所与性样式，既未被也不应被太阳的任何位置，钟表或任何物理手段所度量。

在这段论述中，自然态度下理解的客观时间（客观自在地流淌、可以被物理计算的一维时间序列）被排除在现象学时间之外；现象学的时间，完全是作为体验本身展开的内在领域。这条研究进路很容易让现象学被批评为一种主观主义（subjectivism）、内在主义（internalism）或关联主义（correlationism）的哲学，即无法研究一个完全独立于所有主体关联的实在。尤其在关于时间的问题上，一个典型的批评是胡塞尔难以正确地讨论先于人类存在的远古时间或者个人出生前的历史时间。[①] 对这些批评者来说，因为胡塞尔错误地把时间还原到意识的内在性之中，因此错失了很多客观时间的重要面相。[②]

然而，现象学是否真的不谈论，甚至不能谈论自然态度下的客观时间？事实上，胡塞尔早已说明，现象学还原只是把还原的对象置入括号之中：“它［被还原之物］仍然在那里，正如被置入括号者在括号中一样，正像被排除者在包容范围之外一样。我们也可以说：设定［事物客观存在］是一种体验，但我们不‘利用’它，而且这当然不被理解作我们失去了它……”（胡塞尔，1996：96）因此，我们不应把对客观时间的还原理

① 当代最明确地提出这个批评的是思辨唯物论者 Meillassoux，他在《有限性之后》中把这个问题称为祖始化石问题。（2008：ch. 1；2014：12f）认为，一切关联主义者，即“认为一切有意义的 X 都必须是一个思想的相关项”，包括胡塞尔等现象学家，都难以给予“祖始的陈述一个含义，或一个意义”。与 Meillassoux 相类似的也有法国技术哲学家斯蒂格勒（2020），他认为胡塞尔把时间意识奠基在原初回忆之中，忽略了时间意识建构所依赖的外在的技术世界。这些批评都指向于胡塞尔错误把时间完全还原到意识的内在性之中，忽略了在意识之外，或比意识更早的时间。

② 比如，斯蒂格勒认为胡塞尔透过内时间意识的滞留（Retention）或第一持存来奠基时间意识，忽略了人类依赖技术的第三持存来进行记忆的重要性。在这个脉络下，第三持存正是如文字、照片、电影等存在于客观外部世界的技术产物。

解为对客观时间的排除，仿佛唯一真实的时间是体验流中的时间而已。毋宁说，胡塞尔（2009：34）在1905年关于内时间意识的讲座开首就明确了现象学的任务是“试图确立客观时间和主观时间意识之间的合理关系，并且试图理解：时间的客观性，即个体的客观性一般，如何能在主观的时间意识中构造出来”。因此，尽管在胡塞尔看来自然态度下的客观时间不是不证自明的，也不是最基本的时间形态，但这并不妨碍现象学合法地追问我们日常意义下理解的客观时间是什么？它是如何被意识经验和建构的？

## 一 时间的客观性问题作为另一个理论起点

笔者认为，客观时间问题在胡塞尔的时间意识研究中具有重要的地位。虽然从胡塞尔学术发展史的角度来看，胡塞尔1905年的讲座是继承《逻辑研究》而来①，但从讲座的内容和1905年前后的手稿看来，奥古斯丁的时间问题是另一个不可忽略的理论起点。即使奥古斯丁在整部《内时间意识现象学》中只出现过一次，笔者认为奥古斯丁的问题意识一直贯穿着胡塞尔的思考。在1905年讲座的开首处，胡塞尔就引用了奥古斯丁的名言：“［关于时间］，没人问我，我还知道；若有人问我，我想向他说明时，便又茫然不知了。”（胡塞尔，2009：34）在这个文本的脉络里，胡塞尔呈现出来的时间意识研究是回应着奥古斯丁的，因此很难想象胡塞尔会在接下来的研究里完全回避奥古斯丁（1991：232）提出的时间问题：“如果过去已不存在而未来尚未存在，则它们如何存在？然而，如果现在永远是现在，它不消逝到过去，则没有时间而只有永恒。”

这个著名的时间问题提出了日常意义下的时间三相（过去、现在、未来）构成的一个逻辑悖论。根据这个悖论，如果过去和未来不存在，则时

① 在《逻辑研究》中，对观念和意义的追问导向了作为意义根源的意向行为的考察，因此作为意向性的意识成为现象学的首要议题；追问这个意识如何构成和把握自身，就引出了内时间意识现象学的问题。从《逻辑研究》到时间意识研究过渡的内在逻辑，可参考马迎辉（2020）。

间不存在；然而如果它们存在，则没有任何变化，也就没有时间。因此无论过去和未来存在与否，都会导致矛盾。①

然而，这个矛盾不允许我们马上用归谬法得出“时间是不真实的”这个结论；② 时间在经验之中是如此清晰明了，乃至于我们根本不可能想象一个没有时间的经验。哪怕是对一个物理对象最简捷的感知，都预设了经验的前后延绵，我们永远无法“看到”一个只在经验中出现了一瞬间（这个瞬间完全没有时间跨度）的东西。因此可以说，一切经验都预设了某种时间。正是在这个意义上，奥古斯丁才会说“没人问我，我还知道”。

由于时间在经验之中是明了的，问题只在如何表达它而不会导致矛盾，因此在西方哲学的传统中一直都有一条思考时间问题的线索，以“没人问我”之前的直接的时间经验作为出发点。比如，在提出时间悖论后，奥古斯丁马上获得的结论就是，所谓的过去、现在、未来其实都是某种意义上的现在：过去是现在的回忆、未来是现在的期望。这条思路一直延续到胡塞尔的老师布伦塔诺（Franz Brentano）。布伦塔诺认为，我们之所以能经验到过去是因为在每个当下的感知中都伴随着一个原初联想（ursprüngliche Assoziation），它再造着过去的经验对象，并与当下的感知对象同时被经验到。③ 布伦塔诺与奥古斯丁的一个共通点是，回忆是一个当下对过去之物的表象，并且我们通过这个回忆意指到过去。

---

① 时间三相悖论的一个著名的现代版本是英国哲学家 McTaggart（1908）提出的“时间不真实性”（The Unreality of Time）论证。麦克塔加先区分了两个时间概念：A－序列和 B－序列。A－序列是关于事件由将来过渡至现在，再流逝到过去的时间序列。B－序列是众多事件按先后次序排列而成的序列。麦克塔加论证说，B－序列自身是无法构成时间的，因为 B－序列不涉及变化。例如，“汉朝在秦朝之后建立”这个事实，无论时间过了多久都是不会改变的。如果时间必然涉及变化，那么 A－序列就是必要的概念。然而，麦克塔加认为，A－序列是不可能成立的，因为它会导致一个矛盾：如果 A－序列成立，那么它要求同一个事件能被三个互相对立的时态（过去、现在、未来）所描述，这是不可能的。因此 A－序列是不成立的，推论时间也是不真实的。

② 虽然麦克塔加明显地接受了这个结论，但大部分哲学家都无法接受这个结论，因此麦克塔加的论证引发了过去一个多世纪分析哲学中关于时间的辩论。

③ 参考 Brentano（1995）。原书出版年份为 1891 年。

胡塞尔明确地批评了这个进路。[①] 胡塞尔认为，如果过去只是一个当下的表象，那么我们无法区分回忆和想象。胡塞尔（1996：18－49）如此批评布伦塔诺关于一个过去的音符 A 的原初联想：

> A（至多可以把强度的减弱除外）根本没有过去，而是始终当下的。全部的区别就在于：联想也应当是创造性的，并附加了一个被称作“过去”的新因素。这个因素连续地发生渐次的变化，随变化的多少，A 或多或少地成为过去。因此，只要“过去”还存在本原时间直观的领域内，它就必定同时也是当下。“过去”这个时间因素必定也在同一个意义上是一个当下的体验因素，就像我们现时地体验到的红色的因素－这是一个明显的背谬。

从这个批评可见，胡塞尔关注的远不只是对时间的主观经验。如果我们只满足于对时间经验的心理学描述，“原初联想”完全是一个充分的理论。我们可以设想，在目睹一支我小时候用过的笔时，我生起一系列对这支笔的回忆（Wiedererinnerung/ recollection）。这个回忆是当下发生的，它是被这支笔的感知所触发的。在这个意义上，我们完全可以说这个回忆是一个当下的经验。然而为什么胡塞尔认为把它认作当下的体验因素是背谬的？因为如果这个回忆没有真正的记忆（Erinnerung/memory）作支撑，它就完全有可能是当下产生的像既视感（déjà vu）一般的错觉。更进一步说，这个心理学描述完全没有说明时间的构成，反而，它预设时间已经自行消逝了，“原初联想”只是在时间消逝之后重新激活某些个别的体验内容而已。在这里，时间的流逝本身就已经被预设为是真实的了。因此布伦塔诺的理论并没有真正解释时间本身是如何被构成的，而且，它恰好没有

① 这里指的是胡塞尔在 1905 年讲座中对布伦塔诺的批评。学界对于胡塞尔批评时所使用的文本有分歧。胡塞尔全集第十卷《内时间意识现象学》的编者 Rudolf Boehm（1962）认为胡塞尔依据的是布伦塔诺讲座的纪录稿。Nicolas de Warren（2009，53）则认为，胡塞尔引用的文本来自 Marty（1879，121）。文本问题的争议点在于胡塞尔对布伦塔诺的批评是否公允，比如 Oskar Kraus（1930）在提出 1905 时布伦塔诺已放弃了原初联想的理论。这个文本问题并非本文重点，重点是从胡塞尔对布伦塔诺的批评中显示胡塞尔真正关心的问题。

解决奥古斯丁的时间问题：如果过去的事物已经不存在，那么当下的回忆永远不是那个真实的过去；如果过去只是当下构造起来的回忆，那么就不是一个真正逝去了的东西。

为了解决布伦塔诺的问题，胡塞尔提出构成“过去”的意向性不是联想，而是滞留（Retention）。与联想不同，滞留不是对对象的立义，而是对消逝现象的经验。滞留与原初联想有两个重要区别，首先，滞留牵涉的不是对象的内容，而是对象的相位；其次，对这个相位的意向不同于对过去某一时间的指向，而是对整个消逝的时段的意向：

> 这个声音被给予，这就是说，它是作为现在被意识到，但“只要”它的某一个相位被意识为现在（jetzt），它就被意识为现在。但是，如果某个时间阶段（与这个音声延续的时间点相符）是现时的现在（开始阶段除外），那么一个相位的连续统就被意识为“刚才”（Vorhin），而从开始点到现在点的时间延续的整个片段（Strecke）就都被意识为流逝了的延续，而这个延续的其余片段则尚未被意识到。（胡塞尔，1996：56）

两个差别都指向布伦塔诺的问题。首先，“滞留”针对的是相位或相位的变化而不是内容本身，因此它是构成“过去”本身的意向性，而不是意指“逝去的事物”的意向性；对相位变化的意向性构成了根源的时间意识，在此相位的变化之上，才有可能谈论各种具体内容的变化。从内容到相位的过渡表示，内时间意识现象学已经从描述的心理学过渡到超越论的现象学（即使这时期胡塞尔的超越论现象学尚未成熟）；它针对的是时间本身的超越论构成而不是在时间中的时间经验。其次，“滞留”把意识的当下拓展成一个有宽度的延续，因此滞留不只描述了回忆的现前化（Vergegenwartigung），还作为原初记忆（primärer Erinnerung）解释了记忆与回忆的差别。正是基于这个区别，回忆和想象的差别就在于当下现前化的内容有没有一个真实的记忆作为支撑。如果这个对象能连续地追溯到过去的某一个当下的印象，则这个回忆是真实的；否则，它就只是一个当下的想象而已。

从这个对布伦塔诺的批评可见，胡塞尔进行的不是对回忆的心理学描述，而是在内时间意识中思考奥古斯丁的时间问题：被回忆的过去如何是真实的？如果没有了这层考虑，就无法理解胡塞尔对布伦塔诺的批评。

## 二　从时间的真实性问题到时间的客观性问题

从胡塞尔对回忆真实性的追问可见，胡塞尔实际上没有排除时间的客观性问题：他除了希望证明时间的流逝现象在意识内部是可能和明证的，也希望说明为什么在时间意识之中的呈现的对象可以是客观的。

事实上，胡塞尔（1996：250）在一篇1904年的手稿中明确提出这个问题："（客观地说：）对此是否有明见性，是否不可能出现这样的情况：我现在具有意识：A曾在（以直接回忆的方式），同时A实际上根本不曾在（没有前行的感知），或者我现在具有'清新的回忆'，而刚才却并没有感知？"这个问题证明了胡塞尔不只考虑回忆的内容，更考虑到回忆的客观真实性问题。正是因为在心理学意义上的回忆内容不足以说明回忆的真实性，才有需要把研究拓展到时间的超越论构成问题。可是笔者认为，这个从心理学到超越论现象学的过渡实际上并没有完全解决时间三相的悖论，只是把时间的真实性问题转化为时间对象的客观性问题。这个问题的转化需要进一步说明：奥古斯丁的时间问题只是形式地涉及过去、现在和将来这三个时态的最一般定义，因此这个问题可以衍生出多种形式。当我们预设这三个时态指涉客观时间中过去、现在和将来的事件，时间问题就展现为对这个客观时间的真实性的质疑。① 奥古斯丁和布伦塔诺把过去、现在和将来还原为回忆（联想）、感知和期待，问题就演变成当下的回忆是否与客观时间中的过去之物相合的问题。为了解决这个相合的问题，胡塞尔进一步把客观时间还原成内时间意识的建构，根据这个理论，奠基性的不是客观时间，而是超越论的内时间意识流，这个流不断地透过对原印

① 例如对 McTaggart（1908）来说，时间之所以是不真实的，是因为一个"事件"（event）不能同时被三个互不相容的时态描述。此处的"事件"就是发生在客观时间中的。

象的滞留扩展成一个序列，所有被经验的事物都被有序地编写入这个滞留的尾巴之中，构成了最原初的时间秩序。

从内时间意识现象学的层面来说，时间的真实性问题是被消解了，因为过去、现在和未来作为内时间意识的基础时间视域（Horizon）——“滞留”“原印象”和“前摄”是具有第一身的明见性的。如果连这个视域都不存在，意识就根本不存在，我们甚至不可能下一个“时间是不真实”的论断。然而，把时间还原为意识的超越论构造并没有完全解决问题；理论上，我们可以把奥古斯丁的问题再次套用在内时间的体验流之上，问题就变成：“过去”的原印象已不是“当下”的原印象，那么我们还能对象化地反思这个“过去”的原印象吗？如果反思原印象时原初的体验被对象化为一个“过去”，那么对反思的反思又是一个新的体验，如此以往，则原印象的体验内容如何被对象化地把握？①

反思的无穷后退问题不是本文的重点，在这里只需要看到，不论是自然态度下的客观时间对象、心理学意义上回忆的对象还是现象学意义上反思的内在对象，只要它被对象化为一个存在于由“过去”—“现在”—“未来”组成的序列之中时，奥古斯丁的时间问题都能复制到这个序列之中，产生新的问题。在超越论现象学的脉络下，时间流逝的现象是明证了，但时间的客观化问题依然表现为：在内时间意识里构造的对象，如何在变化之中维持其同一性，使得它在任何时候能为任何主体理解。②

由于这个问题的症结在三相的矛盾性中，因此一个可能的解题思路是：被对象化的时间是否必须具有这个三相结构？正是在《贝尔瑙手稿》中，胡塞尔提供了一个崭新的客观时间理论，试图证明在时间意识中把握的对象可以客观化为不同形式的刚性时间秩序，避免奥古斯丁的时间问题。

① 事实上，胡塞尔在《内时间意识现象学》时期一直没有完美地摆脱这个反思当下意识引起的无穷后退问题。如 Zahavi（2004）恰当地指出，胡塞尔一直到写于 1917—1918 年的手稿中仍然在处理这个问题。

② 时间的客观性问题可以从不同的角度被提出，本文只在这个意义上讨论所谓的时间客观化问题。

## 三 《贝尔瑙手稿》中的客观时间理论

在《贝尔瑙手稿》中，胡塞尔（2016：154）把时间从一维的流动拓展为一个二维的时间结构[①]："如果我们回忆起构造一个原素的延续统一性的意识的系统化结构，那么它就是一个两维的行为连续统一体……"换句话说，意识流与对象分属于两个不同的维度。这两个维度分别可以进行两种对象化的过程。

首先，胡塞尔区分了时间客体（Zeitobjekt）和时间对象（Zeitgegenstand）。[②] 在《贝尔瑙手稿》中，时间客体指在意识流中占有确定时间相位的东西："时间客体是在一个感知中本原被给予的。这个感知有一个开始相位，在其中，时间客体具有原涌现的现前，它是现在当下的，并且这个原当下是一个只是通过抽象才能突显的、不独立的相位。"（胡塞尔，2016：95）胡塞尔举例说，想象可以"生动化"一个过去的对象，"但是，这对时间客体行不通，因为过去之物绝不可能成为现实当下的"（2016：95）。由此可见，虽然时间客体是从活的当下连续涌现的（如一个刚刚逝去的感知），但它同时通过滞留的方式伫留在"过去"，因此它拥有一个绝对的现象学时间的相位。当下经验的客体化表明，没有两个当下的体验是一模一样的，当我们听两次同一样的声音，第二次经验作为第二次是与第一次区别开来的。这种客体化在某经验被对象化的把握之前就发生了，这个客体化保证了意识流是一个不能被任意打乱的序列。

与此相对，当我们在谈论一个时间对象（Zeitgegenstand）的时候，我们并不需要穿越回过去的体验，在体验流中把握这个对象，因为作为另一个维度，时间对象被给予为在不同时间形式之中的对象，它在意识流中没

① 在汉语学界，马迎辉（2014a；2014b；2015；2020）对此时间意识的二维模型提供了不少新近的研究。在英语学界，Warren（2009）也有专门的分析。

② Moran 和 Cohen（2012：228）在《胡塞尔词典》里对胡塞尔哲学中"客体"（Objekt）和"对象"（Geganstand）做出了如下区分："'客体'是一个广泛的范畴，它可以包括实在的，观念的，具体的，抽象的，个体的和种属的客体。胡塞尔保留'对象'一词专指知识的对象，即作为'站在对面'……面向主体的认知行为的对象。"

有占据确定的相位，相反：

> 对内在对象来说，我们没有一个对一个完成之物的单纯拥有，而是具有一个存在，这个存在作为在一个生成中的统一性，而且作为一个展示的杂多性［流形，Mannigfaltigkeit］的‘统一性’，这个杂多性由统一性的被给予性的样式组成，如此等等。（胡塞尔，2016：174）

比如说，一个杯子可以被感知、想象、回忆，这些意向行为在超越论意识当中都能够被构造为不同的时间客体；然而在这些不同的意向行为之中，杯子作为同一个杯子被意向为同一个意向对象，它首先呈现在外部物理时空的流形之中。这个区分就使胡塞尔（2016：162）明确看到，意识的时间和对象的时间属于不同的维度，即使它们在数字上可以是同一的。

基于这个区分，胡塞尔（2016：134）进一步发现，虽然对象一直在流逝，但其中被给予的时间对象可以被客观化为一个“刚性的时间秩序”（Zeitordnung）；“时间作为个体的秩序是刚性的，时间样式［模态，Zeitmodalitäten］在流淌，并且在这里只在标明了的方向中在流淌。”胡塞尔（2016：180）再举例说，“伯罗奔尼撒战争是一个事件，这个事件充实一个确定的时间片段……没有事件能够跳出其时间位置或其确定的时间片段”。由此可见，伯罗奔尼撒战争作为一个历史事件不是一个实项的存在于意识之中，被不断地推入滞留之中的客体；它有一个固定的时间位置（比如公元前431年）。在这个意义上，对象的时间是一个形式：“所有时间对象被嵌入时间，并且每一个对象通过其延续，通过其特殊、属于它的形式从这个时间切掉一个块片；时间是世界的一个实项要素。”（2016：382）① 换句话说，时间是对象所属的“世界”的形式，比如历史事件属于历史时间，自然物属于自然时间，虚构的对象属于虚构的时间等等。这些时间是刚性的，不流动的时间形式（Zeitform）。

这并不表示这些时间形式是先天实存的，而是在意识之中被构造出来

① 在这个意义上，胡塞尔（2016：421）甚至同意康德说“时间是感性的形式，因而是每一个可能的客观经验世界的形式”。

的，这个构造过程主要通过想象（Phantasie）完成。[①] 在此，想象并不是虚构，也不是如布伦塔诺的“联想”，因为它并不带来新的材料。胡塞尔（2016：227）说：“想象内容是相应感觉材料的变异之物，它们自身不是感觉材料，只是不同地被立义。”通过材料的想象变异，我们可以找到一个具体对象背后的多重流形。[②] 这些流形是对象的一个可能性的领域。比如，一首乐曲并不需要整首听完（它的感知素材完全给予）才能被立义为一首乐曲，它当下就能被立义为一首还没放完的乐曲，有其尚未充实的可能性部分。如此，乐曲的整体就可以是一个音符背后的流形。同样，一个声音也可以被立义为一个发生在外部物理时空的事件，物理时空也有其尚未充实的可能性部分。如此我们可以构造出不同的流形作为一个声音的时间形式。[③]

虽然流形的构造使用到想象力，但却不是任意的，我们可以区分两个流形是不同的，如果它们彼此之间“没有关系”。[④] 胡塞尔举例说：“询问是否一个童话中的格雷特尔（Gretel）与另一个童话中的一个格雷特尔是同一个格雷特尔……这是无意义的。”[⑤] 因为“一个世界的‘事物’，进程，‘现实性’于另一个世界的‘事物’，进程，‘现实性’‘没有关

① 想象力是主要的，但不是唯一的，比如说，当形式是牵涉到本质领域时，还需要本质直观等等。这里只谈论想象力因为想象力本身足以说明“刚性”的来源，以理解刚性的对象维度是如何可以构成的。

② 胡塞尔对“Mannifaltigkeit”的理解可以追溯到黎曼的几何学。根据钱立卿（2020），虽然胡塞尔的“流形”至少有四种用法，但可以这些流形都可以概括为“一切纯粹可能关系组成的纯粹形式结构”。

③ 笔者特别感谢其中一位审稿人指出了“流形”在胡塞尔哲学中的多样性，上注中钱立卿的文献也提供了详尽的说明。为集中讨论，今只列两例。笔者大概同意钱立卿的观点，笔者认为虽然“流形”一词在胡塞尔哲学里指称多个结构，但这些结构都有一个共同点，就是它们在某种意义上都是可能性关系组成的结构。比如本体论意义上的流形是关于对象的可能判断空间（胡塞尔，2012），物理时空的流形是动觉的可能空间，音乐的整体形态是可能的音符组成的整体等等。关于胡塞尔的“流形”观念能否有一个一致的形式定义不是本文关注的重点，对本文的论证目标来说，我们只需要知道任何“流形”都具有某种刚性的结构，并且使某对象能通过在此结构中的位置来定义即可。

④ 这一点与流形在数学上的意义相似，在拓扑学上，两个流形是等价的如果它们之间存在共形变异。关于胡塞尔如何使用共性变异这个概念，可参考王知飞（2018）。

⑤ 见胡塞尔（2016：404）。另一个例子是：“我们现在虚构的这个半人半马怪与我们此前曾虚构的一只河马彼此没有时间状况。”（2016：419）

系'。"（2016：419）这种"关系"或者本质关联决定了对象所在的流形的边界。由于这些"关系"只是理念中被发现的形式，因此它们是刚性的。①

胡塞尔认为，我们日常理解的客观时间，其实是一个复合的结果，时间对象的客观性首先来自于与对象本质相关的流形和世界整体，但这些客观的形式是刚性的，日常经验体验到的时间流动性来自于这些可能性的流形的充实。这个充实的过程一方面产生了时间流动的现象；另一方面在众多可能世界里充实出一个唯一的"现实世界"，它的时间是"现实时间"。②（我们因此可以区分诸多的、刚性的客观时间和唯一的、流动的现实时间，胡塞尔认为日常自然态度下讲的客观时间只是后者，它是"客观"形式和"主观"经验的综合结果。）③

现实时间是这样构成的：胡塞尔（2016：194）认为只有当一个"现时的主体"出现时，我们才可以谈论流动的现象；"没有某一个现时的主体，一个时间对象就是不可设想的，就这个主体来说，'现在'或'过去'或'未来'是被构造的。"这个过程可以用完整时间图的构作方法来表示。首先，我们有一些刚性的时间形式，每个可能对象按其所属的世界或者流形有固定的时间形式。比如，当一个音符响起时，同共被意向的整个乐曲的形式流形。这个由音符的前后相对位置构成的整体是刚性的。这些流形可以表现为图一。其次，如果这些秩序可以按一定的方式"下沉"，转变成另一个。这是可能的，因为胡塞尔强调现实世界只有一个（2016：378－383）。不同的时间形式因此能勾连成一个统一的现实时间的秩序。因此有图二。

---

① 这种"关系"有时候也称为"时间状况"。（胡塞尔，2016：150）

② 胡塞尔（2016：412）认为这其实是"现实世界"的本质规律："如果一个世界实存，那么它就排除所有其他世界……所有这些世界必须是一个时间世界，至少它们按照时间具有统一性。"简单来说，如果有一个主体可以先后充实两个可能世界，那么两个世界至少有一个"先后"的时间关系，按照这个关系就能统一两个世界为一个世界。比如说，一部小说的世界与一部电影的世界是两个可能世界，但如果有一个人先读了小说再看电影，那么他就会意识到两个可能世界都是虚构的，它们能统合在一个更大的现实世界时间里。

③ 当然，这里的"客观"和"主观"是打引号的，这是对象化以后的产物，并不表示胡塞尔预先接受了这个二分法，但同时不能忽略的是，这个二分作为构造的结果还是可能和有意义的，这点经常为现象学研究者忽略。

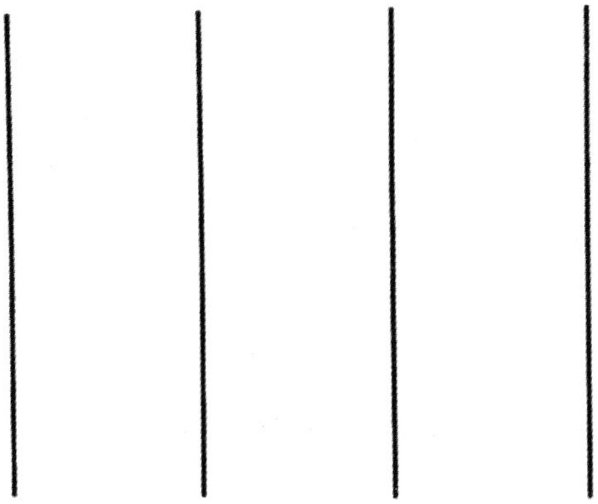

图一 固定的序列（胡塞尔，2016：68）

此时，仍未见任何变化的现象，因为这里还不能表示出任何过去、现在、未来。时间三相的出现要求有一个认识的主体站岗，在其意向充实的顶端画出一个现在，这样，当主体“参与”进这个原进程时，就能画出一个由现前构成的水平线，因此就有了完整的时间图（见图三）。

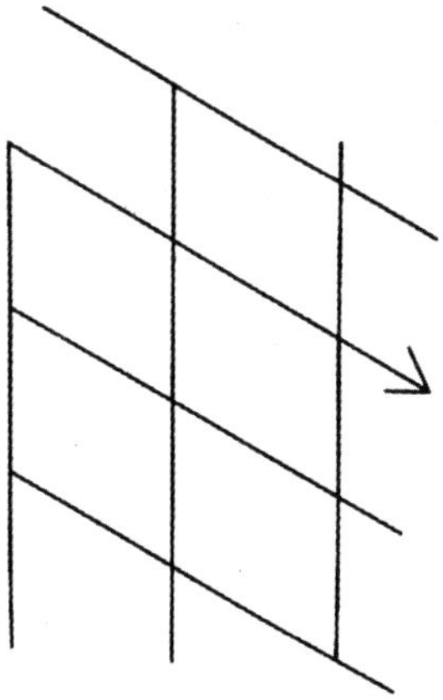

图二 下沉的序列

（胡塞尔，2016：68）

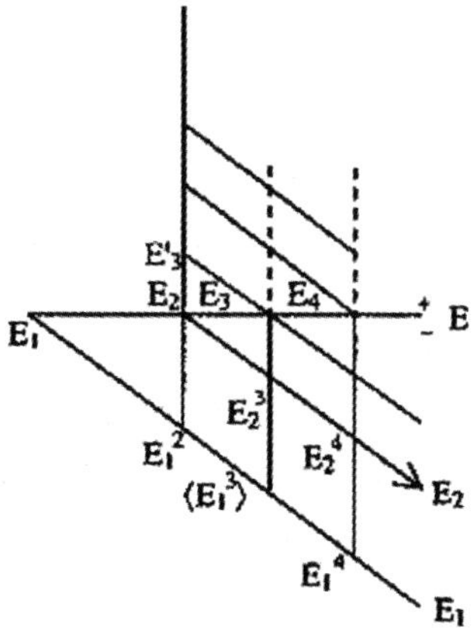


图三 完整的时间图

（胡塞尔，2016：58）

在图三中，上半部是尚未被充实的，作为前摄和可能性的部分；下半部是被充实了的部分。比如在 $E_2$ 这一点时，我们按照该对象的时间形式，

预判会有一个 $E_3$' 即将在下一刻到来。当这个意向被充实时，就成了一个新的现前 $E_3$。[①] 这个过程就构成了主体的体验流。[②] 基于这个站于现前的体验流，就可以画出相对的过去和未来，同一个事件，就能先被前摄，再被充实为现在，再滞留到回忆之中，因此就能经验到流逝的现象。但就时间形式（垂直线）来说，它并没有经历这个三相的变异。因此胡塞尔（2016：182）说，“客观时间片段的全面的形式是刚性的……”，真正流淌的只是事件的时间模态（Zeitmodalität）和被给予方式而已。[③]

该注意的是，这个“原进程”并不表示在现象学的时间上有此先后，实际上，体验流和时间对象是一同构成的。从超越论的角度来说，只有一个活的当下，它是一个本原的视域。（胡塞尔，2016：188）但当这个活的当下运作起来，它就一方面把原素构造成为时间客体，组成一个延展的体验流；另一方面通过想象力构造诸种可能的时间、世界形式和其中的时间对象。体验流和时间对象只是同一个超越论的发生过程展开的两个维度而已。

## 四 时间问题的一个解决方案

正是这个“原进程”提供了一个回应时间客观性问题的方案。首先明确可见的是，胡塞尔认为日常自然态度下所谓的客观时间（现实时间）其实只是世界的时间形式在体验之中充实的结果。这表示胡塞尔至少是交出了一个关于客观时间（而不只是内时间）的现象学（这点经常被忽略）。其次，胡塞尔认为虽然时间是由意识构造的，但它能通过各种刚性的时间形式被构造成独立于意识之外，因为构造它只需要对象本身的本质关联允许的自由变更而已。

① 更完整的对时间图的解读可以参考 Dodd（2005）。

② 我们在此处区别体验流和意识流，体验流专指在充实发生后的这个主观的体验过程，意识流是在超越论现象学底下整个发生的过程，在《贝尔瑙手稿》中，胡塞尔又把意识流称作原过程（Urprozess），以避免误会。

③ 中译本把“Zeitmodalität”译作“时间样式”，这个翻译容易与“时间形式”（Zeitform）混淆，况且“Modalität”一般译为“模态”，意指将来的模态是可能的，过去的模态是已实现的，所以笔者主张译为“时间模态”比较合适。

这个时间的对象化或者观念化的理论提供了一个回应奥古斯丁时间问题的进路：首先，超越论的时间意识保证了流逝现象在内意识层面是明见和真实的。但真实的时间不只停留在体验内部，它可以被客观化。被客观化地表述的时间只是一些刚性的时间秩序，因此它们首先不会牵涉到过去、现在、未来的问题。当一个时间对象从前摄的可能性转变为被充实的现实性，从体验流的角度来看，它是经历了未来、现在、过去的转变，但这个转变只是“主观”体验到的时间模态的转变而已，如果我们要“客观”的描述这个过程，我们完全可以依靠一个刚性的时间形式。比如说，当我们听一段音乐的时候，整个被给予的是作为乐曲形式的流形，它包含着一个尚未被充实的部分。当乐曲听完了，乐曲整体被充实了，但乐曲本身的形式并没有任何改变。作为一段旋律 A – B – C 中的 B 音，还是处在 A 和 C 之间，无论这段旋律被充实与否。[①] 因此，通过时间形式而被对象化的时间和时间对象，是不必要牵涉到时间三相的。整个时间形式，不在时间之中，而只是一个拟时间而已[②]，因此不会遭遇到奥古斯丁时间问题的挑战。

当然，这个理论并不是为了解决一个形而上问题而构思出来的理论，它是有严格的现象学基础的。这个客观时间的现象学还是排除了日常自然态度下的客观时间。在日常的自然态度下，我们认为时间是客观现实的、流逝的、唯一的；但经过现象学的还原，胡塞尔发现所谓的客观时间是奠基在诸种可能的时间形式之上的，因此它不只是现实的，而且是观念的。[③]

---

① 当然这个形式的首次构造需要立义、充实等流动的意识行为，但一旦对象被构造了，描述这个对象的语言可以只牵涉对象的形式而忽略流动的体验内容。

② 在与《贝尔瑙手稿》同期的另一本手稿中，胡塞尔（1980：505）说：“在想象之中，我们不可能合法地把对象直观为现实，为现在、过去、未来等等。相反的，我们把它连同它的内容意识为‘正如’它是现前的。对我们来说，它是现实地‘正如’。”

③ 值得注意的是，虽然时间形式是观念的，但胡塞尔（2016：245）认为时间最终是现实的，因为“实在世界的现实存在不是通过主体的观念可能性得到保证的，这些主体可能感知这个世界，并且它不仅要求观念的可能性，而且要求现实性”。因为胡塞尔（2016：246）认为，超越论的主体必须是绝对而实存的，如果这里谈论的只是一个观念可能的主体，那么谈论它的构造也只能是可能的构造。如果超越论主体是实存的，那么它充实的世界也是实存的。本文先不讨论这个说法是否合理，关键是指出现实世界的观念也必须是一个主体建构的观念。

如果同情的理解这个说法，我们就能发现其实大部分我们日常用以交流客观时间的概念其实都是刚性的。比如说，日历上的日期和钟表上的时间刻度，都是刚性的数学形式。我们并不需要把自己从昨天到今天所经历的一切都客观化地表达出来，才能指明“昨天”；我们只需要一个彼此都理解的日历。当我们用日历来交流的时候，其实并没有意指任何流逝的现象。2021 年 3 月 3 日这个日期不论作为过去、现在或者未来，都是可以在日历系统里被理解。正是这些刚性的概念让我们在日常生活之中不必遭遇奥古斯丁的时间问题，就能领会某种意义上的时间客观性。

当然，日历和纪年法是一种比较粗浅的形式，严格意义上的客观时间是指自然科学里的时间。自然科学里的时间的客观性，仍然是由诸种可能的刚性时间形式或时间模型构成的。比如说，牛顿的线性可微分时间只是其中一种可能的客观时间形式之一。这个形式是完全刚性的理念形式，比如自由落体的位移可以以公式 $s = (1/2)\ gt^2$ 表示，其中 s 是位移的距离，g 是重力加速度，t 是时间。同一个公式完全可以描述一个相反的过程：物体被抛起来的过程，因此这个刚性的时间形式是没有方向的。[①] 在牛顿时间之外，我们还可以由多种可能的客观时间模型，比如相对论和量子力学所建立的时间形式，都能成为整个宇宙的时间模型，但这些模型却不尽相同。它们彼此按系统内的概念的本质关联形式构成，互不相干。比如，加速度公式“$s = (1/2)\ gt^2$”无法描述电子的运动轨迹，因为电子的运动不具备牛顿力学描述的时间形式，但这种差异并不妨碍牛顿力学和量子力学各自都能成为客观的理论，并描述一个具有客观性的时间。

因此，虽然现实时间只有一个，但我们可以用不同的客观时间概念来构造和沟通这个现实时间。日常自然态度下，乃至自然科学里认为只有一个客观时间，恰好是遗忘了现实时间有无限种被客观化地把握的可能性。

这一点正好体现了现象学在思考客观时间时比自然主义的优越性。对胡塞尔的批评者经常预设存在一个纯物质的自然远古时间，是现象学无法谈论的。殊不知，这种自然主义的时间观非但不能面对奥古斯丁时间问题

---

① Sudarshau（2017）甚至认为在这种模型中没有任何事件的发生。

的诘难，而且无视了我们用以理解这个远古时期的概念工具。比如说，我们通过考古学的碳定年法理解的“过去”与物理学理解的“过去”就不是同一个“过去”，如果知道这个所谓的“过去”是奠基于不同的学科对象观念化后的时间模型，那么我们就永远有更多理解这个“过去”的可能性，而不是刻板的承认了“过去”只是一个既定现实。

表面上看来，现象学仿佛多此一举的认定“过去”只是当下主体的构造①，但事实上，如果没有一个当下的主体去定义“现在”，“过去”是不能被定义的。“十万年前”对某个古人类来说是“现在”，对一个现代人来说是“远古”；因此当我们说“过去”或者“十万年‘前’”时，一定是相对于某主体的。这不是关联论的偏见，而是一个语法规律。相反，自然主义者既要说“十万年前”，但又不承认这个“前”是相对于一个主体，这就是个悖谬。客观时间的现象学表明，这个“十万年前”只能是主体对过去的想象，这表面上仿佛取消了“过去”的客观性，但其实这只是表明了我们平时用于理解世界的时间模型，其实都只是假设性的。从牛顿的绝对时间、爱因斯坦的相对论，到量子力学，其实都是不同的时间客观化的结果。我们通过这些模型才能立义一个“过去”，这些模型都有自己的边界，也能因应不同的素材被修改。其实这种对时间客观性的理解才是与科学相一致的。科学不正是不断推翻以前的时间模型；考古学不正是不断推翻以前对远古的想象吗？因此，胡塞尔的客观时间现象学比自然态度的时间观更符合现实里科学思考时间的实况。

## 五　结语：胡塞尔的客观时间现象学

从以上分析可见，胡塞尔除了建立了一套关于内时间意识的现象学，还提供了一套关于客观时间的现象学。这并不是说胡塞尔在此接受了一种

① 比如胡塞尔在全集第三十六卷（2003）里说：“假如一个主体性存在并通过他的经验与思考从周遭呈现的周围世界开始构造起这个世界，一个作为基底的物质世界，包括世界最早的延绵，就可以符合认知的条件。世界最早的时期，包括一个纯物质的自然，都能够透过理性被反向地构造。”同段落也被 Zahavi（2017）引用来证明胡塞尔有处理远古时间的问题。

主客二分的二元论哲学；毋宁说，在二维的连续统一体中，对象的时间和体验流的时间是同一个原过程构造出来的两个不同方向而已。[①] 然而，这并不妨碍我们可以独立地理解胡塞尔的客观时间现象学。

这个客观时间现象学让我们看到，日常自然态度里被认为是客观地自然流逝的一维时间序列其实是一个复杂的意识建构的产物，它是各种通过想象构造的刚性时间形式在体验中被充实的结果。这个发现提供了一个解决奥古斯丁时间问题的思路：时间流逝的现象是主观的，但这并不妨碍体验的内容可以被客观化为不同的时间对象，在刚性的时间形式里能够被客观地通达和理解。当然，这并不表示时间问题被完全解决了，比如，胡塞尔认为内在的流逝体验也可以在主体间性之中被通达理解的，这些牵涉时间三相的构造过程如何能获得主体间意义上的客观性，是胡塞尔后期如 C 手稿中的主要内容。这方面的内容，包括流逝本身能不能有绝对的客观性的问题，都不在本文的讨论范围之内。本文也不能完整呈现二维时间结构的整个发生过程的所有细节，包括不同阶段的对象化和客体化，乃至不同流形和可能世界的构造过程和时间形式。本文的目的只在于指明现象学可以提供一个独立于主体体验的客观时间现象学。这种客观时间现象学并不是在假设了有一个客观时间的前提下的后设研究，而是研究当下体验的诸种被客观化的可能。在这个意义下，虽然现象学不一定能证明我们一直在日常自然态度下经历的“现实时间”肯定永远是真实的，但它对时间客观性的来源的说明至少是可理解的（comprehensible）。

可理解的意义是指它开辟了这么一种思路：通过客观时间的现象学，我们能够排除独断的自然主义时间观，并在日常自然主义的时间观里发现各种已经在起作用的时间形式（比如，化学物衰变期、物理—数学模型、历史叙事等）。通过分析这些时间形式，我们不但能理解各种时间观念是如何被建构和沟通的，更能发现这些时间形式的限制和边缘，并针对未来新的经验素材建构新的时间模型。这种往前建构，而不只是往后还原的现象学维度，正是长期被忽略的现象学可能性。笔者认为，如果现象学对科

① 事实上，在胡塞尔后期哲学如 C 手稿中，世界、历史等超越于经验主体之外的领域都被收入在超越论主体性的发生之中。参见方向红（2014）。

学来说仍然是有反思意义的，那么一种朝向客观性的现象学正是必要的和可能的①。

**参考文献**

方向红，2014，《时间与存在：胡塞尔与海德格尔现象学的基本问题》，商务印书馆。

胡塞尔，1996，《纯粹现象学通论》，李幼蒸译，商务印书馆。

——，2009，《内时间意识现象学》，倪梁康译，商务印书馆。

——，2012，《形式逻辑与先验逻辑》，李幼蒸译，中国人民大学出版社。

——，2016，《关于时间意识的贝尔瑙手稿》，肖德生译，商务印书馆。

马迎辉，2014a，《意向性，绝对流与先验现象学》，《江苏社会科学》第四卷，第23—30页。

——，2014b，《范畴，现象学还原与被给予性》，《南京社会科学》第九卷，第38—43页。

——，2015，《意向性：从立义到意向流形》，《安徽大学学报》第六卷，第36—43页。

——，2020，《时间性与思的哲学》，江苏人民出版社。

钱立卿，2020，《胡塞尔的'流形论'观念是如何形成的？——一个数学思想史角度的综观》，《中国现象学与哲学评论》第二十六卷，第215—269页。

斯蒂格勒，2020，《技术与时间：迷失方向》，赵和平译，译林出版社。

王知飞，2018，《从集合到流形——论胡塞尔现象学的现代数学起源》，《中国现象学与哲学评论》第二十二卷，第372—392页。

Augustine, 1991, *Confessions*, Henry Chadwick (trans.), Oxford: Oxford University Press.

Brentano, F., 1995, *Descriptive Psychology*, Benito Müller (trans.), Routledge.

Dodd, J., 2005, "Reading Husserl's Time Diagram from 1917/18", *Husserl Studies* 21 (2), 111-137.

Husserl, E., 1962, *Zur Phänomenologie des inneren Zeitbewusstseins (1893-1917)*, ed., by Rudolf Boehm, Martinus Nijhoff.

——, 1977, *Ideen zu einer reinen Phänomenologie und phänomenologischen Philosophie*, ed., by Erstes Buch. Karl Schuhmann, Martinus Nijhoff.

——, 1980, *Phantasie, Bildbewusstsein, Erinnerung. Zur Phänomenologie der anschaulichen Vergegenwärtigungen. Texte aus dem Nachlass (1898-1925)*, ed., by Eduard Marbach, Martinus Nijhoff.

——, 2001, *Die Bernauer Manuskripte über das Zeitbewusstsein (1917/18)*, ed., by Rudolf Bernet and Dieter Lohmar, Springer.

① 感谢文章的两位评审提供了宝贵的修改意见和评语。

——, 2003, *Transzendentaler Idealismus. Texte aus dem Nachlass (1908 - 1921)*, ed., by Robin D. Rollinger, Kluwer.

Marty, A., 1879, *Die Frage nach der geschichtlichen Entwicklung des Farbensinnes*, Gerold.

McTaggart, J. M. E., 1908, "The Unreality of Time", *Mind* 17 (68), 457 - 474.

Meillassoux, Q., 2008, *After Finitude: An Essay on the Necessity of Contingency*, Ray Brassier (trans.). Continuum.

——, 2014, *Time Without Becoming*, Mimesis International.

Moran, D. & Coren, J., 2012, *The Husserl Dictionary*, Continuum.

de Warren, N., 2009, *Husserl and the Promise of Time: Subjectivity in Transcendental Phenomenology*, Cambridge University Press.

Kraus, O., 1930, "Zur Phänomenognosie des Zeitbewusstseins", *Archiv für die gesante Psychologie* 75, 1 - 22.

Sudarshau, E. C. G., 2017, *Time in Physics and Time in Awareness. Space, Time and the Limits of Human Understanding*, ed., by Shyam Wuppuluri & Giancarlo Ghirardi, Springer.

Zahavi, D., 2004, "Time and Consciousness in the Bernau Manuscripts", *Husserl Studies* 20 (2), 99 - 118.

——, 2006, *Subjectivity and Selfhood: Investigating the First - Person Perspective*, The MIT Press.

——, 2017, *Husserl's Legacy: Phenomenology, Metaphysics, and Transcendental Philosophy*, Oxford University Press.

# 金岳霖回答了真之符合论的问题吗？

## ——兼谈当代真之符合论问题与金氏符合论的建构

陈邦臣（CHEN Bangchen）*

**摘要：**真之符合论是历史最悠久的关于真的认识方式，至今仍旧有许多学者倡导不同版本的真之符合论。但符合论带来的困难和质疑也非常多，不同学者对符合论给出了不同的责难和回应。在诸多版本的符合论中，金岳霖综合了融洽、有效、一致等方法，提出了自成体系的金氏符合论，为我们回答各位学者对符合论提出的问题提供了有力的支持。以下我将首先简要说明当代符合论发展的情况，包括其存在的一些问题与回应；然后我将对金氏符合论中的真之载体、真之制造者与符合关系进行分析，说明其具有的特点；最后我将根据前述符合论一般的问题和回应，论证金氏符合论不仅能够回应这些问题，还具有其独特的竞争力优势。

**关键词：**真；符合论；金岳霖；命题；事实

* 陈邦臣，清华大学哲学系。

# Did Jin Yuelin Answer the Question of Correspondence of Truth?
## ——On the Contemporary Correspondence Theory of Truth and Jin's Correspondence Theory

**Abstract**: The theory of correspondence of truth is the oldest way of understanding truth. So far, many scholars advocate different versions of the theory of correspondence of truth. However, there are many difficulties and queries brought by the theory of correspondence, and different scholars have given different criticisms and responses to it. In many versions of the theory of correspondence, Jin Yuelin integrated coherence, effective and consistent methods, and put forward his own system of the theory of correspondence, which provides strong support for us to answer the questions raised by scholars. In the following, I will first briefly introduce the situation of contemporary correspondence theory, as well as the relevant refutation and response; Then I will analyze Truth - bearer, Truth - maker and the relationship between Correspondence in Jin Yueln's correspondence theory; Finally, according to the general problems and responses of the above correspondence theory, I will demonstrate that Jin Yuelin's correspondence theory can not only respond to these problems, but also has its unique competitive advantage.

**Key words**: Truth, Correspondence, Jin Yuelin, Proposition, Fact

真之符合论是哲学史上历史最悠久的关于真的认识方式，也是最符合我们日常经验认知的一种判断方式。而根据 2009 年 PhilPapers 杂志的调查①，针对排名前 99 个哲学系的所有普通教职工，对于“承认哪种真理

① Bourget and Chalmers (2014).

论：符合论、紧缩论还是认识主义？”这个问题，选择符合论的占50.8%，紧缩论24.8%，认识主义6.9%。这说明了在当代哲学研究者中，符合论仍然具有其认可度和普适性。在传统上，真之符合论的竞争对手主要是真之实用主义、真之融贯论、证实主义，而在当代，它则要面对真之紧缩论、真之同一性理论、真之多元论的竞争。显然，符合论本身具有许多产生争议的问题，才使得它无法满足我们对真的认识要求；同时，它又具有独特的优势使我们无法放弃这种理论。因此，对于真之符合论的支持者而言，如何克服符合论本身被责难的问题，并且显示出其独特的竞争力，是最核心的困难。

在近代的中国学者中，金岳霖在其《知识论》一书中表达了他对真之符合论的认可，他将融贯、有效、一致等方法进行综合，提出了独具特色的金氏符合论，表达了其对于“真”的独特认识。笔者认为，金氏符合论较好的回应了对于符合论的大部分责难，并且在对于真之理论的竞争中，具有其独特的优势。因此，在下文中，我将首先简要说明当代符合论发展的情况，包括其存在的一些问题与回应；然后我将对金氏符合论中的真之载体、真之制造者与符合关系进行分析，说明其具有的特点；最后我将根据前述符合论一般的问题和回应，论证金氏符合论不仅能够回应这些问题，还具有其独特的竞争力优势。

## 一　各版本的真之符合论

传统符合论的核心在于对“真”的定义，认为把“真”作为一种关系属性，从而说明一个真之载体（Truth - bear）与真之制造者（Truth - maker）之间产生的符合关系。而随着符合论的不断发展和扩展，符合论对真之载体与真之制造者的各种不同用法和理论的认识，衍生出了许多不同版本的符合论。但归结起来，在当代符合论中，最常见的符合论版本可以做出如下区分：

事实符合论（以下简称CF）：若x是一个p，则x是真（假）的当且仅当 x（不）符合一个事实（fact）。

事态符合论（以下简称 CS）：若 x 是一个 p，则 x 是真（假）的当且仅当 x 符合一个（不）获得的事态（state of affairs that obtain）。

这两者的区别主要在于对虚假（falsehood）的处理，CS 对于虚假的定义是存在而未被获得的实体，例如存在一个“绿的雪”的事态是我们未获得的；CF 的虚假定义则没有对未获得的事态的存在进行确定，例如我们说“我们没获得一个事实”就意味着不存在这种事实，因此在 CF 定义下就不存在一个“绿的雪”的事实。（当然，“事实”和“事态”的术语并不是标准化的，如阿姆斯特朗用“事态”的概念其实在说的这里的“事实”。）① 由此可以看出，CS 更倾向于柏拉图主义，它预设了先在但未知的某种实体，而 CF 更倾向于亚里士多德主义，即它不承认有某种未知而存在的实体的承诺。但事实上，这两者不是矛盾的，CS 的支持者通常会认为事实就是获得的事态，因此 CF 的概念也可以转化为 CS 的概念，从而使得 CS 具有更大的范畴。

有些哲学家认为，我们有更好的理由来支持 CS 而不是 CF 的定义：1. CS 并不意味着真之载体范畴外的事物是假的，而仅仅只认为它们不符合任何事实，这给可能世界留下了空间。2. CS 允许真之载体的范畴中有非真非假的项。3. 如果主要的真之载体是句子或精神状态，那么事态可以是其含义和内容。而相反，CF 提出的事实对于错误的句子和信念没有相对应的意义和内容。4. 在析取命题“p 或 q”中，p 真 q 假的结果是无法对应一个析取事实的，然而 CS 允许其符合的事实是获得的事态与未获得的事态组合成的事态，这满足了析取命题的符合论要求。当然，也有些哲学家认为 CF 要好于 CS，理由是：如果不预设未获得的事态是现实的组成部分，那么也就不存在对于本体论预设的诟病了。

除了这两个版本外，CF 与 CS 的区分还产生如下一个混合的版本：

---

① 参见 Armstrong（1997）。

C′：x是真（假）的当且仅当x（不）符合一个存在的事实。

这个版本实际上不是很好区分，比如维特根斯坦在《逻辑哲学论》4.25中的阐释的，英文版[①]给出的是："如果基本命题为真，则存在［符合的］事态；如果基本命题为假，则不存在［符合的］事态。"把"事态"替换为"事实"则足以说明这是维特根斯坦的C+版本。然而在德文版中，则陈述为"如果基本命题为真，则事态被获得（besteht）；如果基本命题为假，则事态不被获得（besteht nicht）。"

第四种版本曾经十分流行，但如今已不受欢迎[②]。这是通过同意（agree）代替符合，C+：若x是一个p，则x是真（假）的当且仅当x（不）同意一个事实。这种模式避免了无法获得事态和事实不存在的承诺问题，但却带来了更大的麻烦，比如"同意"这种关系的神秘性是怎样的，同意的谎言是真的吗？

以上是传统的符合论各版本的定义区分，但除了传统的这些版本外，还有一些被修改过的版本，例如逻辑原子主义和逻辑亚原子主义。维特根斯坦（1921）与罗素（1918）提出了以事实为基础经过修改的真之符合论，作为逻辑原子论的一部分。这分为两种情况，第一种是基础的真之载体，所谓基本的或原子的真之载体的"真"在于其与原子事实的符合关系：如果x是基础的，则x是真的当且仅当x符合原子事实。第二种是对于非基础性的"真"，根据逻辑结构和逻辑真值来进行递归解释，如"p"真那么"非p"假。逻辑原子主义利用真值表中包含的熟悉规则，根据其更简单的成分来评估复杂的公式。这些规则可以通过两种不同的方式来理解：（a）追踪复杂事实和构成简单事实之间的本体论关系，或（b）追踪逻辑语义关系，展示如何用以下方式解释复杂句子的真值，即它们与较简单的构成句子的逻辑关系，以及简单、基本的句子与原子事实的符合和不符合。逻辑原子论者主要采用了选项（b）的方式。

逻辑亚原子主义将真之载体如句子，分析成其实体的组成部分，并将

---

① Wittgenstein（1961/1921）.

② 参考Russel（1918：177－281）；Austin（1979：117－133）。

符合关系分解为适当的语义子关系：名称指的是对象，（开句子的）谓词则由对象满足。复杂谓词的满足可以通过逻辑结构和更简单谓词的满足进行递归处理，例如：对象 o 满足“x 不是 F”当且仅当 o 不满足“x 是 F”；o 满足“x 是 F 或 x 是 G”当且仅当 o 满足“x 是 F”或者“x 是 G”，诸如此类。对于一个单称句子，其“真”被定义为名称表示的对象满足谓词。塔斯基提供的“T 语句”[①] 逻辑机制可用于将简化的草图转变成对“真”的更一般的定义——一种处理包含关系谓词和量词的句子的定义，并且还覆盖分子句子。但即使在这种修改的意义上，塔斯基自己对“真”的定义是否可以被视为符合论，也仍有争议。[②]

## 二 真之符合论的反驳与回应

虽然有不同版本的符合论，但是其产生的问题和反驳也是非常多的，下面我们先来看关于传统符合论定义的一些反驳。它们可以被大致归纳为如下三个问题：

> 1. CS 和 CF 的定义太狭窄了，它们只能针对某些领域（比如科学），但是有些领域不包含在内（比如道德），没有说明道德事实。反驳者承认道德真，但是拒绝现实包含道德事实作为道德真符合的对象的观点，这类似于逻辑实证主义者承认逻辑真[③]而拒绝逻辑事实的观点。

对于这个反驳的回应有几种应对方式：1a. 非认知主义（noncognitivism），即认为这些领域从一开始就无法进行真值评估，例如道德主张属于情感上的宣称，其本身无法称为“真”。1b. 错误理论，即认为这些领域中

① Tarski（1935）.

② 可参考 Popper（1972）；Soames（1999）；Patterson（2008）。

③ 休谟给予了逻辑真与非逻辑真的定义：真或假在于对观念（ideas）的真实（real）关系的同意或不同意，或“关于真实存在（existence）和事实的问题”。详见 Hume（Treatise, 3.1.1, cf. 2.3.10）。

都为假，不存在真。1c. 还原论，来自这些领域的事实能够还原为没有问题的领域的事实，比如道德领域的真可以还原为社会行为现实，逻辑领域的真还原为语言事实。1d. 坚持论者，认为这些领域已经在谈论之中了，并没有更多的领域区分。

事实上，有一些反驳者认为，在不同领域中会有不同的“真”概念，我们在不同的讨论中已经预设了不同领域的前提，这可以看作是对非认知主义的一种回应。这种反对意见被称为“多重可实现性”（multiple realizability），它们认为“真”并不是通过符合事实来定义的，而是通过不同领域的真之载体与事实符合来实现的。当然，它们的观点也并不是反对符合论的观点，而是一种新版本符合论。

> 2. 符合论太明显了，只是空虚琐碎的陈词滥调（platitudes），在日常中我们常把“与事实相符合”与“真”作为习惯替代。像 CS 和 CF 的定义只是将琐碎的语言浓缩为方便的公式，它们本身没有什么理论的分量。①

对此，有些学者给出的回应指出：2a. 类似 CF 和 CS 这样的微型理论是常见的，它们是模型化的常见用法。2b. 有些版本的符合论事实上超越了这些定义。2c. 这两种定义事实上是被广泛接受的，以至于它们兼容了大部分的深度理论，我们找不到拒绝的理由。

> 3. 符合论太模糊了。这是最常见的反驳，符合论的核心概念存在着无法让人接受的承诺。具体可分为符合关系（C1、C2）的问题和事实或事态（F1、F2）的问题。
>
> C1：符合关系是某种相似关系，但真之载体除了和同类的真之载体相似外，和世界上其他东西都不相似。那么并不相似的两者是如何进行符合的呢？

① 可参见 Davidson（1969）；Blackburn（1984）。

C2：符合关系十分神秘，它超越了时空的界限（例如“1984 年的纽约第五大道上的一个人”进行符合是一瞬间发生的事情，这比光速还快），我们该在如何在自然主义的框架下解释这种关系？它们之间存在物理关系吗？

F1：真之载体纷繁复杂，符合论应该承诺于在本体论上无可争议的事实，然而对于否定、析取、条件、普遍、概率、虚拟、反事实等各种命题都难以找到相符合的事实来满足。

F2：所有事实，即便是最简单的事实都是声名狼藉的。“事实”本身就像是一个真之载体，有些人会认为事实就是个用于反映现实的片段的虚构的句子。正如蒯因所说“事实是为了从真句子中投射出来而构造的概念”。①

对于 C1、C2 的问题，一些学者提出了同构符合论的观点来回应这些反驳。同构关系的定义为：如果一个项 K 符合一个确定的事实，则它们具有相同或足够相似的结构。该理论的基本思想是，真之载体和事实都是复杂的结构化实体：真之载体由（其他真之载体，并最终由）语词或概念组成；事实由（事物或事态，最终是事物）事物、属性和关系组成。目的是说明一方面如何从真之载体的最终构成要素，与另一方面其对应事实的最终构成要素之间的潜在关系中产生符合关系。该理论一部分针对符合关系的解释，并走向语义学的路径；另一部分针对事实的认同标准，说明简单成分如何构成复杂整体，并走向本体论路径。

应该指出的是，C1、C2 的观点不独立于人们对真之载体的看法，如果真之载体被认为是普通语言的句子或者心理表征，则符合关系将被认为是语义上的或心理语义的关系的观点是成立的。但若是将命题作为真之载体，则会出现一些复杂的情况：1. 从广义的弗雷格对命题的观点来看，命题是由对象和属性的概念构成的（在逻辑上而不是心理上的“概念”意义上）。在这种观点下，上述观点仍然成立，因为概念之间的关系以及它们

① 参见 Quine（1987）；Strawson（1950）。

作为概念的对象和属性之间的关系似乎是概念语义关系。2. 在所谓的罗素命题观[①]（早期罗素主要从早期摩尔的观点中继承来）中，命题不是由对象和属性的概念构成的，而是由对象和属性本身构成的。按照这一说法，C1、C2 观点可能会失败，因为应用到罗素式命题时，符合关系会崩塌为同一性关系，这也成为对非同一性理论的拒斥。因此，按照罗素这种看法，符合论将被简化为真之同一性理论：命题是真（假）的当且仅当它（不）是事实。

回到同构的方法，如果严格地使用它，符合关系将会是真与事实的一一对应。但这种方法将受到 F1 的反驳，即严格的同构性导致了我们不得不把对应的实体分配给所有不同的真之载体，这些带有逻辑连接词的客体将成为世界的组成部分，然而这是难以被接受的。

对于 F1、F2 的指责，逻辑原子主义和逻辑亚原子主义或许可以回应部分的诘难。逻辑原子主义的设计与本体论观点相一致，即世界是原子事实的整体[②]。原子事实就是所有事实，现实生活中的原子主义者倾向于允许合取事实，认为它们只是原子事实的集合。基本事实是真的，因为它与原子事实相符合，而符合关系仍然是同构，但是仅在基本事实和原子事实之间存在。而在非基本的分子事实的层面上，真与事实之间是不匹配的，即分子命题并不与分子事实产生符合关系。这就避免了说逻辑复杂的命题不存在符合的实体的反驳。观念的复杂性是属于语言的结构，而非世界的特征。亚原子主义者基于对象符合的回归，认为反对 F2 的符合论者应该赞成这种观点：即使是最基本的真之载体也没有分配真之制造者。符合关系本身让位于真之载体与对象之间的两种语义关系：指称（reference）与满足（satisfaction）。戴维森[③]认为，有序的满足是传统的对事实的符合概念的全部内容。他认为指称和满足是不需要因果关系或任何解释的“理论结构”。

然而，即便逻辑原子主义和亚原子主义都做出了一些回应，其中也产

① Russell (1903).
② Wittgenstein (1961/ 1921: 2.04).
③ Davidson (1969), (1977).

生了一些新的问题。对于逻辑原子主义的问题如下：（a）基本的真之载体究竟是什么？他们是如何确定的？（b）有些分子真之载体（由原子组成），例如虚拟语气和反事实分子，往往会引起反对，但不能用简单的真条件子句来处理，因为它们的真值似乎不是由其构成的原子命题真值决定的。（c）是否存在与真的普遍命题相符合的普遍事实？维特根斯坦（1921）不承认有普遍事实，他认为应该用无限合取的方式对普遍命题进行分析；而罗素[①]和阿姆斯特朗则拒绝了这一分析，他们承认普遍事实。（d）“否定的（negative）真”是最臭名昭著的问题，因为它们与一个吸引人的原则“真之制造者原则”相冲突，这一原则认为世界上每个真都必须有某种东西使它成为事实，即，每个真之载体都必须有一个真之制造者。然而存在这种情况：假如 p 是基础的，非 p 为真当且仅当 p 是假的当且仅当 p 没有一个符合的事实；那么非 p 为真的情况并不存在一个真之制造者。

逻辑亚原子论的问题如下：（a）亚原子论与原子论一样，也解释了分子真之载体的真值；因此，具有“真”功能的分子真之载体仍然面临与原子论相同的问题。（b）信念归因（attribution）和模态要求引起的特殊问题，例如“相信”是一关系谓词，在句子“约翰相信雪是白的”为真当且仅当“相信”满足约翰和对象指称的“雪是白的”这一情况中，后者是一个事态，它使得亚原子主义无法进行处理。（c）指称不确定性现象有可能破坏以下观念：基本的真之载体的真值总是由其外延或构成要素的满足决定，例如相对论中的“质量”缺乏确定的指称，即无法说明其是相对的质量还是绝对的质量。

## 三　金岳霖版本的符合论

金岳霖建立在其知识论体系之上，综合了融洽、有效、一致等真理论的一些观点，提出了一种新的符合论学说。对于真，金岳霖给出的定义非

---

① Russel（1918）.

常直接：符合是“真”的所谓，本书以符合为真的定义，所谓真就是符合。我们常识如此接受是因为我们接受一独立于知识者的客观的外界，我们要求命题与那外界的情况符合。[①] 围绕着关于真即符合的定义，金岳霖如同其他版本的符合论一样，对于符合论的三部分概念也分别给出了自己的定义和论证。

首先是对于真之载体，金岳霖将命题作为真之载体，并给出了命题的定义：命题的定义就是思议[②]内容之有真或假者，或意思内容中之肯定事实或道理者，或一句陈述句子之所表示而又断定事实或道理，因此而为有真假的思议的内容者。[③] 在金岳霖看来，命题通过句子进行表述，而这个句子必须是陈述句，对于疑问句，祈使句这些句子都不能表示一个命题，这就把句子和命题进行了区分。除了用肯定句来表示命题之外，金岳霖还进一步规定了表示命题的是句子样型（types）。句子可以区分为样型和凭借（tokens），它们是两者相互依靠联系起来的。要区分这两者可以用一个例子来说明：“aaaa”就样型说仅表示一个字母，而就凭借说则表示四个字母。句子凭借表现的是命题的显现，它是一个特殊的事体，有某时某地某环境的问题，而句子样型表现的是命题本身，它具有普遍性，不存在某时某地的局限问题。金岳霖把真之载体认作命题，可以看出其首先认为真之载体必须要具有普遍性、客观性的特征，信念具有特殊性和主观性的特征，因此必然是不被接受的。而通过对句子进行凭借和样型的区分，清楚地区分出了句子凭借用来表现命题显现的部分和想象上的寄托，而句子样型表达了命题本身和思议的内容。

从形式上看，金岳霖还给出了基于谓词逻辑的命题的共同形式“Φx”，这个形式体现了命题的主谓结构，并且其形式是可以延伸为“Φx · Φx……”的合取式。他清楚的区分出所寄托的句子层面的主谓与命题层面的主谓的不同：句子或表示命题的句子有时有主词和谓词，命题也有主体

① 金岳霖（2017：947－948）。

② 需要澄清的是，在金岳霖的知识论中，“思想”需要被划分为两个概念，思是思议，想是想象，思议的内容是意念或概念，思议的对象是普遍的抽象的对象；想象的内容是意象，想象的对象是具体的个体的特殊的东西。

③ 金岳霖（2017：866）。

和谓念。我们现在要表示文法上的主词不必表示命题的主体。[①] 在形式上，Φ 表示的是命题的谓念，而 x 则表示命题的主体。我们举一个简单的例子来说明金岳霖的这种命题形式的看法，例如“这个人是学生”这个句子，其按照共同形式“Φx”的改写不是将 x 当作“这个人”，Φ 当作学生，这样的划分。而是要化归为“Φx · Φx”的合取式，即 x 当作这个主体，Φ 为“是人”和“是学生”，于是这个句子应该改写为“x 是人且 x 是学生”。在这个新改写的句子中能看出，主体是 x，而谓念有两个，分别是“是人”与“是学生”。所以单看一个句子的主谓结构并不能一下子就将主体和谓念对应清楚，这也是为什么金岳霖特别强调主词有时候不必表示主体。

命题还有特殊和普遍之分，金岳霖认为特殊命题是对于特殊有所肯定或否定的命题，用句子表示时的主词指示一个特殊的东西或事体。所谓指示，意思是要利用文字以外的工具去衬托某一特殊的东西或事体出来。例如“这个人是学生”中的主词“这个人”是限于某时某地的特殊的人，就必须在文字以外说明清楚这个人的特殊性，否则无法说明“这个人”的意义和指称，也就无法判断这个句子的真假，因而也就称不上是个命题了。而普遍命题不同于特殊命题，它既不肯定或否定特殊的事实，也不肯定或否定限于时地的普通情形。句子中表示普遍命题的主词所表示的是抽象的，“就所思的内容说，它是意念，或概念，就所思的对象说，它是种类或共相”[②]。意念或概念都是抽象的，它们都不是象。金岳霖特别强调这一点，抽象的意念如“无量大”，本身找不到一个具体的意象，即不能把意念当作意象。意念是普遍的，它可以被普遍的引用，而象是特殊的，不存在“普遍的象”的说法。有些意念有相应的意象以为寄托，如“红”意念可以寄托在“红”意象上，但二者是有分别的。总之，金岳霖认为普遍命题之为普遍是就它所断定[③]的对象说的，它所断定的对象是普遍的；特殊

---

① 金岳霖（2017：868）。

② 金岳霖（2017：873）。

③ 断定是判断中一主要活动，在金岳霖的概念中它专指命题的断定，即活动只限于命题。断定者就是判断者，而断定不就是判断。

命题之为特殊是就它所断定的对象说的，它所断定的对象是特殊的。命题无论就普遍或特殊说，总是思议的内容，总是意念或概念的关联或容纳一呈现，或意象于一意念或概念范围之内。

其次是对于真之制造者，金岳霖和大多数符合论者一样，给出的是“事实”这一概念①。金岳霖对于事实给出的定义是“事实是接受了的或安排了的所与”②，它总是客观的，它的材料总是所与③。事实实际上是一种意念与所与的混合物，它是套上意念的所与或者填入所与的意念。它既然是接受、安排了的所与，就意味着已经有意念去接受它，在接受中我们也少不了进行判断，因此作为混合物的事实既有所与成分，也有接受成分。只有正确的接受才能称之为事实，而事实又不是普遍的，既没有普遍的个体也没有普遍的事实，因此金岳霖直言“事实是特殊的真命题之所表示或肯定的”④。事实总是已经发生或者正在发生的，也就是说，事实总牵扯到时空，因此我们描述一个事实总是离不开说出它的一时一地，这是事实特殊性的表现，也是其限制。

金岳霖还指出了事实没有正负的问题，即不存在负事实的说法。传统的真之同一性理论认为，命题与事实是同一的，然而它们很快就遇到了很大的困难，即一个正（肯定的）命题是一个正的事实，那么一个负（否定的）命题是否是一个负的事实呢？例如“这是个学生”无疑能找到这个事实，但说“这不是个学生”是事实就让人难以在经验上接受。金岳霖认为，正的真命题表述一个事实应该是没有问题的，无论是一个正的普遍的真命题表示或肯定固然的理⑤，还是一个正的特殊的真命题表示一特殊的

① 金岳霖认为用“事实”来讨论命题符合与否的情况是为了方便，实际上这个真之制造者应该是“实在”，客观的情形并不有命题而已，普遍命题所符合的是固然的理，特殊命题所符合的是所断定的事实，历史总结命题所符合的是一时一地的普通情形。详见金岳霖（2017：955）。

② 金岳霖（2017：770）。

③ 所与的概念在金岳霖的知识论中是较为核心的概念，他的知识论从正觉即正常的官觉出发，认为正觉的内容是呈现，而呈现中客观的部分称之为所与。所与是客观的，相对于官觉类的（如人类、狗类），它是知识的材料。

④ 金岳霖（2017：787）。

⑤ 固然的理是把自然律的对象综合起来说的，固然表示此理本来如此，它不是官觉者或知识者创造的，也不同于必然的理，它并非逻辑命题。

事实都没有问题。但是负的真命题依然是肯定一事实的，但事实本就没有正负一说，就金岳霖的观点看，完全没有官觉上根据的压根就不能称之为事实，当然也不会有负事实的说法了。负的特殊的真命题仍然有事实上的根据，至少与之矛盾的命题肯定不是事实，我们可以判断其为假。鉴于金岳霖的这种判断，他反对真之同一性理论，坚持了符合论的观点。

金岳霖把事实作为真之制造者，其最大的特点是承认一个实在论的前提，即存在一个本然的世界作为我们所与的来源。本然的世界是所有不同的官觉类所共有的世界，这区别于自然的世界而言，自然是相对于不同的官觉类的。就本然说，人类和狗类都有同样的本然世界，但就自然说，人类和狗类的自然是不同的。然而事实并不就是本然或自然的世界，事实是受时空限制的特殊的真命题，其限于一时一地的特征更接近于“事态”的概念，并且它不假设存在着不被获得的事实，因为事实还有被意念接受的成分。由此看来，金岳霖对于事实的理解更接近于事态符合论的观点，即 CS：若 x 是一个 p，则 x 是真（假）的当且仅当 x 符合一个（不）获得的事态（获得的事态就是事实）。

最后是对于符合关系的理解，金岳霖坚持符合论的观点，并且把真定义为符合：符合与否是真假的定义，所谓真就是符合。符合不是求真的工具，它是理解真的概念。[①] 把真当作符合，那么真就是一种关系质，它是命题与客观的实在（即事实）的关系所赋予命题的关系质，而不是命题自身带有的性质。它也不是命题与命题之间的关系，也不是所谓的一致，因为单一的命题是有所谓真的，但是可以没有命题间的一致关系。把真作为符合还意味着我们不可能用情感意志去改变这种关系，因为实在本身是客观的，而命题就金岳霖看来，也是客观的，那么这个符合当然就是一种客观的关系，不由主观的意志去改变了。把真作为符合也表示一种独立性，一个命题的真不会是说某时某地为真，它是独立于时空的真，它不是相对的真，而是绝对的真，从这也可以看出以真为符合具有一种超越性。通过把真当作符合，金岳霖想表现的是真所又具有的客观性、独立性和超

① 金岳霖（2017：956）。

越性。

除了符合的定义外，符合还有标准的问题，即用什么样的标准去判断一个命题与实在是否是符合的。金岳霖综合了融洽、有效、一致三种判断的方式，作为符合的标准。第一种判断方式是融洽，金岳霖认为应该关注的是一时一地的感觉上的经验上的融洽，而不是大范围的融洽，例如用水洗脚，因太冷或太热大喊一声便是不融洽，温度适中便是融洽。融洽还分积极与消极，积极的融洽才是属于真假的标准，它是把注意力集中在真假的问题上，是从正觉出发的；倘若是感觉迟钝、缺乏训练而注意力不集中在真假上，便是消极融洽的情况。融洽也有程度、范围的不同，知识愈多，理论愈严，工具也愈精，而所感觉到的融洽范围愈广，程度愈高。总之，融洽是符合的必要条件而不是充分条件，真可以推出融洽，但是融洽无法推出真。第二种判断方式是有效，由于感觉上的融洽有一定的时间限制性，对于一些假设的命题等无法马上得出融洽与否，因此采用有效的判断方式是必要的。所谓有效是相对于假设[①]说的，假设在没有事实上的障碍或者思想上的不一致时是一种暂时的有效，而当命题得到证实之后，假设便完全有效。在有效性上，也具有时空的限制性，在不同的时期内，只要知识有进步，有效和融洽一样也成为范围加大，程度加高的有效。和融洽一样，一个无效的命题虽是假的，但是有效的命题也不必是真的，它是符合的必要不充分条件。第三种判断方式是一致，金岳霖定义一致为：所谓一致就是多数命题的彼此无矛盾。宽义的一致是命题（多数）的无矛盾，狭义的一致是相干的命题的无矛盾。[②] 所谓相干是就真值蕴涵（entailment）说的，倘若命题 p 和 q 彼此不蕴涵彼此，或没有蕴涵关系，则 p，q 不相干，否则相干。金岳霖认为，用来作为符合标准的一致不是形上的一致。真的命题的确一致，但一致的命题不一定真。不一致的命题有真有假，假的命题可以一致并且还可以一致的假。假的命题可以一致是说 p，q，r……可以一致又都是假的，一致的假是说它们彼此有蕴涵关系，成为

① 此处的假设按金岳霖说，应该是 hypothesis，是有待于证实的，它不是 assumption 即假设它的人都认为真且不必证明证实。

② 金岳霖（2017：966）。

有系统的假命题集合。（金岳霖只承认命题可以一致地假，但不承认有一致的“假”的逻辑）与一命题一致的命题虽不必真，然而与真命题一致的命题确是真命题。一致这一标准不同于融洽和有效求之于命题范围之外（融洽是命题和对象在感觉上的融洽，有效是命题在行为或作或结果上的有效），它只是就命题一方面而说的，不是就命题和它的对象的关系而说的。那么为什么命题的一致能作为符合的标准呢？按金岳霖的推论：所与本来是有法有则的，事实既是接受了的所与，也本来是有理论结构的；理没有冲突，事与事之间也没有冲突；此所以与真命题相干而又一致的命题也是真的。[①] 一致与融洽、有效还有一个区别，一致是样型，它是没有时空限制的，因此不会有一时一地的一致。一般我们认为有一时一地一致的是对应于命题显现的一致感，这和一致是有区别的，一致是不需要为感觉者所感觉的。但一致仍旧与融洽、有效一样，都是符合的必要而不充分的条件。

## 四　金氏符合论是否足以回应反驳？

金岳霖版本（下称“金氏”）的符合论显然是符合 CS 定义版本的符合论的，但其符合论的版本是否能够应对学者们对于符合论的各种反驳呢？首先在 CS 定义上狭窄的问题上，金氏符合论已经做出了一定的回应，按金岳霖说，命题所符合的对象是实在，普遍命题所符合的对象是固然的理，它是可以被证实或证明的；特殊命题所符合的对象是断定的事实；历史总结的命题所符合的对象是限于一时一地的普通情形。[②] 可以说，金氏符合论中的实在考虑了有无时空限制的各种情况，是比一般 CF 或 CS 定义中事实和事态概念更精确、宽泛的真之制造者。而对于诸如道德等领域的命题，金岳霖虽然没有谈论其是否应该被纳入符合论之中，但是根据他对命题的理解为“思议内容的有真有假者”，我们可以推断，与道德相关的句子本身可能并不符合命题的标准，因为其本身不能判断真假，从而也就

① 金岳霖（2017：968）。
② 金岳霖（2017：955）。

无法被纳入符合论的范围之中。由此看来，对于这个问题，金岳霖的回应应该是拒绝道德等无法判断真假的句子作为命题，从而避免这一责难。

其次，在符合论太显然的问题上，金岳霖也可以说其定义也不是简单的浓缩公式。他清楚的说明“真是符合”的真的定义，并且给出了融洽、有效、一致应用于具体不同情况的必要而不充分条件，提出了一个完整而全面的符合论体系。显然，金氏符合论将传统的真之理论竞争者都当作判断是否“符合”的标准，从而囊括进符合论之中。因此也是超越了一个简单的定义，具有丰富内涵的符合论，这一责难对金氏符合论并不有效。

再来看对于符合论模糊的指责。在 C1 中，相似关系的指责在金氏符合论中并不成立，因为无论作为其真之载体的命题，还是作为真之制造者的事实，都是来自于所与的。命题是思议内容之有真有假，而思议的原料就是所与，因此命题作为内容是从所与而来的；而事实是接受了或安排了的所与，是所与和意念的混合物，因此根本上也是来自于所与的。所与是客观的呈现，命题与事实同样是客观的，它们之间的相似关系是符合关系当然也就不是问题。同样的对于 C2，金氏符合论也不存在神秘的符合关系一说，因为命题与事实的关系并非是一种主客二元的截然划分，也没有鸿沟一说。金岳霖在《知识论》中直言：本书认为有经验之内的客观事实，这主要在于本书以正觉[①]为出发点。正觉所供给的所与本来就是客观的，它是客观的呈现。事实是以意念去接受了的所与，就所与说，它是在客的，在外的；就以意念去接受说，它是在我的，在内的。命题与事实本来就没有鸿沟。[②] 前文说到，把“真”作为符合也表示一种独立性，一个命题的真不会是说某时某地为真，它是独立于时空的真，它不是相对的真，而是绝对的真，从这也可以看出以真为符合具有一种超越性。由此看来，金氏符合论并没有 C2 指出的问题。

对于 F1 的问题，前述已经说明了没有负事实即否定性事实这么一说，而对于析取、条件、普遍、概率、虚拟、反事实等各种事实是否存在的问

① 正常的官能者在官能活动中正常地官能到外物或外物的一部分即为正觉。详见第三章所与或知识的材料 I 正觉的分析。

② 金岳霖（2017：955）。

题，金岳霖没有给出相应的说法。但是就其对于事实的概念看，显然也不存在以上列举的不同种类的事实。就金岳霖看来，事实是受限于时空具有特殊性的，完全没有官觉上根据的压根就不能称之为事实，因此以上所列的不同类型的事实本身并不存在这种说法。按金岳霖的话语说，事实本身没问题，但这种事实的学说有问题。在这个问题上，金氏符合论与逻辑原子论的观点类似，都只承认"正事实"。对于 F2 的问题，金氏符合论也可以说这种指责是无力的，因为事实本身是意念和所与的混合物，并不能简单的将其看作是意念随意的一种安排，更不能说其是从句子中投射出来的虚假的概念。句子是命题的表示工具，我们也通过句子对事实进行判断。事实和命题之间差异在金氏符合论中也很显然，因此 F2 的指责也是无力的。

尽管在金岳霖的知识论体系中，真之符合论是能够自圆其说的，对于多数问题也能够进行有力的回应，然而其一些基础概念的前提设定依然会让人诟病。例如一个"本然"的世界存在的可能，是类似于像康德式的"物自体"的存在，金岳霖并没有提供一个其为何存在与如何可能的有效论证，而只将其当作预设前提，这对于一些不接受这一前提的怀疑论者或许依旧是无法满足的。外部世界与内在世界的鸿沟在多数学者看来，依然无法进行弥合。然而金岳霖用于符合事实的并非是信念或主观的主张，而是客观的命题。如果说在主客之间存在着鸿沟的问题，那么在金岳霖符合论中应该是不成立的，有这个问题的不是"符合"，而是命题本身的获得与事实本身的获得的问题。命题与事实的获得与否是否合适，金岳霖没有明确指出，只是略微提到了依靠"正觉"来进行应付。但即便如此，金氏符合论依然给现代符合论提供了存在的空间。

综上所述，金氏符合论应该至少是对大多数对于符合论的问题都能够做出回应的，虽然其还存在着"本然""正觉"等难以说明的本体论预设，但是其对于真之承载者、真之制造者以及符合关心的充分解释，使得其仍旧提供了足够强有力的符合论版本来回应已有符合论的困难。而其对于真之融贯论、有效论等竞争者，都将它们归结为符合的标准之一，作为必要而不充分的条件，而不是作为真之定义去看待，这就把真之定义与真之标准进行了区分，使得其具有更强的竞争力。

**参考文献**

金岳霖，2017，《知识论》，商务印书馆。

Armstrong, D. M., 1997, *A World of States of Affairs*, Cambridge: Cambridge University Press.

Austin, J. L., 1950, "Truth", reprinted in*Philosophical Papers*, *3rd*, Oxford: Oxford University Press 1979.

Bourget, D. and Chalmers, D., 2014, "What Do Philosophers Believe?" *Philosophical Studies*, 170, 465 - 500.

Blackburn, S., 1984, *Spreading the Word: Groundings in the Philosophy of Language*, Oxford: Clarendon Press.

Davidson, D., 1969, "True to the Facts", *The Journal of Philosophy* 66, 748 - 764.

——, 1977, "Reality Without Reference", *Dialectica* 31, 247 - 253.

Popper, K., 1972, "Philosophical Comments on Tarski's Theory of Truth", *Objective Knowledge: An Evolutionary Approach*, Oxford: Clarendon Press.

Patterson, D., ed., 2008, *New Essays on Tarski and Philosophy*, Oxford: Oxford University Press.

Quine, W. V. O., 1987, *Quiddities: An Intermittently Philosophical Dictionary*, Cambridge, Mass.: Harvard University Press.

Russell, B., 1903, *The Principles of Mathematics*, London: Allen and Unwin.

——, 1918, "The Philosophy of Logical Atomism", *Logic and Knowledge: Essays 1901 - 1950*, ed., by R. C. Marsh, London: George Allen and Unwin 1956.

Strawson, P. F., 1950, *Truth*; reprinted in *Truth*, ed., by G. Pitcher, Englewood Cliffs: Prentice - Hall 1964.

Soames, S., 1999, *Understanding Truth*, Oxford - New York: Oxford University Press.

Tarski, A., 1935, "The Concept of Truth in Formalized Languages", *Logic*, *Semantics*, *Metamathematics 2nd ed.*, Indianapolis: Hackett 1983.

Wittgenstein, L., 1961 [1921], *Tractatus Logico - Philosophicus*, trans., D. F. Pears and B. F. McGuinness, London: Routledge.

# 实践哲学
# Practical Philosophy

# 欲望、文学与审判

## ——但丁《神曲》的一种哲学解读

威廉·E. 卡洛（William E. Carroll）*

吕鹏（LV Peng）/译（trans.）**

**摘要**：解读但丁的伟大诗作是一项艰巨的任务。但丁既是诗人又是心灵的朝圣者，他既是这首诗的作者，也是这首诗的主题。在全部文本中，诗人坚持他的地狱、炼狱与天堂之旅的现实性特征。诗人但丁不时向读者讲述应如何理解他所写的内容，以及遇到他的故事时应避免的各种危险。在阅读伟大作品时迷失的危险是但丁与弗朗西丝卡和鲍罗在欲望之地狱层会面的重要部分。在讲述心灵朝圣者（但丁）对弗朗西丝卡读兰斯洛特和吉内维尔的故事的反应时，诗人但丁提供了如何阅读他自己的诗的重要线索。

**关键词**：但丁；《神曲》；维吉尔；《埃涅阿斯纪》

## Lust, Literature, and Damnation: Reading Dante's *Divine Comedy*

**Abstract**: Reading Dante's great poem is a daunting task. Dante is both poet and pilgrim, since he is both the author of the poem and the subject of the po-

* Distinguished Visiting Professor, School of Philosophy, Zhongnan University of Economics and Law.

** 吕鹏，武汉大学，武汉晴川学院犹太文化研究中心。

em. Throughout the text, the poet insists upon the "realism" of his journey through Hell, Purgatory, and Heaven. Dante, the poet, from time to time addresses the reader concerning how to understand what he has written and the dangers to be avoided in encountering his story. The dangers of losing one's way when reading great texts is an important part of the pilgrim's meeting with Francesca and Paolo in the circle of the lustful in Hell. In telling the story of the pilgrim's (Dante's) reaction to the story Francesca relates of her reading the story of Lancelot and Guinevere, Dante the poet offers important clues about how one ought to read his poem.

**Key words**: Dante, *Divine Comedy*, Virgil, Aeneid

我的重量就是我的爱；无论我被带到哪里，都是我的爱把我带到那里。

奥古斯丁《忏悔录》卷十三

但丁和维吉尔在地狱里遇见了亚里士多德！对现代人来说，这是一个多么令人兴奋的故事。然而，这位身处地狱的伟大哲学家亚里士多德，被但丁称为“哲人中的大师”（*il maestro di color che sanno*）[《地狱篇》4：131]。在这些评价中，我想称赞另一位大师——但丁。他理所当然地配得上这个头衔——“诗人中的大师”（*il maestro di color che poetanno*）。虽然我教学和研究的主要领域是科学史以及科学、哲学与神学之间的关系，但在美国我每隔一年就要教授一门关于但丁诗歌的课程。我的教学特色之一，尤其是关于知识史的课程，是带学生阅读西方文明的一些伟大作品，包括荷马、维吉尔、但丁、弥尔顿。从数学与自然科学，到社会学与心理学，不同学科的大学生能够与人文学科的学生一起阅读并讨论但丁的《神曲》等叙事诗，这是美国教育的一个亮点。当然，不是所有的学生都读但丁或其他伟大的叙事诗人的作品。但是那些读过的，可以通过接触一些关于自然、人性和上帝的最好的作品来丰富他们的教育经历。像荷马、维吉尔、但丁和弥尔顿这样的诗人要求我们深刻地思考我们自己和我们所居住的世界，我认为接触他们的作品应该是教育的一个重要组成部分，尤其是任何试图让人们了解何为人类的教育。事实上，我认为诗歌，包括索福克勒斯、埃斯库罗斯和莎士比亚等作家的伟大悲剧作品提供了遇到深刻哲学、神学问题之最佳途径的起点。诗歌既能激发想象力又能激发理智，这是哲学和神学等抽象作品所不能做到的。

尽管是尝试性的，但我期待与大家探索一些问题，即关于阅读但丁的伟大诗作意味着什么。众所周知，这部写于 14 世纪早期的《神曲》是一部关于但丁·阿利吉耶里在异世界的旅程——地狱、炼狱和天堂。这一百首诗歌分为三个部分：地狱、炼狱和天堂。在这三部分中，但丁分别见到了古代历史上著名或不太著名的人物，以及那些在但丁有生之年去世的人们。他们中有君主与帝王、哲人与诗人、主教和教皇们，还有商人、律师和政治家。《神曲》是一部关于中世纪文化的大百科全书，它汇集了希腊和罗马的主题，包括古代世界的神话人物，以及新旧约圣经的主题。在许多方面，这部诗歌是对古典文化与基督宗教之间关系的一个细致的评注——在理性与信仰之间。诗人但丁讲述了他自己的旅程，自始至终都有许多向导者襄助他。他第一个向导是罗马诗人维吉尔，其史诗《埃涅阿斯纪》是但丁的重要灵感来源。我不打算对《神曲》做一个概述——事实上，我预设大家对这部诗歌的总体结构是有一定熟悉程度的①。对于那些可能对这部伟大的诗歌知之甚少的人，我希望我的论述能激发他们更多的学习兴趣。

当天路客但丁离开地狱第一层的候判所（Limbo）进入地狱的第二层（这里是纵欲者被刑罚之处），他和维吉尔遇到了克里特岛传说中的国王，在维吉尔《埃涅阿斯纪》中曾被提到的冥界死者的审判者米诺斯。在但丁的《地狱篇》中，米诺斯检查了每一个被判罪人的过犯，然后把他或她打

① 《神曲》最好的英文译本和评论是 Charles Singleton 的。Allen Mandelbaum、Anthony Oldcorn 和 Charles Ross 为整首诗编辑了一段段的评论（Lectura Dantis），每卷一本分为三卷，分别对应《地狱》《炼狱》和《天堂》（加州伯克利，1998 年）。在但丁逝世 700 周年（2021 年）期间，又出现了许多新书和文章。也许到目前为止最著名的是 Giulio d'Onofrio 的 Per Questa Selva Oscura：La teologia poetica di Dante（Roma，2020）。两个极佳的在线资源分别是 Dartmouth 和 Princeton 的但丁项目。

入地狱里应得的层级里。米诺斯暂停了他的工作，对但丁说："你这来到受苦之境的人……要谨慎如何进入，留心所信任的，不要因入口的宽阔迷惑你"［《地狱篇》5：16－20］。这个警告不仅针对但丁，也针对我们这些读者，因为我们也和他们一道进入了这个"受苦之境"（*doloroso ospizio*）。但丁既是诗人亦是朝圣者。诗人但丁邀请我们（事实上，在某种意义上是迫使我们）与朝圣者但丁一起旅行，因为但丁是诗歌的中心人物。诗人邀请我们进入朝圣者的随行行列，与他一起经历地狱、炼狱与天堂的旅程。

但丁如此被造就了，所以他在《天堂篇》中告诉我们，他是一个宏大主题的诗人［《天堂篇》10：22］，他祈祷当他要把所见所闻写下来的时候他的记忆不会失效。我们该如何看待诗人对自己所见异象的真实性及其作品之先知性的执着？这些说法是否是但丁为了创作一部精彩的诗歌而特意使用的手法？因此，换句话说，这首诗在严格的意义上来说是虚构的吗？[①] 抑或我们又必须从其他方面来看待他的主张呢？

美国伟大的但丁研究专家查尔斯·辛格尔顿（Charles Singleton）指出："神曲的虚构性在于说它不是虚构的。"[②] 但我认为我们应该摒弃虚构与非虚构的二分法。这首诗是一个中世纪文学传统中的预言性文本，属于异象文学。这些文本不适于我们关于虚构或非虚构的分类范畴。现代读者可能的确难以将《神曲》视为非虚构之物。而这些只能告诉我们更多关于现代读者的事情，而不是诗歌本身，这点毫无疑问。当我们断然拒绝考虑但丁所说的现实时，我认为这种拒绝表明了我们对现实的狭义认识。现代性所主张的现实主张，尤其是作为一种排斥预言性和灵性——甚至排斥形而上学与神学的不真实的现实主张。它最多把它们放在想象的领域，这种平庸的现实主张实在无法从更深刻的维度去理解何为真实。

---

① 意大利伟大的但丁学者 Bruno Nardi 在《但丁的中世纪文化》（*Dante la cultura Medium*，Barii，1949）中的"但丁老师"（*Dante profeta*）中列出并讨论了但丁坚持自己所谓旅程真实性的所有主要段落，见第 336—416 页。

② Singleton（1957：129），也可以参考 Hollander。

1335 年，在佛罗伦萨举行的多明我会分会会议上，该社团的成员被正式禁止阅读但丁的《帝制论》（*De monarchia*）和《神曲》[①]。人们可以理解他们对《帝制论》的这一反应。因为在这部著作中，但丁支持那些主张神圣罗马皇帝自治权力的人的主张——而这一主张反对教皇权是基督教世界的最高权力。但是《神曲》又有什么危害呢？

会议前五年，多明我会神学家，里米尼的奎多·韦纳尼（Guido Vernani of Rimini）写信给大学校长博洛尼亚主教，呼吁关注他的观点——他认为但丁写了第五部福音书。不仅因为但丁声称知道被诅咒者和被拯救者的最终命运，且根据韦纳尼的看法，他写了一部关于神圣旅程的真实描述。

但丁最早的评注者，从他的儿子彼特罗·阿利吉耶里（Pietro Alighieri）开始，不遗余力地否认对但丁的异端指控。他们认为但丁的诗仅仅只是一个复杂的隐喻，是一位伟大的富有想象力的作家的作品而已[②]。因此，正如一位评论者雅各布·德拉·拉那（Jacopo della Lana）所描述，当但丁把一个灵魂“放置”在三个世界中的其中一个时，唯一真正被宣告的是关于这个灵魂的邪恶或美德。到 14 世纪末，这种评论传统已经确立。薄伽丘曾写道，但丁“带来了奇异、闻所未闻的心灵创造。《神曲》用一件妥帖合身的虚构外衣来隐匿真理”（*De genealogia deorum* 14.7）[③]。几乎六个世纪以来，这一传统观点占据了至高无上的地位：认为《神曲》的真理是隐喻式的，由但丁在“一件妥帖合身的虚构外衣”中阐述出来。比如即便在今天，这些评论家们会告诉我们，维吉尔代表理性，有一个大写的 R，贝阿特丽切则代表恩典。

如果把人物当作抽象物来看待的话，我认为这首诗是不可理解的。如

---

① Folena（1965：4）.

② Alighieri 写道：“有些事情不能从字面上理解，因为从字面上看，这样的事情会导致错误而不是指引。因为除了允许我区分比喻的说话方式之外，有哪个头脑健全的人会相信但丁是这样经历的，并且看到了这样的事情呢。”［《评注》第 8 页，引用于彼得·德朗克《但丁和中世纪拉丁传统》（1986：126，n.8）］德朗克的这篇笔记包含了关于这首诗的比喻和现实主义之解读的各种辩论中极好的论战。

③ For these commentaries on Dante，see the on－line Dartmouth Dante Project. 这些关于但丁的评注，请参看 on－line Dartmouth Dante Project。

果我们相信维吉尔因为我们认为他在某种程度上代表了理性，那我们就不会理解在地狱里对罪人的刑罚，也不会理解地狱或炼狱的结构。尽管但丁极度敬重维吉尔，但维吉尔的视野并不能取代诗人或朝圣者的视野，亦不是理性的化身。

这部神曲是一个“美丽的谎言”（*bella menzogna*）吗？我们如何解读它？它到底是什么样的著作？

为了寻找答案，让我们回到“地狱”，即但丁文中的地狱。作为对米诺斯警告的回应，朝圣者的向导维吉尔告诉米诺斯，但丁的旅程是一次“命定之旅”（*fatale andare*）[《地狱篇》5：22]。它是来自上天的意志，在那里能力与意志是同一的。由于维吉尔是他的向导，我们常常想起但丁的旅程与埃涅阿斯旅程的对比。公元前 1 世纪维吉尔所写的伟大罗马史诗《埃涅阿斯纪》讲述了特洛伊王子从被希腊人征服的城市的火焰中出逃的故事。被维吉尔称之为“命运之逃亡者”（*fato profugus*）的埃涅阿斯 [《埃涅阿斯纪》1.2]，在众神的带领下，在西边建立了一座新的城市，这座城是朱庇特神所许诺的永远的帝国（*imperium sine fine*）[《埃涅阿斯纪》1.279]。罗马这座城市的起源，通过维吉尔的史诗，追溯到了古特洛伊城，并发现它的英雄奠基者埃涅阿斯，已注定由众神立为一个天下城邦（cosmo－polis）的根基。这个城市是一个真正的世界之城。

但丁和埃涅阿斯之间的对比在《神曲》中很明显。与米诺斯相遇之前，当维吉尔向但丁宣布他必须进行的另一个世界之旅时，但丁反对说：“我为何要到那里去？又是谁容许我这样？我不是埃涅阿斯，我也不是保罗。”[《地狱篇》2：31－32] 毕竟，埃涅阿斯建立罗马的使命，其中一个使命包括访问亡者的世界，是众神许可的。而圣保罗升入天堂的出神经历，正如他在写给哥林多人的书信中所描述的 [《哥林多后书》12.4] 是上帝特别恩典的结果。虽然有几十种以文学形式被记录下来的中世纪的天堂和地狱景象，但没有其他作者如但丁一样叙述。“在但丁之前，没有一位中世纪的作家将自己与埃涅阿斯和圣保罗相比，认为他是受上帝恩典的驱使，为了人类的利益而进行另一次世界之旅，以便在世界历史的关键时刻纠正其中的不公。”①

随着《神曲》的展开，我们看到但丁变成了一个新的埃涅阿斯和一个新的保罗。希腊和罗马的精神遗产，特别是通过维吉尔和《埃涅阿斯纪》的调和，与希伯来及基督教圣经的传统结合在一起，形成了但丁诗歌的根基。因此，在某个重要意义上，《神曲》是西方文明的灵魂诗作。但是当我们进入诗句时，正如米诺斯告诉但丁的那样，“要谨慎如何进入，留心所信任的，不要因入口的宽阔迷惑你”。(《地狱篇》5：19－20）危险是真的，但并不比地狱这“痛苦之处所”（abode of pain）中的更真实。我们必须学会如何在诗句中航行，这样我们才能安全抵达旅程的终点。

在整部《神曲》中，诗人不时地直接对他的听众讲话，唤起我们对一个特别事件的注意，或邀请我们进入一个更深刻的视野。在《天堂篇》的第二篇，有一个特别令人困惑的警告。但丁对他的这群读者们说：“在一桅小舟中，渴望倾听的你们呀，跟随在我的船舰后面，歌唱着驶向她的航路。回头再看看你们的海岸吧，不要在深渊中贸然前进，因为也许失去了我，你们会坠入迷茫（*rimarreste smarriti*）。我要经过的水域，前人从未航行过。”［《天堂篇》2：1－6］我们如何避免诗人所暗示的危险？我们如何避免迷失和困惑？② 的确，我们应该像但丁建议的那样回头是岸吗？我们在诗句中的航行是否有可能像但丁在《地狱篇》第26篇中如此雄辩地描述的，尤利西斯的“疯狂飞行”（*folle volo*）？在荷马《奥德赛》里面那个著名故事的中世纪版本中，但丁笔下的尤利西斯讲述了他如何牺牲自己的责任回到希腊的妻子和家庭，并诱使他的船员航行到地中海世界以外的未知之地③。然而，尤利西斯的航行以海难和诅咒告终。我们在诗句中的航行也有类似的危险。

最后，我想，我们已经准备好和但丁一起在地狱的第二层里遇到纵欲之徒了。我想说，这篇诗文很重要。与其说是为了理解对放纵的惩罚，不如说是因为这篇诗文揭示了文学的危险，即相对应地，当我们读者遇到

① Peter Dronke（1986：2）.

② 动词 smarire 的过去分词是诗人在地狱之初用来描述旅程开始前的状况的分词。

③ Charles Singleton（1970：456－457，n.56）.

《神曲》本身时，应该避免的危险。事实上，我们可能会发现欲望、文学和审判之间的关联。

当我们回到第五篇时[①]，我们与维吉尔和但丁一起听到了哀号的“悲哀音符”，旋风的风暴，罪恶之灵魂的尖叫、呻吟和哀叹——那些被地狱之狂风掀翻的灵魂“上下旋转、左右翻腾”。［《地狱篇》5：23ff］地狱的天气反映了主宰这里受罚之罪人生活中不安的激情。在欲望的地狱层里，一对罪人“如同被欲望召唤来的鸽子”，离开了“狄多所在的队伍”，穿过“恶毒的气流”向着天路客但丁而来。拉文纳领主吉多·达·波伦塔的女儿弗朗西丝卡，嫁给了里米尼领主吉安西奥托·马拉泰斯塔。不幸的是，她和自己已婚的小叔子鲍罗相爱了。弗朗西丝卡讲述了她和鲍罗如何在他们激情四射的拥抱中惊异，然后被她丈夫杀死的故事。她言辞中的魅力吸引了但丁，使但丁问道：“弗朗西丝卡，你的痛苦令我悲伤怜悯而哭泣，但是请告诉我，在甜蜜叹息的时候，爱情是怎样使你知道你可疑的欲望的？”［《地狱篇》5：116 - 120］弗朗西丝卡透露回应说，当她和鲍罗一起读到兰斯洛特（Lancelot）和吉内维尔（Guinevere）的故事时，他们被深深地迷住了，以至于他们屈服于彼此的欲望：

> 有一天，为了消遣，我们读到了兰斯洛特的故事，看爱情是如何锁住了他。我们二人单独共处，什么也不怀疑。有好几次阅读让我们的目光相遇，颜容也为之失色。但在突然间，它战胜了我们。当我们读到渴望的微笑是如何被如此伟大的爱人亲吻时，这个永远不能与我分离的人，颤抖着吻了我的嘴唇。这本书和作者就是我们的加莱奥托（Gleotto），那天我们再也没有继续读下去了。（《地狱篇》5：127 - 138）

在亚瑟王的传说中，加莱奥托爵士怂恿了骑士兰斯洛特和王后吉内维尔之间的不当关系。因此，弗朗西丝卡特别恰当地将这本书称作“加

① 关于这首歌的大量评论贯穿于有关《神曲》的文献中。尤其是对弗朗西丝卡和鲍罗的故事，一个特别有见地的分析是 Paolo Valesio（1998）。

莱奥托”。

这段诗句最后描述了天路客但丁对弗朗西丝卡的故事的反应：“当一个灵魂说这话时，另一个灵魂哭了，因为怜悯，我晕倒了，好像死了一样，像死尸一样倒下。”［《地狱篇》5：139－142］[①] 弗朗西丝卡和鲍罗因为激情而失去了意识，但丁却因为同情而失去了意识。

在这篇诗歌的前面，维吉尔为但丁列出了其他在纵欲地狱层里受到惩罚的罪人们：女人中有迦太基的建立者——腓尼基逃亡出来的狄多王后，以及埃及艳后克利奥帕特拉，还有美女海伦——她被帕里斯掳走正是特洛伊战争的起因。在男人中，维吉尔指出了阿喀琉斯，帕里斯和特里斯坦。事实上，维吉尔向但丁展示了“一千多个阴魂，并指出他们的名字”［《地狱篇》5：67－68］。但丁告诉我们：“当我听到我的老师指出旧时的女子与骑士们（*le donne antiche e' cavalieri*）的名字时，怜悯战胜了我，我感到眩晕。”［《地狱篇》5：70－72］注意这句话，就在与弗朗西丝卡相遇之前，预示了她要讲述的故事，以及但丁对此的反应：“怜悯战胜了我，我感到眩晕。”[②] 这些古代女子与骑士的故事，是中世纪宫廷爱情传统的核心，不仅唤起人们对伟大功绩和高尚事迹的回忆，也唤起人们罪孽的激情。正如我们所看到的，弗朗西丝卡揭露了她自己对这样一个故事的解读：“有好几次阅读让我们的目光相遇，颜容也为之失色。但在突然间，它战胜了我们。（*ma un solo punto fu quel che ci vinse*）”［《地狱篇》5：131－132］他们所读的书有自己的韵律，它渐渐占据了恋人们的心。

我认为这篇诗歌有一个核心主题——文学通过文字保存和传播古老的爱情故事，可能会把我们引向罪孽。就像鲍罗和弗朗西丝卡借由阅读他们“自由的加莱奥托”（*libro galeotto*），即兰斯洛特和吉内维尔的传奇，而被引向罪孽一样。文学作品中充斥着“书写下来的荒谬”（falli scritti）——我在这里借用了但丁在《天堂篇》（16：13－15）[③] 里一段文字中所使用的表达方式。事实上，弗朗西丝卡自己的故事本身亦是一个“书写下来的

---

① 这首歌最后一行的节奏是但丁诗歌天才的一个极好的例子：*E caddi come corpo morto cade*。

② 最后一句话是 *fui quasi smariito*，再次呼应了第一章开头所介绍的失落感和迷茫感。

③ Poggiolo（1957：343－344）.

荒谬”。

学者们指出，弗朗西丝卡对兰斯洛特传奇中接吻情节的解释与中世纪传奇本身所描绘的内容之间存在着重大差异。在罗曼史中，颤抖的兰斯洛特被吉内维尔抓住并亲吻。在弗朗西丝卡的版本中，角色颠倒了，弗朗西丝卡颤抖的嘴唇被鲍罗亲吻。弗朗西丝卡误传的爱情故事中的段落反映了她和鲍罗故事中的重要瞬间，这是很有启发性的。熟悉中世纪宫廷爱情传统的读者会发现，弗朗西丝卡在任何宫廷邂逅情节的既定套路中都会被设定在这个重要瞬间中——在宫廷爱情故事的术语中被称为“爱之燃点”（*amoris ascensio*）。正如弗朗西丝卡所说，他们读到了兰斯洛特，“看爱情是如何锁住了他”（*come amor lo strinse*）。弗朗西丝卡和鲍罗对兰斯洛特的“爱之燃点”所展示出的好奇心，与天路客但丁对他们俩自己的“燃点”所展示出的好奇心简直雷同：“爱情是怎样使你知道你可疑的欲望的?”

当诗人但丁把注意力集中在这个重要瞬间（*solo punto*）时，我想他希望他的读者能够注意到 13 世纪晚期流行的兰斯洛特和吉内维尔故事的特别版本。[①] 在这个故事版本中，兰斯洛特被认为是呆傻笨拙的，而吉内维尔是操控性和轻蔑的。实际上在这个版本中，亲吻兰斯洛特的吉尼维尔根本不是亚瑟王的妻子，而是个女巫般的赝品。但是因为在接吻的那一刻他们停止了阅读，鲍罗和弗朗西丝卡并不知道她的真实身份。他们也不知晓兰斯洛特因为他对神圣追求的不忠而受到了严厉的惩罚，他的位置由加莱奥托所取代。讽刺的是，弗朗西丝卡和鲍罗所读到的兰斯洛特故事实际上是对骑士精神的信仰批判，为表明私通之爱只会带来不快。鲍罗和弗朗西丝卡正在阅读一篇专为预防潜在通奸者下地狱而创作的作品。而他们身处地狱的事实表明，他们没有聆听他们最需要的指引，却真确地迷失在了字里行间!

弗朗西丝卡的最后一语“那天我们再也没有继续读下去了”（*quel giorno piu non vi leggemmo avante*）也许会让人想起另一个著名的关于罪的自传，但结局却不同。早在 900 年之前，也就是公元 4 世纪末，奥古斯丁

---

① Sommer（1909 - 13：258 - 263）.

用他的笔告诉我们，当他皈依基督教的时候，他是如何听到一个孩子的声音说："拿起来读吧，拿起来读吧!"奥古斯丁记载了他对这个声音的回应。之后，他读到了圣保罗致罗马人书信中那句著名的谴责肉体罪恶的经文。奥古斯丁接着说："我没有再读下去了，这已经够了。"[《忏悔录》卷八：12] 奥古斯丁对圣保罗书信的阅读让我们想起了《忏悔录》中的一个更早的场景。当奥古斯丁写到他早年的教育时，他提到了他学习过的维吉尔的《埃涅阿斯纪》：

> 我不得不背诵一位名叫埃涅阿斯的英雄的流浪故事，而与此同时，我却不知道自己飘荡的生活方式。我学会了为殉情的狄多之死而哀叹，却没有为自己的困境而流泪。而一直以来，在这些事情中，我都朝向死亡行进，而与你，我的上帝、我的生命分离。还有什么比一个不幸的罪人不知道自身的悲惨处境，还为狄多的命运而哀叹更可悲的呢？狄多是为着爱埃涅阿斯而死，我这罪人却没有因为缺乏对你的爱而死，去为自己流泪。因为爱这个世界，就是与你（上帝）断绝关系，然而人们却为之鼓舞，并为违背于此而感到羞耻。我没有为此而哭泣，而是为狄多哭泣，她将自己的生命付与利刃，而我却离弃了你，将自己交给了你创造的至低之物。[《忏悔录》卷一：13]

有趣的是，维吉尔和《埃涅阿斯纪》在《神曲》中具有的特殊位置与奥古斯丁皈依经历中的相反。在《忏悔录》中，奥古斯丁戏剧化地描述了他经历曲折的理智与感官诱惑，从《埃涅阿斯纪》到上帝之书的心灵之旅。《忏悔录》的最后部分包含了奥古斯丁对上帝之书，即《圣经》的系统性解读。在许多方面，但丁拯救了这部伟大的罗马史诗及其作者，使其免受奥古斯丁式的严厉谴责①。事实上，但丁把《埃涅阿斯纪》放在救赎历史的背景下，把特洛伊人和犹太人二者都视为上帝的选民。特洛伊人埃

① 对于维吉尔和奥古斯丁的讨论，因为它涉及理解《地狱篇》第五篇及以后的内容，我要感谢 Giuseppe Mazzotta（1979），特别是第 147—191 页的工作，因为它影响了我在这一节的大部分分析。

涅阿斯是罗马的创立者，他代表着为基督的到来而预备的世界那个遥远的文明起源。

我们不能因为《神曲》蕴含了异教之古典沉淀的重要元素，包括史诗，就觉得但丁对《埃涅阿斯纪》的着迷是不正常的①。但丁展示了他对希腊和罗马诗歌、历史、哲学和神话传统的熟悉。古代世界的遗产是但丁基督教宇宙观的重要组成部分。可是但丁的视角并不是古典与基督教观念的随意组合，他提供了一个纯粹且全面的视域，我们仍可在其中辨识出那些古典元素。《神曲》包含了古典世界的精神遗产，我们可以通过分析来区分这一遗产，但这一遗产也是但丁基督宗教诗歌的完整部分②。但丁不是牵强地使用异教主题，包括诗歌传统，或仅仅给他们穿上基督宗教的外衣。准确地说，借用托马斯·阿奎那的一句话，他把古典时期的水变成了基督宗教诗歌之酒——这部诗歌本身就是要引导诗人和读者走向救赎。

《地狱篇》第五篇中有不少情节提到了《埃涅阿斯纪》，尤其是维吉尔笔下关于狄多和埃涅阿斯相遇的故事。狄多在这篇诗歌中被提到过两次：第一次是在众爱欲之女主角的名单中，她们拥挤在这罪恶之地——“另一个女人是为了爱情而自我了结，她背弃了向着希凯乌斯的骨灰所发的誓言”[《地狱篇》5：61－62]；第二次，在鲍罗和弗朗西丝卡向两位诗人飞来的描述中，她被直接点名——“这从狄多所在的队伍中，穿过恶毒的气流飞到我们这里的人们也是如此，这队伍中有我悲悯的呼喊。”[《地狱篇》5：85－87]

狄多和埃涅阿斯的故事是《埃涅阿斯纪》中较著名的情节之一。埃涅

① 关于狄多与埃涅阿斯故事之于但丁的重要性，参考 Kay（2011），Barolini（1984）以及 Wetherbee（2008）。

② Wetherbee 在一段见解深刻的文章中指出：“但丁的诗比以往任何一首本民族语诗歌都更完整地融入了古代史诗的世界观，正是由于他吸收和挑战罗马诗人悲剧视野的直接性和诚实性，《神曲》及其所描述的超越性体验才产生了超凡的力量。在这部诗中，但丁与这些诗人的私淑定义了一个自我发现的过程，这实际上是一个与作为其主要主题的精神之旅相对应的存在意义的过程。与罗马史诗中的诗人们达成一致被反复证明是朝圣者获得真正理解的必要前提，他们所教授的功课必须不断地重新学习。即使在天堂，他们的智慧仍然与但丁的灵性教育有着广泛的且常常令人不安的关联，并最终提醒着人们他们对历史的看法，从阿尔戈号的旅程到尤利西斯号最后几天的历程，仍然是但丁表达他对天堂之体验的关键。”Wetherbee（2008：4）。

阿斯和他的水手刚刚离开了西西里岛，就在那里他的父亲安喀塞斯失去了生命。一场可怕的风暴又吞噬了他们的船只——这是朱诺女神企图继续挫败埃涅阿斯命运的结果。埃涅阿斯和他的水手们发现他们船只失事的地方在北非海岸，附近有一座在狄多女王带领下崛起的新城市。她也像埃涅阿斯，是从地中海东岸出逃而来的。

维吉尔的故事讲述了迦太基女王和特洛伊英雄的相遇，这个故事让年轻的奥古斯丁如此着迷——这是另一个著名的故事。狄多已经被自己对埃涅阿斯的渴望所燃烧，也被丘比特的飞箭所刺中，她鼓励她的特洛伊客人讲述特洛伊城陷落的故事。埃涅阿斯以这样一段话开始："殿下，如果我要陈明希腊人是如何毁灭特洛伊，并凭吊特洛伊帝国昔日的伟大，这份回忆娓娓，实在痛苦难当。……然而，如果你真的渴望知道我们的境遇，想听到特洛伊最后痛苦的简言，我虽不寒而栗，难以直面其苦，亦将启言说之。"［《埃涅阿斯纪》卷二：3－13］埃涅阿斯的话让我们想起弗朗西丝卡的开场白［《地狱篇》5：124－126］她将讲述与鲍罗的那次罪孽相遇，"就像那个在诉说中哭泣的人"。

埃涅阿斯在书中对特洛伊城陷落的描述引发了狄多的爱欲与最终堕落。狄多爱上了特洛伊英雄埃涅阿斯，于是把他在特洛伊的英勇事迹雕刻在了正在建造的迦太基的神庙墙上。但是在她面前的埃涅阿斯，也就是这个故事的讲述者，不仅仅只是特洛伊的王子，他已注定是罗马的缔造者，在此时已经历了重大的蜕变。狄多拥抱的埃涅阿斯就是她所听到的故事中的埃涅阿斯，这拥抱既是狄多也是迦太基灭亡的种子。当埃涅阿斯离开时，正如他必须离开一样，狄多自杀了。狄多堕落的原因和迦太基堕落的原因如出一辙——欲望。特洛伊也像迦太基一样因贪欲而堕落，即对海伦的贪欲。正如我们所见，这些故事中的诱惑，遑论对个人抑或帝国，之于奥古斯丁来说显而易见。我们也许还记得埃涅阿斯探访冥界时，狄多与埃涅阿斯的另一次相遇，他对狄多的阴魂说"温情地哭泣吧！"［《埃涅阿斯纪》卷六：455］所以但丁在造访冥界的时候，对弗朗西丝卡的阴魂说话时亦充满了怜悯。

奥古斯丁在《忏悔录》（卷十三：9）中提醒我们："我的重量就是我

的爱（*pondus meum amor meus*），无论我被带到哪里，都是我的爱把我带到那里” 弗朗西丝卡徒然地希望通过重复她的故事来获得某种幸福。但她的故事本身就是一种诱惑，一种足以引诱但丁的诱惑，就像弗朗西丝卡和鲍罗被兰斯洛特的故事所诱惑一样。我们在她的故事中看到了真正的危险，“任由文学的体验掌控其想法，就是在伪装激情的真身本体”①。

诗人但丁给我们讲了一个故事，一个他在纵欲之地狱层里遇到的被审判之人的故事。这个故事是他穿越地狱、炼狱与天堂之宏大故事的一部分。这是天路客但丁经历的故事，它建立了但丁作为叙述者的权威。《神曲》中所讲述的故事，在某种程度上，是关于这个故事是如何写成的。《地狱篇》的第五篇是一个关于故事的故事，更是一篇关于故事之危险性与文学之危险性的评论。文学有一种强大而诱人的力量。兰斯洛特与吉内维尔的故事证明了它对弗朗西丝卡与鲍罗来说尤其危险。弗朗西丝卡自己的故事又给但丁带来了困惑，正如埃涅阿斯在《埃涅阿斯纪》中所讲的故事被证明了是狄多之毁灭的导火索。

当一个人读文学作品尤其是那些写得漂亮的故事时，他必须谨慎。心甘情愿地搁置一个人的质疑思考，以想象的方式进入作者所构建的世界是非常容易的。② 为了阅读文学作品，我们的确需要想象力。但这种心甘情愿的暂停质疑思考是有危险的。在文本自动给定的前提中，我们可能会忘记，这些前提的真假取决于一个更高的源头，特别是道德或伦理原则，是有别于作者设定的特定人物与场景的。危险在某种程度上，在于将文学作品视为一个完全自主的实体，独立于自身之外的任何真与善的秩序。因此，文学作品将成为它自身的小宇宙，读者进入其中，心甘情愿地放弃与真理良善之更高秩序的所有秩序，即来自造物者的秩序。

就像但丁和维吉尔在地狱之旅中遇到的其他罪人一样，弗朗西丝卡揭示了她的罪。她仍然被她对鲍罗的情欲所支配。正如她所说：“爱情，没有一个被爱的人可以不去爱，它使我因着他如此强烈地高兴，正如你所看

---

① Kirkpatrick（1987：94）.

② Coleridge 在《*Biographia literaria or biographical sketches of my literary life and opinions*》（1817）中介绍了现在经常使用的表达方式“自愿搁置之怀疑”（willing suspension of disbelief）。

到的，它甚至现在也没有离开我。”［《地狱篇》5：103－105］弗朗西丝卡主张一种激情的决定论，自由意志在其中不起任何作用。进而，她只能想象一种爱的方式，在其间她永远沉沦在想入非非之中。即便在死亡中，即使没有肉体，她的关切仍然是属肉体的。她似乎是在用她的感官欲望来确立自身存在之内核，但这种欲望却只是人类与其他动物所共有的。弗朗西丝卡在绝对意义上爱着自己与自己的身体，她通过鲍罗的眼爱着自己——一个小小的，自我维系的世界，其中没有超越自身价值体系的法则。[1] 这样的欲望确实是被审判的。她的自我之爱模仿了上帝的存在方式，即纯粹的自我之爱。正如奥古斯丁所说：“上帝啊，所有离弃你、抵挡你的人，都以一种不当的方式模仿你。但正是通过这种模仿行为，他们表明你是万物的创造者。而结果没有任何地方可以让人躲避你。”［《忏悔录》卷二：6］

一个基督徒在弗朗西丝卡的行为中发现了骄傲之罪，而撒旦就是这种罪的典型例子。正如但丁在他的诗中告诉我们的，撒旦“未到成熟”便先堕落［《天堂篇》19：48］。他不愿意让上帝的恩典使他成熟，使他充满福乐的景象。撒旦寻求自主，不依赖任何人，甚至不依赖上帝。正如奥古斯丁在《上帝之城》（14：13）中所说：

> 除了渴望一种扭曲的高举之外，还有什么是骄傲呢？因为这是一种扭曲的高举，放弃了心灵应该牢牢固定于其上的基石，变成了仿佛它是一直是基于自身而存在的…现在你们要“高举你们的心”，即高举你们的意念。然而不是在骄傲中崇拜自己，而是尊崇上帝。……这就是最初的罪：人把自己视为自己的光，却从那使他成为光（如果他把心安放其中的话）的真光逃离。

在我们这个时代，提醒人们不要无端地颂扬文学似乎有些古怪，实则因为其中更大的危险在于拒绝与价值判断建立的紧密关联。然而，这种愤

① “第五篇是对爱情故事的美学伦理重新评价，作为激情自主与罪恶他律交叉的典范。” *Paolo Valesio*，80.

世嫉俗的解药不应该是导致美与真分离的不加批判的迷恋。因此，现代读者在阅读《神曲》时可能遇到的另一种危险，在某种意义上，与弗朗西丝卡、鲍罗以及年轻的奥古斯丁所屈从的危险恰恰相反。当我们在阅读《神曲》，心甘情愿地悬置怀疑时，我们倾向于将自己与诗中令人不安的主张隔离开来：关于地狱与天堂的现实性，以及关于审判与救赎的主张。弗朗西丝卡和鲍罗将兰斯洛特和吉尼维尔的故事看得太认真了，而我们往往对但丁的故事又不够认真。但我认为，此中却有一个潜在的相似点。那就是将文学作品视为意义的自主王国：要么不加批判地予以认同，要么被任意地忽略，就像我们现在这样。

但丁提醒我们文学的危险，当然也包括他自己的文学。要谨慎如何进入，留心所信任的。当心那些可能导致混乱、困惑和损失的以及自愿悬置的怀疑。正如我所建议的，阅读《神曲》的一个危险在于，只把作品当作一个封闭的世界，一个我们可以凭想象进入的世界。但是一个只被视为虚构的世界，我们很容易忽视它的主张。相反，《神曲》是一系列的窗口，诗人通过这些窗口邀请我们凝视更高的秩序。这首诗虽美，但我们不应迷失其中。

**参考文献**


Barolini, Teodolinda, 1984, *Dante's Poets: Textuality and Truth in the "Comedy"*.

Dronke, Peter, 1986, *Dante and Medieval Latin Traditions.*

Folena, Gianfranco, 1965, "La tradizione delle opere di Dante Alighieri", A*tti del Congresso Internazionale di Studi Danteschi*, 20 – 27 aprile.

Hollander, Robert, "Allegory in Dante", *Princeton Dante Project* [Allegory in Dante (2.0) (princeton.edu.].

Kay, Tristan, 2011, "Dido, Aeneas, and the Evolution of Dante's Poetics", *Dante Studies* 129, 135 – 160.

Kirkpatrick, Robin, 1987, *Dante's "Inferno": Difficulty and Dead Poetry*, Cambridge.

Nardi, Bruno, 1949, *Dante la cultura Medium*, Barii.

Paolo Valesio, 1998, "激烈之鸽", *Lectura Dantis. Inferno*, 艾伦·曼德尔鲍姆等编辑, 加州伯克利, 63 – 83.

Poggiolo, Renato, 1957, "Tragedy or Romance? A Reading of the Paolo and Francesca Episode in

Dante's Inferno", *PMLA* , June, Vol. 72, No. 3, 313 – 358.

Singleton, Charles, 1957, "The Irreducible Dove", *Comparative Literature* 9, 129 – 135.

——, 1970, *The Divine Comedy: The Inferno. Text and Commentary*, Princeton.

Sommer, H. O. , 1909 – 13, *The Vulgate Version of the Arthurian Romances*, Vols. 7, vol. 3.

Wetherbee, Winthrop, 2008, *The Ancient Flame: Dante and the Poets.*

# 洛克的家庭理论

## ——妻子的屈从与公私领域的二分*

周飞童（ZHOU Feitong）**

**摘要：**自由主义对公共领域与私人领域的二分遭到了一些女性主义者的批判。作为自由主义开创者的洛克，主张在家庭中妻子服从丈夫，这与其自由平等的个人主义政治学说产生了张力。洛克对家庭持有一种神学目的论的观点，他认为生育是家庭的自然的、唯一的目的，是夫妻间唯一的共同关切，并且，生育也是一种自然法所给予的义务。因此，围绕共同关切，夫妻需要统一意志，家庭事务的最终决定权被归属于个人，通常就是丈夫，这被看作能够更好地促进义务的完成。家庭的自然目的使其既不属于公共领域也不属于私人领域，并且，这种自然目的导致的共同关切限制了公共正义对家庭内部事务的干预。洛克的家庭理论无法回应女性主义者对自由主义的公私二分的批判。

**关键词：**洛克；家庭；公私二分；女性主义；自由主义

## John Locke's Family Theory: Wife's Subjection and Public & Private Distinction

**Abstract**: Some feminists have criticized liberalism's dichotomy between the public and private spheres. As a founding father of Liberalism, there are conflicts

---

* 感谢北京林业大学的王瑞雄博士、两位匿名审稿人以及责任编辑对本文的写作提出了许多重要的批评与建议。

** 周飞童，北京林业大学马克思主义学院，作者邮箱：zftbfu@ foxmail. com。

between Locke's family theory and the freedom&equality he advocated. Meanwhile, the relationship between Locke and Feminism is still unclear. This article argues that Locke holds a theological teleology standing towards the family that he considered procreation as the natural, sole end of the family and the sole Common Concern within the conjugal relationship; also, procreation is human's obligation that given by God or natural law. Therefore, for the common concern, husband and wife need to unify their wills, and the last determination right within the family is assigned to an individual, usually the husband. The family's natural end makes it neither in the public nor in the private sphere and hampers state intervention of family affairs. Locke's family theory provides no help for liberalism to respond to feminists' criticism.

**Key words**: John Locke; Family; Public & Private Dichotomy; Feminism; Liberalism

## 导　言

自由主义内部存在着两种公共领域和私人领域的二分的观念。第一种区分将公共领域等同为国家，将私人领域等同为市民社会。国家表现为公共性、强制性。市民社会则被看作追求个人目标的场所，人们在其中以私人的名义自由地联合。古典自由主义者主张市民社会的优先性，国家的主要功能就是保障人们在市民社会中的自由。① 第二种区分是公共性与个人隐私的区分，公共领域既包括国家的政治事务，也包括市民社会。在这里，政治权力的强制性与社会规范的压力都构成了对个人自由的威胁。相比于古典自由主义者，新的自由主义者要求一个能够保护个人隐私的领域。② 这个领域常被认定为家庭。③

① Kymlicka（2002：388 – 389），也可参考 Waheed（2018）。

② Kymlicka（2002：395 – 395），也参见 Kelly 对洛克与其他自由主义者的评价："the family should be preserved as a private realm shielding individuals and intimate associations from public scrutiny."（Kelly，2002：378）.

③ 本文中，家庭与婚姻均表示发生在夫妻之间的关系。17 世纪的英国，仆人常被看作家庭成员，但本文不讨论主仆关系，也不讨论亲子关系。为行文方便，不对婚姻与家庭做概念区分。

一些女性主义者对公共领域与私人领域的区分做出了批判。第一种区分的问题是将家庭排除在市民社会之外，没有保证家庭生活按照平等和同意的原则进行组织，也造成了对女性在家庭内的工作的贬低与忽视。家庭既不属于公共领域，也不属于私人领域。实际上，自由主义继承了传统父权制对公共领域与家庭的区分，公共领域属于男性，而家庭属于女性。在传统的父权制划分中，公共领域既包括政治活动，也包括非政治的社会活动。所以基于这种划分而进行的公共领域与私人领域的划分，只不过是在男性世界的内部进行的划分。[①] 于是，要保证家庭生活同样按照平等和同意的原则进行组织，就要求拒绝传统父权制对家庭与公共领域的区分，将家庭归入市民社会，从而适用于自主原则而不是等级秩序。

第二种区分的问题是容易导致家庭免于公共正义也即国家权力的审查。[②] 因为隐私权被认为属于整个家庭而不是个人。国家权力拒绝对家庭内部事务进行干预，并不一定会保证女性的个人自由与隐私。相反，拒绝干预可能会加剧她们在家庭中的从属地位。金里卡认为，大多数女性主义者所需要的是抛弃传统的家庭自主观，而不是拒斥自由主义对隐私权的主张[③]。“家庭隐私可能非常危险，尤其对于女性和儿童来说”[④]，“这样的隐私权放任男性单独地压迫女性”[⑤]，家庭的隐私至少在一定程度上是家庭暴力发生的原因[⑥]。欧金指出，女性主义者并不是要否认在公共领域与家庭生活之间的区分以及隐私，而是要求家庭内部的平等与安全。[⑦]

对上述两种问题的解决都承认了公共领域与私人领域的区分。前者将家庭归入私人领域，适用市民社会的自主原则；后者将家庭归入公共领域，适用公共领域的正义原则。二者的共同目标，是通过对家庭内部原则的调整维护女性的平等地位。然而，自由主义是否真的将家庭排除在适用

① Kymlicka（2002：388 - 391）.
② Noëlle and Howard（2018）.
③ Kymlicka（2002：394 - 398）.
④ Okin（1989：129）.
⑤ MacKinnon（1987：102）.
⑥ Kelly（2002：363）.
⑦ Okin（1989：128）.

于自主原则的私人领域之外？家庭是否真的不受正义原则的审查?[①] 进一步的问题是，公共领域与私人领域的区分究竟是怎样的一种区分？家庭在其中处于怎样的位置？

显然，“自由主义”是一个“家族相似”的概念，以自由主义作为指责对象，可能导致以偏概全。自由主义的源头可以回溯至洛克。洛克在《政府论两篇》中做出了许多有关家庭的表述，[②] 他的家庭理论的政治哲学意义，集中表现在他对父权制的反驳上。[③] 正是基于对家庭的理解，尤其是对父权与政治权力的区分，洛克反驳了菲尔默所主张的人天生就不自由的观点，以及与之相应的绝对君权（上篇6，下篇1、2）。[④] 与菲尔默相反，洛克认为人自然地处于一种自由而平等的状态，人与人之间不存在从属的关系，一切权力都是相互的（下篇4）。如此看来，不同的性别在自然的自由与平等上应该不存在差别。

的确有学者认为洛克为女性主义奠定了重要的理论基础。玛丽莎·巴特勒认为洛克对女性的观点尽管不是女性主义的，但却打开了将女性看作与男性一样的个人的可能，这表现为洛克的个人主义以及他对女性的理性能力的肯定。[⑤] 沃什对洛克对公共领域与私人领域的区分做出了积极的评价，认为洛克的区分对女性主义者所追求的自由与平等有很大作用。[⑥] 然而，也有学者指出了洛克的性别歧视，洛克所说的平等只是男人之间的平等。[⑦] 沃尔德伦则认为，在洛克对普遍平等的主张与他的父权制性质的主张间存在不可调和的矛盾。[⑧]

那么，洛克的家庭理论与女性主义者的主张之间到底有什么样的关

---

① 欧金认为，自由主义有一种基本的区分，将家庭排除在政治与市场之外。Okin（1989：111）.

② 本文引用《政府论两篇》时，只在文中标出上下篇及节数。中文版本为：洛克（1964）。英文本参见 John Locke（1960），根据英文版本，本文对中文翻译做了细微调整。

③ Simmons（1992：215），也可参见 Myers（1998：204－205）.

④ Pateman（1988：85）.

⑤ Butler（1991）.

⑥ Walsh（1995）. 沃什反对二分，而主张多个领域的区分，如政治、经济、家庭、宗教等，但本文仍采用二分法。

⑦ 如 Clark（1977）。Pateman（1988：52－53）.

⑧ 沃尔德伦（2015：44－54）。沃尔德伦在提出自己的主张前对帕特曼的解读进行了反驳。

系？他的家庭理论能否回应女性主义者对公共领域与私人领域二分的批评？通过重新阅读洛克关于家庭的文本，我将表明，洛克的家庭理论在一定程度上符合女性主义者对自由主义的公共领域与私人领域二分做出的批判，但却不是完全符合。在公共领域与私人领域区分的第一种意义上，洛克的家庭既不属于公共领域，也不属于私人领域；在公共领域与私人领域区分的第二种意义上，洛克将家庭归入公共领域，受正义原则的审查，属于政治权力合法介入的范围，然而这样的介入却有特别的限度。导致上述结果的原因是共同的，那就是洛克对家庭持有一种神学目的论观点，将生育看作家庭的唯一的自然的目的。

在本文第一部分，我回顾了一些围绕洛克家庭理论中妻子是否自然地受丈夫支配的争论。在第二部分，指出家庭中存在一种最终决定权，且这种权力被归属于个人。这是因为，家庭被认为拥有唯一的自然的目的，即生育，而这是夫妻间唯一的共同关切。并且，完成这种自然目的是一种义务。在第三部分与第四部分，以第二部分的结论为出发点，我分别指出，在公共领域与私人领域区分的第一种意义上，洛克的家庭既不属于公共领域，也不属于私人领域；在公共领域与私人领域区分的第二种意义上，洛克将家庭归入公共领域，受正义原则的审查，属于政治权力合法介入的范围，然而这样的介入却有特别的限度。而这都是因为家庭被看作具有自然的目的。第五部分是本文的结论，我指出，因为洛克将生育看作家庭唯一的自然的目的，所以他的家庭理论无法回应女性主义者对公私二分问题的批判。

## 一 洛克主张妻子自然地屈从于丈夫吗

关于洛克的家庭理论，学界存在不少问题与争论。比如，儿童对父母的服从究竟是什么程度的服从？儿童既然不处于自然法的约束之下，如何能够具有权利和义务？财产权的主体是家庭还是个人？① 洛克的家庭理论

① Simmons（1992：187－205）.

中，包含六种角色，三对关系。六种角色分别是妻子、丈夫、父母、儿童、主人、仆人；三对关系分别是夫妻关系、亲子关系、主仆关系。出于本文的目的，在这一节我将集中回顾学界围绕性别平等问题对洛克家庭理论的争论。争论的缘起，是洛克关于人的自由平等的主张与家庭中妻子与丈夫在权力与权利上不平等的主张之间的矛盾。一方面人天生自由平等（下篇4），且子女对父母的服从是等同的（下篇52、53、64，上篇55、61）；另一方面，洛克又认为家庭事务的最终决定权归属于丈夫（下篇82，上篇47、48），教育子女的义务主要属于丈夫（下篇69）。围绕这样的矛盾，学界存在不同的看法。

一些学者认为，洛克主张丈夫对妻子享有一种自然的支配地位。塞利格尔指出，洛克出于传统和自然的原因主张妻子低于、从属于丈夫。“家庭中意志的统一要求统治权，而这种统治权绝大多数情况下自然地归属于男性。”① 帕特曼也有类似观点。② 欧金指出，尽管洛克在反对父权制时主张父亲和母亲在亲权上的平等，但是却认为妻子在家庭中自然地从属于丈夫。所以，洛克的政治哲学的基础是父权制的家庭，而不是成年的个人。③ 同样认为洛克主张女性出于自然原因服从男性的，还有玛丽莎·巴特勒。她认为，对于洛克来说，只要指出妻子对丈夫的服从不存在来自上帝的神圣理由，且没有政治意义，就足够了。④

西蒙斯认为洛克从来没有主张丈夫对妻子拥有任何自然的支配地位。“丈夫的权威既不是自然的也不是必要的。”⑤ 至于洛克为什么认为丈夫在家庭中对妻子享有权威，西蒙斯给出了两点解释。第一，洛克认为丈夫在力量与能力上优于妻子（当然，现在看来这并不是真的），而我们在一些方面的确尊崇更强壮、更有能力、更聪明的人，所以，妻子给予丈夫在家庭中高于自己的权威。第二，在自愿结成的联合体（unions）中，总需要一些办法来解决分歧。家庭也是如此，总需要有最终的决定权。而一个联

---

① Seliger（2020：212）.

② Pateman（1988：54，93）.

③ Okin（2013：199－200）.

④ Butler（1991：82－83）.

⑤ Simmons（1992：174）.

合体中的决定权属于力量最大的那个部分，于是，决定权就被给予“更有能力和更强壮”的丈夫。西蒙斯认为，如果抛弃洛克对女性在能力体力等方面弱于男性的错误假设，那么对婚姻中道德关系的洛克式契约解释并没有什么不理性或不自由。[①] 也就是说，西蒙斯将洛克主张女性在婚姻中服从男性的原因，归结为洛克的时代对女性的错误认知，这是洛克的历史局限性。丈夫并不因为其丈夫身份而拥有对妻子的支配地位。看来，与其说西蒙斯反对妻子自然地服从于丈夫，不如说他进一步解释了夫妻间的自然差异如何被转变为妻子对丈夫的服从。不过，西蒙斯还提出了另一个理由来反对妻子自然地服从于丈夫：婚姻中的关系来源于契约的规定，妻子完全可以在契约中主张自己拥有最终的决定权。[②] 梅耶斯也认为，洛克主张诉诸契约内容而不是诉诸自然，来解决夫妻在婚姻中的分歧。[③]

克拉克也不认为妻子自然地服从于丈夫。她提出，洛克主张的丈夫对妻子的支配并不是自然的产物，而是习俗的产物。习俗指的是仅属于男性的私有财产权。要维护这样一种财产权，就需要丈夫对妻子的支配，这样才能保证财产的继承人是丈夫的后代。“只有当一个男人能够控制一个女人时，他才能确定所有她的后代都同样是他自己的。”所以，女性在生育方面的自然禀赋“必须被转化为经济与社会方面的劣势，来保证她们对男性的依附地位”，进而维护这种财产权体系。[④] 但是，克拉克的解读与洛克的文本间存在着张力。洛克并没有否认妻子的财产权，甚至认为对共同财产的处理权力也能够根据契约进行调整，只要符合生育抚养子女的目的即可（下篇 83）。[⑤] 就是说，妻子也可以根据契约拥有处理共同财产的权力。

## 二 家庭的自然目的——生育的义务

无论是诉诸自然事实、习俗，还是诉诸契约的内容来解释洛克给予丈

① Simmons（1992：173－175）.
② Simmons（1992：174）.
③ Myers（1998：202）.
④ Clark（1977）.
⑤ Walsh（1995：264）.

夫在家庭事务上的优先于妻子的权力,[①] 除克拉克以外，上述的论者都默认了一件事，那就是作为一个共同体（community）的家庭中存在一种最终的决定权，且这种决定权需要被归属于夫妻中某一个人的意志。尽管他们使用了不同的术语，如支配、决定、统治，以及服从、从属，但其意思都指围绕家庭事务存在一种最终决定权。而上述论者只是在争论这种决定权的归属的原因，却并未质疑为什么要有这样一种决定权，以及追问这是怎样的一种决定权。

洛克这样主张丈夫的最终决定权：

> 但是，虽然夫妻只有唯一的共同关切（common concern），然而由于各有不同的理解，他们不可避免地有时也会有不同的意志；因此有必要使最后的决定——即统治——有所归属，这就自然而然地落在较为能干和强健的男子分内了。但是这只限于有关他们共同利益和财产的事情……（下篇 82）

我们可以将洛克的论证重构如下：A 因为夫妻间存在唯一的共同关切；B 又因为夫妻间围绕共同关切可能存在不同的意志；C 所以围绕共同关切的最终决定权需要被归属于夫妻中某一个人的意志；D 又因为丈夫是较为能干和强健的；E 所以最终决定权归属于丈夫的意志。

我们先假设 ABC 没有问题，来看条件 D 和结论 E。丈夫较为能干和强健使得丈夫的意志具有对家庭中共同关切的最终决定权，这种最终决定权的获取方式，不同于本文第一部分提到的西蒙斯所说的联合体中最终决定权的获取方式。后者指决定权归属于联合体中力量较大的部分，但这种归属体现的是洛克主张的多数统治原则，这一原则是针对政治共同体而言的。政治共同体的目的是保护与促进共同体中所有成员的共同利益（下篇 131）。洛克认为，大多数人的同意决定政治共同体的行动（下篇 96），同意加入一个政治共同体的人，就有义务服从大多数人的决定（下篇 97）。

① 上述论者主要在与人为相对的意义上言说自然，不过巴特勒的自然还有与神启相对的含义。

可以看到，政治共同体的行动决策是在各方的意志（利益）相互折衷之后共同做出的。少数人的意志仍然对决策产生了不可忽视的影响。但是，由于夫妻二人只能算作两个意志，不能加总折衷，所以说最终决定权属于丈夫，并不是说丈夫的意志在量的意义上大于妻子，而是说丈夫的意志优先于妻子的意志。于是，家庭中围绕共同关切的决定并不是建立在夫妻二人意志的妥协的基础上。由此可见，家庭中围绕共同关切的决定不同于政治共同体中围绕共同利益的决定。最终决定权被归属于夫妻中某一个人的意志。塞利格尔敏锐地指出，对于洛克来说，家庭中“要么就是丈夫支配，要么就是妻子支配”，没有共同支配（co - dominion）这回事。[①] 国家所维护的共同利益能够被洛克还原为每一个个人的具体利益，它是罗尔斯所说的作为交叠共识（overlapping concensus）的共同利益[②]。因此，洛克的国家显然是共同支配的，不可能在国家中要求一种最终决定的意志。当不同的意志无法调和时，每一方都有权利“诉诸上天”，也就是诉诸武力（下篇 168、240、241）。

那么，家庭中的共同关切是什么呢？在洛克看来，家庭的共同关切是生育繁衍。洛克将生育看作婚姻的唯一目的，[③] 不以生育为目的的契约不是婚姻契约。[④] 由此可见，尽管家庭是通过同意也即契约结成的（下篇 78），可家庭的目的却并不来源于同意，而是自然的。[⑤] “自然目的是婚姻关系的前提，它使得并不是所有的和最重要的与其相关的义务能够由契约双方根据意愿决定。”[⑥] 也就是说，婚姻契约的内容不能与自然的生育目的相冲突，夫妻二人所订立的婚姻契约的内容受到生育目的的限制。[⑦] 正是

---

① Seliger（2020：211）.

② 参见 Rawls（2005：482 - 483）。

③ 虽然洛克有时会说生育是婚姻的主要目的，而不是唯一目的（下篇 78、80），但他明显地暗示了这一点。见下篇 79、82、83 节：“男女间结合的目的既不仅是生殖，而是种族的绵延”；“夫妻只有同一的共同关切”；“婚姻所要达到的全部目的…即生儿育女和在他们共同生活时的相互支持和帮助”；“只要与生育和抚养儿女直到他们能自立谋生为止的精神相符合就行”。本文提到生育时，也包含抚养、教育。

④ Simmons（1988：170）.

⑤ 本文所说的自然指与人为相对的自然。

⑥ Myers（1998：205）.

⑦ 参见 Kelly（2002：370）。

这种自然目的解释了洛克为什么说“夫妻只有唯一的共同关切”。

家庭中的共同关切不同于国家中的共同利益。既然家庭的共同关切也即婚姻的目的是生育繁衍，那么这种关切就无法被夫妻双方中的任何一个人单独完成。对洛克来说，国家的共同利益可以被还原为每一个人的个人利益，国家是保护个人权利的工具。而家庭中的共同关切不仅不能由个人完成，而且这种共同关切似乎被洛克看作一种义务：“男女间结合的目的既不仅是生殖，而是种族的绵延”（下篇 79）；“夫妻间只有唯一的共同关切”（下篇 82）；“婚姻所要达到的全部目的……即生儿育女”（下篇 83）；并且，上帝要求人过社会生活，[1] 而最初的社会就是夫妻社会（下篇 77），人类的生育与繁衍是上帝的目的（上篇 33、41）。这样看来，生育就成了上帝给予人的义务，而夫妻二人就是为了完成这种义务而组成家庭。

家庭的共同关切及其义务属性，看上去能够解释为什么洛克认为家庭中存在最终决定权，且归属于夫妻中的某一个人。因为生育被看作家庭的自然目的，且家庭的共同关切是个人所不能单独完成的，因此家庭需要统一行动，这就要求统一家庭中的意志。而家庭中客观上存在两个意志（尽管它们可能正好相同），所以就需要有一个意志拥有最终决定权，否则难以处理两个意志出现分歧的情况。[2] 当洛克说丈夫“较为能干和强健”时，他并不是认为丈夫是家庭中力量较大的部分，而是认为丈夫在能力上优于妻子，由丈夫做最终决定能够更好地促进家庭的共同关切，也即生育，这也是促进义务的完成。妻子对丈夫的服从具有一种“自然的基础”（上篇 47），这种服从仅是婚姻中的（上篇 48），也就是与生育相关的。洛克所说的妻子对丈夫的自然服从，并不是说妻子与丈夫间存在自然的等级。而是说基于一些自然事实，妻子服从丈夫能够更好地促进婚姻中的自然目的。妻子的服从不是因为她的妻子身份。

---

① Locke（1954：158）.

② 当然，这并不是一个逻辑上严格的结论，但我想这是对洛克为什么主张妻子服从丈夫的一个合理解释。当出现分歧时，夫妻二人之间不能以民主决策的投票方式进行意志加总与妥协，因为只有两个意志，无法寻找分歧中的多数意志。这时，客观上存在着解决分歧的其他可能方法，如通过理性对话寻求共识、骰子、仲裁等。但是，洛克没有提到这些方法，而是说最终决定权要有所归属，且他将最终决定权归属于了丈夫这个个人。

遗憾的是，洛克对家庭内部有一个自然目的、存在唯一的共同关切的假设，却没有得到应有的质疑。尽管洛克对女性相对于男性的自然劣势的认知现在看来似乎并不正确，但是仅仅否定女性的自然劣势却不能否定家庭中存在的支配关系。接下来我将以家庭的自然目的为出发点，考察洛克的家庭理论能否回应自由主义女性主义者对公共领域与私人领域二分的批判。我将表明，家庭的自然目的也即生育繁衍，使得家庭在公共领域与私人领域二分的第一种意义上既不属于国家也不属于市民社会；在二分的第二种意义上，家庭受到公共正义原则审查，但是这种审查非常有限，不能保障女性在家庭中的隐私权。

## 三　家庭既不是公共领域也不是私人领域

自由主义对公共领域与私人领域的第一种划分是国家与市民社会之间的划分。需要注意的是，公共领域与私人领域的区分并不是物理空间的区分，而是不同目的与责任的区分："公共行为就是承担了促进共同利益的责任，是指对每个人利益的不偏不倚的关注。当从事私人行为时，就不要求当事人做到不偏不倚。"① 对应到洛克的理论，国家或者说政治社会与市民社会有不同的目的，因而它们是不同的领域。丈夫与妻子、父母与子女、主人与仆人相互结合的社会"都不能够形成政治社会，假如我们对每种社会的不同目的、关系和范围加以考虑的话"（下篇77），并且，"凡是对结成任何社会的目的并无必要的，对于这种社会就没有必要"，夫妻社会与政治社会也即国家不同，生杀予夺的权力在婚姻中并不存在，这是因为，这种权力并不为婚姻的目的所需要（下篇83）。由此我们可以看出，不同社会的区分在于它们不同的目的，至于关系和范围，则可以看作目的的衍生物。

政治社会或者说国家的目的是保护个人的所有权。②"政治社会的首要目的是保护所有权"（下篇85）；"人们联合成为国家和置身于政府之下的

① Kymlicka（2002：424）.

② 洛克的所有权指的是生命、自由与财产（下篇59、87、135）。

重大的和主要的目的，是保护他们的所有权”（下篇124）；国家的权力“没有别的目的，只是为了人们的和平、安全和公众福利”（下篇131）。并且，政治社会的目的是人为的，而不是自然的。个人的所有权在逻辑上先于国家。在自然状态中，每个人就享有自由平等的权利，在自然法的范围内支配他的财产与人身（下篇4）。由此可见，国家的目的是工具性的，正如汽车的目的也是工具性的。国家的目的所指涉的对象，也即个人的生命、自由与财产，才具有内在价值。国家服务于这些对象。

然而，家庭也即婚姻的目的在于生育繁衍，① 并且这种目的是自然的，并不是来源于人为设定。“自然”的重要意图是“人类滋生和种族繁衍，而在保障婚姻关系下的家庭界限则又是达到以上要求的必需条件”（上篇59）；是上帝使人加入了夫妻社会（下篇77），但上帝并没有要人加入政治社会。在洛克看来，生育繁衍是婚姻的目的，这种目的也是自然目的，它来源于自然，或者说来源于上帝，具有内在价值而不是工具价值。

通过对比可以发现，国家的目的是保护个人的所有权，是工具性的、人为的。而家庭的目的是生育繁衍人类，是自然的、神圣的，具有内在价值。然而，根据自由主义对公共领域与私人领域的第一种区分，私人领域是国家之外的市民社会，是每个人追求自己独特人生价值，也即特殊善的场域。对于个人而言，市民社会中的目的是自由设定的，市民社会中并不存在自然目的。于是，因为家庭的目的是自然的，不能自由设定，所以家庭就既不属于公共领域，也不属于私人领域。并且，既然家庭的目的也即生育是自然的，那么一切与生育相关的家庭事务也是自然的。如果市民社会是市场社会的话，那么女性在家庭中的工作被忽视贬低的原因，就在于其工作的自然属性：一切与养育相关的事务都被排除在经济计量之外。

## 四　家庭受正义原则的有限审查

自由主义对公共领域与私人领域的第二种区分，是包括政治与经济的

---

① 参见本书第137页注释③。

公共领域与个人隐私间的区分。私人领域是隐私领域，不受政府与社会的干预。① 女性主义者对这种划分的批判是，如果家庭是私人领域，那么它将不受公共正义原则的审查，政府将无法介入家庭事务，而这可能加剧女性在家庭中的不平等地位。

那么，根据洛克的看法，政府能否对家庭事务进行干预呢？需要再次说明的是，私人领域不是空间概念，而是关系概念。在私人住宅中进行的谋杀或者虐待显然属于犯罪，理应受到政府的制裁。毫无疑问，既然洛克认为政府的目的在于保护人民的所有权，也即生命、自由与财产，那么，在其领土之内，一切破坏上述目的的行为都应当受到政府的干预。② 问题是，究竟什么算是政府对家庭的干预呢？按照一些女性主义者的主张，政府对家庭的形式与运转产生着重要的影响，讨论政府是否干预家庭是没有意义的，政府必然干预家庭。③ “个人的就是政治的”，这并不是说要取消个人隐私，也不是说个人生活与政治生活完全重叠，而是要说明女性在家庭中的处境受到政治权力深深的影响。④ 所以问题并不是政府是否对家庭进行干预，而是政府如何对家庭进行干预。⑤

政府对家庭的干预可以分为两种类型：“其一是对家庭或家庭中个人在经济和服务上的责任承担和支持，其二是对个体在家庭和婚姻内部基本人权方面的保护。”⑥ 女性主义者对第二种公私二分的批评，针对的是这里

---

① 参见本文导言部分。

② Walsh（1995：251－277）.

③ Olsen（1985：837）.

④ Okin（1989：124－128）.

⑤ 参见欧金对二分的批判，Okin（1989：128－133）。关于这个问 Kelly 存在误解：“Locke's theory of the family provides no enforcement mechanism that might limit the power of the family patriarch.” See Kelly（2002：374－378）。她似乎将公共领域与私人领域的区分当成了空间上的区分。另外，也有学者反对女性主义者对公私二分的否定。劳伦斯认为，公私的区分是存在的。家庭法律应当干预的领域是公共领域，而家庭法律不应当干预的领域则是私人领域。所谓家庭法律，指的是针对人们作为家庭成员的身份而制定的法律，比如子女、父母、监护人等。因此，如果法律不是针对人们的家庭成员身份而制定的，那么法律就没有干预家庭。见 Houlgate（1998：141－146）。但是，女性主义者并不是要区分什么法律是家庭法律、什么法律不是家庭法律，女性主义者要表明的，是家庭受到政府权力的影响，而政府的一些行为可能维护或加剧女性在家庭中的屈从地位。劳伦斯澄清的只是法律概念上的区分。

⑥ 吴小英（2015：22n.）。

所说的第二种干预，即政府对家庭中的个体的保护。家庭关系因其隐私性质而阻碍了政府对家庭中个体的保护。女性主义者所要求的，是政府在涉及基本权利的底线问题上能够突破家庭的隐私屏障，直接用权力对家庭中的个体进行保护。[①]

洛克的家庭理论能满足女性主义者对政府保护的诉求吗？一方面，洛克明确表示，夫妻之间的婚姻是一种契约关系。婚姻在同意的基础上发生（下篇 78），并且，妻子在与丈夫的共同利益和财产的事情之外，"充分和自由地保有由契约规定为她的特有权利的事项"，"在自然权利或他们的契约所许可的范围内，妻子就有和丈夫分离的自由"（下篇 82）。看上去，丈夫与妻子之间的关系受到二者订立的契约的约束，契约关系受到政府保护，自然属于干预的范围。[②] 然而，另一方面，洛克紧接着又主张，政府对家庭的干预的范围，仅限于夫妻之间对"生儿育女"及其相关事务所产生的争执，也即关于如何实现婚姻的目的——生育的争执，而并不能剥夺夫妻任何一方为达到生育目的而需要的权利或权力（下篇 83）。

那么，妻子究竟在生育之外还享有多少订立契约的自由呢？其实，将妻子的角色换成丈夫，上述的疑问也是成立的。因为给定了生育的目的之后，丈夫或妻子为了生育究竟需要具有怎样的权利或权力，却根本说不清楚。洛克论证说，如果绝对主权和生杀之权属于丈夫，且为夫妻关系所必要的话，那么在不允许丈夫具有这种权力的国家中，就不可能有夫妻关系。于是他得出结论：这种权力是婚姻关系不需要的，因为没有这种权力，婚姻关系也能实现其生育的目的（下篇 83）。但是，洛克在这里对婚姻中的绝对主权和生杀之权的否定是不充分的。因为至少在逻辑上，仍有可能论证这种权力能够更好地实现生育的目的。于是，尽管这种权力不是必要的，但它仍有在婚姻中存在的余地。没有必要与不能存在完全是两回事。

可见，在婚姻给定的生育目的之下，夫妻之间的权利与权力关系看似是契约关系，其实却极其混乱不清，充满危险。因为，给定了一个自然的

---

① 吴小英（2015：21）。

② Butler（1991：86）.

目的，则婚姻关系就根本不是完全意义上的契约关系。[①] 契约关系要求自由订立，可婚姻关系的自由度仅限于选择什么样的人发生这种关系，而这种关系的目的却被预先给定。[②] 于是，在这个目的之下，总可以找到很多理由主张不平等的关系。洛克的家庭理论为夫妻二人的关系留下了太多的可能性，以至于既可以容纳自由平等的关系，也可以容纳奴役压迫的关系。因此，尽管家庭受到公共正义的审查，但洛克的家庭理论却无法为女性的个人隐私权与安全提供任何可靠保障。家庭暴力的存在说明公共领域与私人领域的区分"也能够加剧家庭暴力受害者们经常感受到的脆弱与孤立"。[③]

## 五 结论

通过上述分析可以看到，在公共领域与私人领域二分的第一种意义上，洛克理论中的家庭既不属于国家，也不属于市民社会；在公共领域与私人领域二分的第二种意义上，洛克理论中的家庭受到公共正义的审查，然而这种审查非常有限，仅仅限于与生育繁衍相关的事务。因此，洛克的家庭理论不能回应女性主义对公共领域与私人领域二分的批判。

导致上述结果的原因在于洛克对家庭持有一种神学目的论的观点，他将生育繁衍看作家庭的唯一目的，并且，这种目的是自然的，是一种有待完成的义务。因此，在家庭中，围绕共同关切也即生育的最终决定权被洛克认为需要归属于一个个人，而不是将最终决定看作不同个人意志的妥协或合力。于是在家庭中，要么就是妻子处于支配地位，要么就是丈夫处于支配地位，总之没有自由平等。归根结底，洛克并不是将妻子的屈从角色看作自然的，而是将与生育繁衍相关的一切活动看作自然的。西蒙斯正确

① 参见 Kelly（2002：375－376）对洛克婚姻契约的批判，但 Kelly 强调的主要是女性的实际处境限制了她们对是否结婚、婚姻内容以及离婚的选择的自由，而没有指明生育目的对婚姻契约的限制。Clarke（1977：711）对婚姻契约的批判也是如此，她指出了婚姻契约双方地位的不平等。

② 洛克对同性性行为的反对（上篇59），对离婚的限制（下篇79、81）都是为了促进人类的生育繁衍。参见 West（2013）。

③ Kelly（2002：377）.

地指出，关于妻子的自然事实并不为丈夫带来相对于妻子的支配地位。[①]在这一点上，洛克并没有自然主义的谬误。但是西蒙斯却没有发现，洛克诉诸家庭的自然目的，以此将家庭中的支配关系合法化。值得注意的是，洛克并没有说妻子一定要服从于丈夫，通过契约妻子可以免于这种服从（上篇 47）。至于洛克为什么说丈夫对妻子的统治“自然而然”，大概只能归结为洛克因为时代的局限而对女性产生的错误的认知。

洛克对菲尔默的父权制与绝对权力的反驳，要求一种个人主义的自由平等。然而，将生育看作家庭的唯一的、自然的、作为义务的目的，导致夫妻二人间存在着不可还原为个人利益、不可由个人单独实现的共同关切。这种共同关切与洛克的个人主义政治学说间存在着张力。主张这种共同关切的存在，可能导致一个人为多个人做决定，且这种决定的依据并不是每个个人的利益。这与现代自由民主的精神背道而驰。

**参考文献**


沃尔德伦，2015，《上帝、洛克与平等——洛克政治思想的基督教基础》，郭威、赵雪纲等译，华夏出版社。

洛克，1964，《政府论》（上篇），瞿菊农，叶启芳译，商务印书馆。

——，1964，《政府论》（下篇），瞿菊农，叶启芳译，商务印书馆。

吴小英，2015，《家庭背后的主义之争》，《妇女研究论丛》第二卷，第 17—25 页。

Butler, Melissa A., 1991, "Early Liberal Roots of Feminism: John Locke and the Attack on Patriarchy", *Feminist Interpretations and Political Theory*, ed., By Mary Lyndon Shanley and Carole Pateman, Suite C: The Pennsylvania State University Press, 74 - 92.

Clark, Lorenne M. G., 1977, "Women and John Locke; Or, Who Owns the Apples in the Garden of Eden?" *Canadian Journal of Philosophy*, Vol. 7, No. 4, 699 - 724.

Kelly, Kristin A., 2002, "Private Family, Private Individual: John Locke's Distinction Between Paternal and Political Power", *Social Theory and Practice*, Vol. 28, No. 3, 361 - 380.

Kymlicka, Will, 2002, *Contemporary Political Philosophy: An Introduction*, *2nd ed.*, Oxford: Oxford University Press.

Locke, John, 1960, 1967, 1988, *Two Treatises of Government*, ed., By Peter Laslett, Cambridge: Cambridge University Press.


① Simmons（1992：173 - 175）.

MacKinnon, Catharine A., *Feminism Unmodified: Discourses on Life and Law*, Harvard: Harvard University Press.

Myers, Peter, C., *Our Only Star and Compass: Locke and the Struggle for Political Rationality*, Lanham: Rowman & Littlefield Publishers.

Noëlle, McAfee, & Howard, Katie B., 2018, "Feminist Political Philosophy", *The Stanford Encyclopedia of Philosophy*, Edward N. Zalta (ed.), URL = <https://plato.stanford.edu/archives/win2018/entries/feminism-political/>.

Okin, Susan Moller, 1989, *Justice, Gender, and the Family*, New York: Basic Books.

——, 2013, *Women in Western Political Thought*, Princeton and Oxford: Princeton University Press.

Olsen, Frances E., 1985, "The Myth of State Intervention in the Family", *University of Michigan Journal of Law Reform* 18, No. 4, 835 - 864.

Pateman, Carole, 1988, *The Sexual Contract*, Stanford: Stanford University Press.

Rawls, John, 2005, *Political Liberalism*, New York: Columbia University Press.

Seliger, M., 2020, *The Liberal Politics of John Locke*, London and New York: Routledge.

Simmons, A. John, 1992, *The Lockean Theory of Rights*, Princeton: Princeton University Press.

Waheed, Hussain, 2018, "The Common Good", *The Stanford Encyclopedia of Philosophy*, Edward N. Zalta (ed.), URL = <https://plato.stanford.edu/archives/spr2018/entries/common-good/>.

Walsh, Mary, 1995, "Locke and Feminism on Public and Private Realms of Activities", *Review of Politics* 57, No. 1, 251 - 277.

West, T. G., 2013, "Locke's Neglected Teaching on Morality and the Family", *Society*, 50 (5), 472 - 476.

# On The Supposed Importance of Intrinsic Value in Animal and Environmental Ethics

Yunjie ZHANG*

**Abstract**: The idea of intrinsic value is pervasive in environmental ethics and animal ethics. In fact, the view that certain non - human animals and the environment have intrinsic value is the basis of many ethicists' claim that we are morally obligated to treat these non - human animals and the environment well. In this paper, I argue that these ethicists often conflate intrinsic and final value. If something is finally valuable, then it is valuable for its own sake or in its own right either in virtue of its internal or external properties. To be intrinsically valuable is just to be finally valuable in virtue of one's internal or intrinsic properties. Given this understanding of intrinsic value, many animal and environmental ethicists end up committing themselves to the view that the source of the moral status of certain non - human animals and the environment is some set of their respective internal or intrinsic properties. However, I argue that the value that they are often concerned with is based on non - human animals' and the environment's external or extrinsic properties (sentience, rareness, uniqueness, diversity, etc.). This means that these ethicists need only defend the claim that certain non - human animals and the environment are extrinsically finally valuable as opposed to intrinsically valuable.

**Key words**: Intrinsic Value, Animal Ethics, Environmental Ethics, Final

* Yunjie Zhang, PhD candidate, Philosophy Department, University of Glasgow.

Value, Christine Korsgaard

## Introduction

To say that something is intrinsically valuable is usually to say that it is valuable in itself, on its own, for its own sake, in its own right, as such, or as an end. The idea of intrinsic value is pervasive in environmental ethics and animal ethics. But it is unclear exactly what philosophers working in environmental ethics and animal ethics mean by intrinsic value. I think having a clear definition of intrinsic value will help us better understand what exactly environmental and animal ethicists are arguing for. My argument is that environmental and animal ethicists have conflated two kinds of value: intrinsic value and final value.

In this paper, I do three things. First, I examine how animal ethicists and environmental ethicists understand intrinsic value. Second, I will briefly review the concept of intrinsic value in the history of meta-ethics and introduce Christine Korsgaard's distinction between intrinsic and final value. Finally, I argue that when the animal ethicists and environmental ethicists talk about whether animals or nature has intrinsic value, they actually mean final value.

## Section I Intrinsic value in environmental ethics and animal ethics

The concept of intrinsic value plays an important role in debates in both animalethics and in environmental ethics. In particular, these debates concern how we ought to treat certain entities (e. g., non-human animals and nature). A crucial part of this debate concerns whether certain entities (i. e., non-human, sentient, animals and nature) have intrinsic value. The main idea is that we ought to treat whatever has intrinsic value with respect and so if non-human animals or the environment has intrinsic value, then we ought to treat non-human animals or the environment with respect.

In animal ethics, there is a debate about the extent to which it is morally permissible to engage in animal experimentation, i. e., experimentations on non-human animals. ① On the Utilitarian view, animal experimentation is morally permissible just so long as it has the right consequences overall, i. e., just so long as it leads to the maximisation of overall happiness or pleasure in the world. ② Moreover, on the Utilitarian View, animals do not have intrinsic value. The only thing that has intrinsic value for utilitarians is the pleasure that agents are required to maximise. On the Moral Rights View, animal experimentation is never morally permissible. This is because animals have moral rights which limit the ways in which they can be morally permissibly treated in the same way that humans have moral rights that limit the ways in which they can be morally permissibly treated. ③ The source or foundation of the moral rights that these animals have is their intrinsic value. As Tom Regan argues, "We are to treat those individuals who have inherent [i. e., intrinsic] value in ways that respect their inherent [i. e., intrinsic] value." ④ Thus, the debate about the moral permissibility of animal experi-

---

① Hugh LaFollette and Niall Shanks discussed about the use of animals on medical research needs to be concerned more ethically in "The Origin of Speciesism", Hugh LaFollette and Niall Shanks argue that people should be concerned with the ethics of how animals are used in medical research.

② Jeremy Bentham developed the first systematic defence of utilitarianism in Principles of Morals and Legislation (1789). He writes that "By the principle of utility is meant that principle which approves or disapproves of every action whatsoever, according to the tendency which it appears to have to augment or diminish the happiness of the party whose interest is in question: or, what is the same thing in other words, to promote or to oppose that happiness. I say of every action whatsoever; and therefore not only of every action of a private individual, but of every measure of government."

③ Regan argues that animals are sentiment beings that have inherent/intrinsic value like human beings in *The Case for Animal Rights*. More importantly, Regan thinks that animals have moral rights in virtue of having inherent worth value. This is the main idea of Regan's moral theory concerning animals.

④ Regan (1983: 48).

mentation is partly a debate about whether animals have intrinsic value. The Utilitarian View denies that animals have it and the Moral Rights View claims that animals have it.

In environmental ethics, there is a debate about how we' re morally required to treat the environment. While it is agreed that we' re morally forbidden from treating the environment any way we please, there is a substantial disagreement about why the environment matters morally. And, the reason the environment matters morally determines exactly how we' re morally required to treat it. According to Anthropocentrism, only humans are intrinsically valuable and therefore only humans are morally important in their own right. ① This means that the environment is valuable only insofar as it can benefit humans and thus it is not intrinsically valuable. Thus, the question of how we' re morally required to treat nature is fully determined by how our treatment of nature affects humans. According to Non-anthropocentrism, however, it is false that only humans have intrinsic value. In particular, non-anthropocentrists argue that nature itself is intrinsically valuable. ② They argue that this means that how we' re morally required to treat nature is determined by the effects our treatment has on nature itself and not just on how it affects humans. Thus, like the debate between the Utilitarian View and the Moral Rights View in animal ethics, the debate between Anthropocentrism and Non-anthropocentrism in environmental ethics is partly a debate about what has intrinsic value.

Given that the concept of intrinsic value is at the heart of these debates, it is

---

① Bryan Norton discussed the differences between anthropocentrism (human-centred environmentalism) and non-anthropocentrism (not human-centred environmentalism) in paper "Environmental Ethics and Weak Anthropocentrism". Although he claims there are core differences between them, he argues they might suggest same policy making and human behaviours.

② In non-anthropocentrism, there are different scopes that philosophers discussed; some say a plant, a river or one individual creature has intrinsic value like one human being, but others also agree on nature as a system or a group of animals as a kind have intrinsic value. I will not discuss the details about these differences here but just keep them in mind that all of them agree on not just human or human kind has intrinsic value.

essential that ethicists working on these issues get clear about what intrinsic value is, how it differs from other ways of being valuable, and what kinds of entities can have intrinsic value. Thus, this paper argues for a particular view of what it takes for something to have intrinsic value. While spelling out exactly what it means for something to be intrinsically valuable, it will be helpful to start with a rough idea. To say that something is intrinsically valuable is usually to say that is valuable: in itself, on its own, for its own sake, in its own right, as such, or as an end. Crucially, being intrinsically valuable is not being valuable as a means for something else that has value. More specifically, I will argue that something has intrinsic value if and only if it has final value solely in virtue of some set of its intrinsic properties.

# Section II

## Section II. i. Subjective vs Objective Value

Intrinsic value is a kind of objective (i. e., mind-independent) value. To say that something has mind-independent value is to say that it is valuable in virtue of something other than the beliefs (or other attitudes) of persons. That is, the source of the value is not the beliefs, perceptions, desires, etc. of any person. Thus, something can be objectively valuable even if no one believes it is or wants it to be valuable. For example, the COVID-19 vaccine is objectively valuable because it saved the lives of millions of people. ① Even if no one believed that the vaccine is valuable, it would still be valuable. Even if no one believed that it actually saved millions of lives, it would still be valuable, because, as a matter

① I'm assuming here that human lives are objectively valuable and that something that is an effective means of protecting human lives is also objectively valuable. I thank a referee for this journal for helping me be clear about this.

of fact, it saved millions of lives.

Objective value is to be contrasted with subjective value. Subjective value refers to a set of "valuing" attitudes that people can have toward various objects, regardless of whether those objects are objectively valuable. For example, a person may desire nothing more than to count the blades of grass on his lawn. Counting blades of grass has subjective value—at least for this person. The subjective value of counting blades of grass in this case clearly depends on the attitudes of at least one person. However, something can be both subjectively valuable and objectively valuable at the same time. In such cases, what one values is also objectively valuable, i. e. , it has value that doesn't depend on one valuing.

## Section II. ii Is Intrinsic Value Just Non-Instrumental Value?

Anthropocentrism views nature as only being instrumentally valuable, i. e. , valuable only as a means to something else with value. Should we view the opposing view (i. e. , Non-anthropocentrism) as holding merely that the environment is non-instrumentally valuable? That is, when Non-anthropocentrists claim that nature is intrinsically valuable, should we understand them as claiming that nature is merely non-instrumentally valuable? Likewise, given that the Utilitarian View sees animals as being merely instrumentally valuable, should we see the opposing view (i. e. , the Moral Rights View) as holding merely that animals are non-instrumentally valuable? That is, does the Moral Rights View hold that being intrinsically valuable is just being non-instrumentally valuable? I will argue that neither Non-athropocentrists nor the Moral Rights View should hold that being intrinsically valuable is the same thing as being non-instrumentally valuable. However, in order to do this, I will first consider the view that being intrinsically valuable at least sometimes means merely being non-instrumentally valuable. I will argue that this view is untenable because it conflates intrinsic value with what philosophers call "final" value.

## Section II. iii. Intrinsic Value is Sometimes Non-Instrumental Value

Perhaps something can be intrinsically valuable, at least sometimes, if it is merely non-instrumentally valuable. Monroe Beardsley suggests that something might be intrinsically valuable in the sense of being valuable for its own sake in virtue of having a certain extrinsic or relational property. That is, a property that something has in virtue of being related to something external to it. For example, whether a person is tall depends upon the height of other people. If everyone is the same height, then no one is tall. Beardsley thinks that things can be intrinsically valuable in virtue of relational properties like uniqueness or rareness. Beardsley offers the case of a rare stamp as an example of something that has intrinsic value because it is non-instrumentally valuable. ① Imagine that the central figure of a stamp is mistakenly inverted during the printing process. The wrong printing leads to its rarity and the value of this stamp comes from this uniqueness. We can say that because its uniqueness is a property that the stamp now has and belongs to it or is part of it, then the value of this rare stamp is not for anything else but for itself, especially from the view of philately value. But if the post office were to print millions of inverted stamps, it would be able to eliminate its value without changing the original inverted stamp, i. e., without changing any of the stamp's "internal" properties. Notice that while the property that makes the stamp valuable is intuitively an extrinsic property (i. e., rareness), the stamp is not clearly instrumentally valuable. Or at least, the stamp is not just instrumentally valuable. For example, if even the stamp couldn't be sold for money or traded for something, it still seems to have value over and above its market or trade value, because it is extremely rare. If this is a case of intrinsic value, then it looks like intrinsic value is sometimes just a case of non-instrumental value.

---

① Beardsley (1965: 1).

However, one might not be convinced that the rare stamp is valuable for its own sake. Perhaps it is valuable to stamp collectors (i. e., they value it), but it doesn't follow that the stamp itself is valuable. ① To assuage this concern, let us look at a different example. Shelly Kagan offers an example in which something appears to be intrinsically valuable in the sense of being valuable for its own sake in virtue of one of its extrinsic properties. He gives the example of the pen that Abraham Lincoln used to sign the Emancipation Proclamation, which led to the freeing of millions of slaves. ② Kagan explains that if Lincoln's pen possess any intrinsic value, then this is because this pen played an important causal role in human history. However, the pen still seems valuable and valuable for its own sake and not just as a means to something else valuable. Of course, the pen might be instrumentally valuable in the sense that it is worth a lot of money, viewing it might give history buffs pleasure, or it might remind us of the value of human freedom. But the point is that, even if it were stipulated that the pen couldn't be used as a means to other valuable things (e. g., because it's currently hidden or lost), it still seems valuable. Therefore, Kagan concludes, "non-intrinsic properties (and, in particular, instrumental properties) [are] relevant to intrinsic value as well." ③

## Section II. iv. Intrinsic Value is Not Non-Instrumental Value

Moore denies that intrinsic value is merely non-instrumental value. In order to determine what has intrinsic value, Moore proposes a certain kind of thought-experiment: to imagine a thing existing entirely by itself (1903: 187). ④ If it would still have value under such circumstances, then its value is intrinsic. Moore

① I thank a referee from this journal for this concern.

② Kagan (1998: 294).

③ Kagan (1998: 294).

④ Moore (1903: 187).

writes:

> *In order to arrive at a correct decision on the first part of this question* [ *i. e.* , "*What has intrinsic value?*" ] , *it is necessary to consider what things are such that, if they existed by themselves, in absolute isolation, we should yet judge their existence to be good* [ *or valuable* ] ;①

Here, Moore argues that as long as something exists in absolute isolation and is valuable, it is intrinsically valuable. This is because given that the object is isolated from other objects and extrinsic properties, the only thing that could explain its value are its internal or intrinsic properties. ② This thought experiment is not only offered as a way to determine whether something has intrinsic value but also a way to elucidate the concept of intrinsic value better by pointing to the fact that intrinsically valuable things seem to be valuable in virtue of their intrinsic properties.

However, it is not clear that Moore's isolation thought experiment is successful at showing what has intrinsic value. One potential problem with this thought experiment is that it's not clear that many things that are intrinsically valuable can be absolutely isolated. For example, let's grant that the state of affairs, "feeling pleasure" is intrinsically valuable. So, if we were to imagine this state of affairs in isolation, we would judge it to be valuable. However, Noah Lemos argues that "feeling pleasure" cannot exist in absolute isolation. Someone must be experiencing the pleasure and therefore there cannot only exist the feeling of pleasure. This problem seems to arise for a wide arrange of things that seem valuable for their own sake (e. g. , knowledge, experiencing beauty, love, etc. ). For example, even if we grant that knowledge is intrinsically valuable, it cannot be considered in isolation from the knower just as love cannot be considered in isolation from the

① Moore (1903: 112).
② Moore (1922: 260), (1993: 286).

lover, and so on. So, it's not clear that all things that might be intrinsically valuable can be isolated in the right way. As Lemos concludes, "this sort of ontological isolationism is not very helpful since there are certain sorts of things that are intrinsically good but simply could not be the only things that exist."①

However, it is not clear how much of a threat this objection is. Moore might simply argue that only concrete (i. e., non-abstract) things can be intrinsically valuable. Thus, while "feeling pleasure" might not itself have intrinsic value, instantiations of "feeling pleasure" do have intrinsic value. That is, it is not that "feeling pleasure" is intrinsically valuable, but something or someone experiencing pleasure is what is intrinsically valuable.

A more pressing problem for Moore's thought experiment is this: it is not clear that it can distinguish between things that are valuable in virtue of their intrinsic properties and certain non-instrumentally valuable things. For example, it seems to me that Lincoln's pen is valuable even when considered in isolation. But we know from the discussion above that the pen's value is derived from its extrinsic properties, e. g., the role it played in freeing millions of slaves. This is a problem, because it looks like Moore's thought experiment fails to do what it was designed to do: distinguish what has intrinsic value from what does not have intrinsic value.

Perhaps Moore would object that considering something in absolute isolation means that one must exclude from thought the object's history and thus treat it as the only thing to ever exist or the first thing to exist. But in these cases we might be judging the value of something based on extrinsic property of the object, i. e., the property of being the only thing to ever exist or the first thing to ever exist. In this case, we might judge that the isolated object is valuable not in virtue of its intrinsic properties but in virtue of some extrinsic property, e. g., rareness or uniqueness. After all, if something is the only (or first) thing to exist, it's quite

---

① Lemos (1994: 10 - 11).

rare and unique.

A better way to reject the claim made by Kagan and Beardsley that there are objects with intrinsic value in virtue of extrinsic properties is to show that these philosophers seem to be conflating two distinct ways of being valuable. Let me explain. Korsgaard argues that intrinsic value and instrumental value are not contrasting kinds. That is, intrinsic value is not merely non-instrumental value. Thus, she argues, the contrast between intrinsic and instrumental value is misleading and false. ① According to Korsgaard, A is instrumentally valuable if and only if it is valuable as a means. The obvious contrast with being valuable as a means is being valuable as an end in itself or for its own sake and not as a means or for the sake of something else. She calls such value final value. This is the kind of value that Beardsley and Kagan seem to have in mind when they argue that the misprinted stamp and Lincoln's pen are valuable for their own sake. That is, their value is not a means to anything else.

We can see the difference between instrumental and final value also by looking at how people value things. If one values something instrumentally, one values it for the things it can bring about. The natural contrast to a thing that is valued instrumentally or as a means is a thing that is valued for its own sake or as an end in itself. ② For example, I might value my car instrumentally as a means of getting from point A to point B or my hat as a means of keeping my head warm. If my car stops running, I would cease valuing it and if my hat were to cease keeping my head warm, I would cease valuing it. However, I surely value certain things (e. g., close friends and family) finally, i. e., for their own sake. ③ That is, I do not value my friend or family just because of what they can do for

① Korsgaard (1983: 169).

② Korsgaard (1983: 171 - 173).

③ It's important to note that just because I value something for its own sake, it doesn't follow that I will *always* value it—even if it doesn't cease to be valuable. For example, if a friendship or romantic relationship ends, I will most likely eventually cease valuing that person for their own sake even though they are still valuable for their own sake. I thank a referee from this journal for helping me be clear about this.

me, but for their own sakes.

Importantly, Korsgaard argues that final value is not the same thing as intrinsic value. Whereas the instrumental/final value distinction concerns whether something is valuable for the sake of something else or for itself, intrinsic value concerns where value comes from, i. e., on which properties value supervenes. Thus, to see the difference between final and intrinsic value, it will be helpful to briefly explain what supervenience involves. What does it mean for some property (or properties) to supervene on another property (properties)? At its core, supervenience is a claim about metaphysical dependence. In particular, A-properties supervene on B-properties if and only if no two things can differ concerning A-properties without differing concerning B-properties. In this way, A-properties are dependent on B-properties. The concept is often explained in part by the slogan "there cannot be an A-difference without a B-difference."

For example, thin moral properties (e. g., right/wrong, good/bad, optional/non-optional) are thought to supervene on certain non-moral, but morally-relevant, properties (e. g., causing/reducing harm, respecting autonomy, increasing/decreasing pleasure, lying/telling the truth). Take the case of stabbing a friend in the back. Grant that it is morally wrong to betray a friend. In this case, the property of wrongness supervenes on the property of being an act of betrayal. To say that wrongness in this case supervenes on the property of being an act of betrayal means that there could not be two acts that differ on whether they are wrong without differing concerning whether they are acts of betrayal.

Many philosophers also think that mental states supervene on (physical) brain states. This means that no two people can be in the same mental state without also being in the same brain state. For example, if being in the mental state of pain supervenes on the brain state of C-fibers firing, then there are no two people who differ with regard to whether they are experiencing pain without differing with regard to whether they have C-fibers firing. ①

Thus, to say that someone is intrinsically valuable is to make a claim about the kind of properties on which that thing's value supervenes. In particular, Korsgaard argues that A is intrinsically valuable if and only if it is valuable in a way that supervenes only on the intrinsic or internal properties of A. Importantly, if A is intrinsically valuable, then A is finally valuable. This is because if something is valuable in virtue of its internal properties, it is at least somewhat valuable in its own right or for its own sake.

While the natural contrast with instrumental value is final value, the natural contrast with intrinsic value is extrinsic value in general and not merely a particular instance of extrinsic value (i. e., instrumental value). Given the above account of intrinsic, we can say that A is extrinsically valuable if and only if it is valuable in a way that supervenes only on the extrinsic, external, or relational properties of A.

According to Korsgaard, the intrinsic value of a thing is considered to hold and remain in any or all situations because the intrinsic value only comes from its own properties and depends on its own properties and will not be changed by different extrinsic situations.

# Section III

## Section III. i Final value in environmental ethics and animal ethics

As the above sections clarified, when something is finally valuable, it is valuable for its own sake or in its own right. That is, final value is the opposite of instrumental value. And, there are two ways that something can be finally valuable:

① Kripke (1980: 98).

in virtue of some set of its internal/intrinsic properties or in virtue of some set of its external/extrinsic properties. In this section, I will show that both animal ethicists and environmental ethicists regularly conflate intrinsic value and final value.

To see where animal ethicists have conflated intrinsic and final value, consider the following:

> (*1*) *To say that animals have intrinsic value is to say that they do not only have instrumental value, i. e., that they are not only valuable as means to an end, but also in themselves or for their own sake. This sense seems to be derived from the sense in which the term 'intrinsic value' is used in the consequentialist tradition (see e. g. Moore, 1922). It seems to refer primarily to the type of value that attaches to animals (and not to duties we might have on the basis of this value).* (2) *To say that animals have intrinsic value is to say that they ought never to be treated solely as means. This sense is reminiscent of the meaning of 'intrinsic value' in the Kantian deontological tradition.* (*DeVries, 2008: 376*).
>
> [*T*] *hose concerned about animals and nature began to use the term "intrinsic value"; by using this term they sought to indicate that it is not only humans who have moral status. Other natural entities are said to have moral status as well: they have a "value of their own" independent of their utility-value for humans.* (*Verhoog, 1992: 148*).
>
> *Something has intrinsic value if its existence is a good thing in itself, apart from its role asa means to other goods.* (*O'Neil, 2000: 185*)

First, notice that these authors always contrast "intrinsic value" with instrumental value. DeVries writes, "To say that animals have intrinsic value is to say that they do not only have instrumental value." As we saw above though, the natural contrast of instrumental value is final value. Second, notice that the authors say nothing about the internal or non-relational properties of animals. Rather, they just argue that animals are valuable "for their own sake" or that they have a "value of their own."

Moving onto the environmental ethics, we can see a similar trend of conflating intrinsic and final value. Consider a few representative quotations:

*Something is intrinsically valuable if it is valuable in and for itself—if its value is not derived from its utility, but is independent of any use or function it may have in relation to something or someone else. In classical philosophical terminology, an intrinsically valuable entity is said to be an "end-in-itself," not just a "means" to another's ends.* (*Callicott, 1989: 131*)

*The principle of intrinsic value states that, regardless of what kind of entity it is in other respects, if it is a member of the Earth's community of life, the realization of its good is something intrinsically valuable. This means that its good is prima facie worthy of being preserved or promoted as an end in itself and for the sake of the entity whose good it is. Insofar as we regard any organism, species population, or life community as an entity having inherent worth, we believe that it must never be treated as if it were a mere object or thing whose entire value lies in being instrumental to the good of some other entity. The well-being of each is judged to have value in and of itself.* (*Taylor, 1981: 198*)

*One of the most important ethical issues raised anywhere in the past few decades has been whether nature has an order, a pattern, that we humans are bound to understand and respect and preserve. It is the essential question prompting the environmentalist movement in many countries. Generally, those who have answered 'yes' to the question have also believed that such an order has an intrinsic value, which is to say that not all value comes from humans, that value can exist independently of us: it is not something we bestow. On the other hand, those who have answered 'no * have tended to be in an instrumentalist camp. They look on nature as a storehouse of Resources' to be organised and used by people, as having no other value than the value some human gives it.*

(*Worster*, *1985*: *xi.*)

*It can be said that, if X is valuable for the sake of something else, it is instrumentally valuable, but if X is valuable for its own sake, then it is intrinsically valuable.* (*Bayram*, *2012*: *1088*).

As with animal ethicists, these environmental ethicists contrast intrinsic value with instrumental value. For example, Callicott writes, "an intrinsically valuable entity is said to be an 'end-in-itself,' not just a 'means' to another's ends." In fact, Bayram explicitly equates something's being valuable for its own sake with it being intrinsically valuable. Moreover, notice that the authors say nothing about the intrinsic or extrinsic properties of nature.

## Section III. ii Extrinsic Final value in environmental ethics and animal ethics

Now that we' ve seen both animal ethicists and environmental ethics conflate intrinsic value and final value, we must answer the question of why this matters. I think it matters for at least two reasons. First, it is important for the clarity and accuracy of their arguments that they distinguish these two theses about value. For example, because there can be extrinsically finally valuable things, Bayram's claim that "if X is valuable for its own sake, then it is intrinsically valuable," is simply incorrect. Second, once they see the difference between intrinsic value and final value, they can also see that non-human animals' or nature's extrinsic final value can provide a reason to treat them well. This means that there are at least two kinds of value that deserve respect: extrinsic final value and intrinsic final value.

In the rest of this section, I will motivate the claim that proponents of the Moral Rights View and Non-anthropocentrism needn't argue that animals or the environment have intrinsic value, just final value, in order to show that we morally ought to treat animals or nature with respect. I will do this by providing examples of how something's being extrinsically finally valuable can provide us a reason to treat that thing with respect.

First, notice that, intuitively, we' re morally required to treat things that are extrinsically finally valuable with respect, e. g. , we' re morally forbidden from destroying or damaging them. For example, we morally ought not to destroy or damage Lincoln's pen—even if we' re the last person on earth and thus we won't be preventing anyone else from getting something of value from the pen. Or, imagine the original score of Beethoven's 5th symphony. We don't need the original score in order to ensure that this piece of music survives and it's not as if reading this particular written score is any more pleasurable to the people that can read it than reading a copy. But again, it would be wrong to damage or destroy it.

Second, notice that many think animals are finally valuable because they are sentient and they have desires, beliefs and emotions. ① However, these properties needn't be intrinsic to a particular animal. The internal/intrinsic properties of something are such that if they were removed that thing would cease to exist. For example, "having three sides" is an internal property of triangles. If you were to remove or add a side to a triangle, it would cease to be a triangle. Now imagine a particular animal, e. g. , a dog. This dog's sentience, desires, beliefs, and limited rationality are not internal properties of that dog. That is, this particular dog would still exist even if it lost its sentience, desires, beliefs, and emotions. If this is true, and we have reason to respect these animals because they have these non-intrinsic properties, then we do not need to appeal to intrinsic properties to argue that we have reason to respect certain animals.

Third, sometimes what intuitively makes it especially wrong or bad to harm or destroy certain animals is that they are rare, e. g. , they belong to an endangered species. But being part of an endangered specifies is a relational (i. e. , extrinsic) property. An animal is part of an endangered species only because there are rela-

① Regan (2001: 243).

tively few other members of that species. So, part of the reason we should treat certain animals with respect is that they have relational property of being rare. ①

Turning to nature, we can also see that some of the properties that make nature finally valuable are extrinsic properties. For example, environmental ethicists value biologically diversity, the rareness of species, and the uniqueness of species. All of these properties come from species' relations to other species and thus are external properties.

We can also imagine that some piece of land is finally valuable because of its role in historically important events (e. g. , the ground on which Lincoln delivered the Gettysburg Address), because of its role in human history (e. g. , the land on which there was the earliest-known civilization), because of its role in certain cultures (e. g. , scared grounds), or because of it inspired great works of art (e. g. , Walden Pond inspired Henry David Thoreau to write Walden and ponds in Giveny, France inspired Claude Monet's famous water lilies). All of these are relational (and thus extrinsic) properties.

If what I've been arguing is correct, then animal and environmental ethicists should either (1) stop talking about intrinsic value and start talking about extrinsic final value or (2) clearly indicate whether their arguments concern the internal/intrinsic or external/extrinsic properties of animals or nature.

**References**

Bayram, Selma Aydin, 2012, "On the role of intrinsic value in terms of environmental education", *Procedia-Social and Behavioral Sciences* 47, 1087 – 1091.

Beardsley, Monroe C. , 1965, "Intrinsic value", *Philosophy and Phenomenological Research*, Vol. 26, No. 1, 1 – 17.

Bradley, Ben, 2002, "Is Intrinsic Value Conditional?" *An International Journal for Philosophy in the Analytic Tradition*, Vol. 107, No. 1, 23 – 44.

Butchvarov, Panayo, 1989, *Skepticism in Ethics*, Indianapolis: Indiana University Press.

Callicott, J. Baird, 1989, "On the Intrinsic Value of Nonhuman Species", *Defence of the Land Ethic*:

① This point is also made by Tenen (2020).

*Essays in Environmental Philosophy*, New York: State University of New York Press.

Chisholm, Roderick M., 1968, "The Defeat of Good and Evil", *Proceedings and Addresses of the American Philosophical Association*, Vol. 42, 23.

De Vries, R. B. M., 2008, "Intrinsic Value and the Genetic Engineering of Animals", *Environmental Values* 17 (3), 375 - 392.

Kagan, Shelly, 1998, "Rethinking intrinsic value", *The Journal of Ethics* 2 (4), 277 - 297.

Korsgaard, Christine, 1983, "Two Distinctions in Goodness", *The Philosophical Review*, Vol. 92, No. 2, 169 - 195.

Kripke, Saul, A., 1980, *Naming and Necessity*, Cambridge, MA: Harvard University Press.

Lemos, Noah, 1994, *Intrinsic Value: Concept and Warrant*, Cambridge University Press.

LaFollette, Hugh, & Shanks, Niall., 1996, "The Origin of Speciesism", *Philosophy*, VOL. 71. No. 275, 41 - 61.

Moore, G. E., 1903, *Principia Ethica*, Cambridge: Cambridge University Press.

McLaughlin, P. B., 1995, "Varieties of Supervenience", *Supervenience: New Essays*, ed., by E. Savellos, and U. Yalcin, Cambridge: Cambridge University Press.

Norton, Bryan, 1984, "Environmental Ethics and Weak Anthropocentrism", *Environmental Ethics*, Vol. 6, No. 2, 131 - 148.

O'Neil, Rick, 2000, "Animal Liberation versus Environmentalism: The Care Solution", *Environmental Ethics* 22, 183 - 190.

Palmer, Clare, 2003, "An Overview of Environmental Ethics", *Environmental Ethics*, ed., by Holmes Rolston & Andres Light, Blackwell Press.

Regan, Tom, 2001, *The Case of Animal Right*, Berkley: University of California Press.

Ronnow-Ramussen, Toni and Zimmerman, Michael J., 2006, *Introduction of Recent Work on intrinsic value*, Springer.

Ronnow-Ramussen, Toni, 2015, *Intrinsic and Extrinsic Value in The Oxford Handbook of Value Theory*, ed., by Iwao Hirose and Jonas Olson, Oxford: Oxford Handbooks.

Ross, W. D., 1932, "The Right and the Good", *The Monist*, 42, 157 - 196.

Taylor, Paul, 1981, "The Ethics of Respect for Nature", *Environmental Ethics* 3 (3), 197 - 218.

Tenen, Levi, 2020, "No Intrinsic Value? No Problem. Why Nature Can Still Be Valuable for Its Own Sake", *Environmental Ethics* 42 (2), 119 - 133.

Thomson, Judith Jarvis, 1992, "On some ways in which a thing can be good", *Social Philosophy & Policy*, Vol. 9, No. 2, 96 - 117.

Verhoog, H., 1992, "The Concept of Intrinsic Value and Transgenic Animals", *Journal of Agricultural and Environmental Ethics* 5 (2), 147 - 160.

Worster, Donald, 1985, *Nature's Economy*, Cambridge: Cambridge University Press.

Zimmerman, Michael, 1999, "In Defense of the Concept of Intrinsic Value", *Canadian Journal of Philosophy*, Vol 29, Issue 3, 389 - 409.

# 道德增强*

托马斯·道格拉斯（Thomas Douglas）**
曾小倩（ZENG Xiaoqian）、
毛兴贵（MAO Xinggui）/译（trans.）***

**摘要**：生物医学增强的反对者们时常声称，即使这种增强对于增强者来说是有益的，也会对他人造成伤害。但是，当所讨论的增强是一种道德上的增强时，该异议则并不具有多少说服力。这种增强有望使得被增强者拥有比以往更好的道德动机。在本文中，我描述了一种可算作道德增强的心理改变。我主张，在不久的将来，我们也许能够通过生物医学干预来诱发这种改变。我还针对未来进行这种道德增强可能面临的质疑为之进行了辩护。我的目的在于将这种道德增强作为生物医学增强总是道德上不允许的这种观点的反例。

**关键词**：生物医学增强；道德增强；生物保守主义；动机

---

* 本文原题为“Moral Enhancement”，发表于《应用伦理学杂志》（*Journal of Applied Philosophy*）2008 年第 25 卷第 3 期，该文与同期其他几篇论文一道提出了“生物医学道德增强”问题，并引领了相关领域的讨论，使得人类增强尤其是道德增强成为近来应用伦理学领域的热门话题。——译者注

我要感谢 Julian Savulescu、David Wasserman、Matthew Liao、Ingmar Persson、Allen Buchanan、Rebecca Roache、Roger Crisp、《应用哲学杂志》的两位匿名评审以及奥塔哥大学、牛津大学和香港浸会大学的听众对本文初稿的评论。——原注

** 托马斯·道格拉斯，牛津大学耶稣学院高级研究员（Thomas Douglas，Senior Research Fellow，Jesus College，University of Oxford）。

*** 曾小倩，西南大学哲学系学生；毛兴贵：西南大学哲学系教授，西南大学西方马克思主义研究所研究员。

# Moral Enhancement

**Abstract**: Opponents of biomedical enhancement often claim that, even if such enhancement would benefit the enhanced, it would harm others. But this objection looks unpersuasive when the enhancement in question is a moral enhancement—an enhancement that will expectably leave the enhanced person with morally better motives than she had previously. In this article I (1) describe one type of psychological alteration that would plausibly qualify as a moral enhancement, (2) argue that we will, in the medium-term future, probably be able to induce such alterations via biomedical intervention, and (3) defend future engagement in such moral enhancements against possible objections. My aim is to present this kind of moral enhancement as a counter-example to the view that biomedical enhancement is always morally impermissible.

**Keywords**: Biomedical Enhancement; Moral Enhancement; Bioconservatism; Motives

生物医学技术通常用于维持或恢复健康。但是，很多生物医学技术也可以用来改变健康人的特征。我将把后面这种改变称为生物医学增强，从而不赋予它任何价值。

生物医学增强在运动领域的运用可能最为明显，在这个领域，药物很久以来就被用来提高成绩。① 但是，生物医学增强在其他领域也相当普遍。一些音乐家会在表演前服用 β 受体阻滞剂来平息自己的紧张情绪，② 相当大比例的美国大学生坦言他们会在学习时服用哌甲酯（利他林）以

---

① Verroken (2005: 29 - 63).

② Tindall (2004).

提高考试成绩,[①] 此外，整容手术也是一种常见的生物医学增强。对可能增强记忆力的药物[②]、复杂技能的维持[③]和机敏性[④]的研究表明，生物医学增强在未来几年内可能会迅速增长。然而，使用生物医学技术来增强我们的素质是否道德仍然是一个有争议的问题。有些人认为，一方面，人们若是能够更加聪颖、长寿和强壮就更好了；另一方面，也没有理由反对使用生物医学技术来实现这些目标。但与此同时，也有许多人认为应当避免生物医学增强。

## 一 生物保守主义命题

反对增强的人并非总是捍卫一个共同且明确的命题。不过，有一些反对者要么会同意下述主张，要么会受它吸引（以下简称**生物保守主义命题**）：即使人们进行生物医学增强在技术上可能，在法律上允许，在道德上也不允许。[⑤]

这个命题的范围需要加以阐明。我所指的"人们"（people），在这里主要包括目前所有现存的人，以及可能出现在不久的将来（例如未来一百年）的人，但却不包括在更遥远的将来可能存在的人。同时，我所指的"生物医学增强"，仅包括在不久的将来在技术上变得可行的增强。对于在遥远的将来所进行的那些增强，或者需要难以置信的技术的那些增强，反对增强的人也许没有什么话可说。

接下来我将论证，经此限定后的生物保守主义命题是错的。

---

① L. D. Johnston, P. M. O'Malley & J. G. Bachman（2003）; C. J. Teter, S. E. McCabe, K. LaGrange et al.（2006）.

② G. Lynch（2002）; R. Scott, R. Bourtchouladze, S. Gossweiler et al.（2002）; T. Tully, R. Bourtchouladze, R. Scott et al.（2003）.

③ J. Yesavage, M. Mumenthaler, J. Taylor et al.（2001）.

④ J. A. Caldwell, J. L. Caldwell & N. K. Smythe（2000）; D. C. Turner, T. W. Robbins, L. Clark, A. R. Aron, J. Dowson & B. J. Sahakian（2003）.

⑤ 有些作者可能只是反对某些类型的增强，但也有人似乎发现所有的增强都是有问题的，或许不应当被允许，他们更倾向于只用生物医学技术来保持和恢复健康。该观点近期最杰出的代表是迈克尔·桑德尔（Michael Sandel）。见 Sandel（2004，2007：47－49）。

## 二 生物保守主义命题的一个可能的反例

生物保守主义命题可以以各种方式得到辩护，但是很多最为流行的辩护都是基于社会的考虑：尽管增强对于被增强的个体来说可能有益，但对他人却很可能有害。① 因此，在智力增强的问题上，可以说，如果一个人使自己变得更加聪明，那么他将对未增强者不利，例如，在就业竞争中他会更胜一筹，或者，他会因为别人智力不如他而歧视他们。②

这些主张在针对最常讨论的生物医学增强（包括体能增强、智力和记忆力增强以及自然寿命的延长）时可能具有一定的说服力。但是，当针对其他类型的生物医学增强时，它们似乎就远远没那么有说服力了。在本文中，我将集中关注一种可能性，即未来的人们可以使用生物医学技术对自己进行**道德**增强。

可以通过多种方式来理解我们应该对自己进行道德增强的建议。仅举几例，比如，我们可以将它理解为：我们应该让自己变得更有美德、更值得称赞、更有道德责任感；或者，我们应该让自己以更加道德的方式行动。但是我不会以这些方式中的任何一种来理解这一建议。相反，我认为这个建议是说，我们应该让自己具有道德上更好的动机（此后我通常会省略“道德上”一词）我把动机理解为一种心理（精神的或神经的）状态或过程，若无对立动机的产生，它将会导致一个人行动。③

由于我只关注动机，所以我不会声称，与之前那个没有得到增强的自己相比，一个人在道德上得到增强，就更为道德了，有一种更为道德的品

---

① 比如，见 Annas（2002）；McKibben（2003）；Mehlman（2005）。

② 基于竞争力来反对增强的观点，见 Buchanan，Brock，Daniels & Wikler（2000：188－191）；McKibben（2003）op. cit.；Farah，Illes，Cook－Deegan et al.（2004：423）；Sandel（2007：8－12）。基于歧视来反对增强的观点，见 Sandel（2007：15）。

③ 我集中关注动机的道德性，因为我认为这是各种主张的一个共同基点。有些康德主义者可能会否认行为或举止是道德评价的恰当对象，而有些把行为视为道德评价最基本单位的人则可能会避免对道德品格做出判断。但我认为，所有人或几乎所有人都会承认，动机也在不同程度上是道德的或不道德的，即便它们的道德性最终源于它们所激发的行为，或源于产生它们的德性，或它们所构成的德性。

格，或者必然会以更为道德的方式行动。我也会尽力避免在什么因素决定了一个动机在道德上是良好的动机这个问题上持任何特定的观点。比如，对于一个动机在道德上好还是不好，有多种不同观点。有人认为这取决于它所激发的是何种行为，有人认为这取决于在一定程度上由它所构成的品格特征，有人则认为这取决于它的后果或者它的内在属性。而我将在这些观点之间保持中立。

做出这些限定后，我要将道德增强定义如下：

> 如果一个人以某种方式改变了自己，以至于我们可以合理地预期，与他没有改变自己的情况相比，这种改变会使得他将来总体上会有更好的动机，那么这个人就在道德上让自己得到了增强。

鉴于我们集中关注的是动机在道德上好不好，这个定义在我看来以一种很自然的方式抓住了道德增强的观念。不过，它有三个值得注意的特征。第一，它比较的是动机的集合，而不是单个的动机。更具体地说，它比较的是一个人得到增强后未来所有动机的集合与他若没有得到增强就会有的动机的集合。第二，它主要关注的是，我们是否可以**合理地预期**一种改变会导致那个行动者有道德上更好的动机（或者如同我将在后文中所说，它是否可以为人预期地让行动者有更好的动机），而不是它实际上是否成功地导致了这些动机。要是没有这第二个条件，我们将很难事先知道某种改变是否构成了一种道德增强。第三，我的定义承认，可以通过非生物医学手段来实现道德增强。在后文中，我将专门集中关注**生物医学**道德增强的情况。

与最经常被提及的各种增强形式不同，符合这个道德增强定义的增强形式不容易被人批评说，一些人的增强会对另一些人不利。在任何合理的道德理论看来，一个人在道德上具有更好的动机都将有利于他人。的确，有些观点认为，正是拥有某种动机往往会有利于他人这一事实使得该动机成为一种道德上良好的动机。诚然，获得一系列更好的未来动机有时也可能会使得一个人对他人施加不利影响，但这只会出现在下面这几种情况下：（a）更好的动机没能产生其典型的效果。例如，一个帮助他人的恰当愿望因为不可预见的情形而造成有害的效果。（b）对他人施加不利影响是为了某种道德目的。例如，对正义的关心致使一个人向做坏事的人施加一种恰当的惩罚。或（c）有一套道德上更好的未来动机集合必然有一些更坏的个别动机。我们不能这样来驳斥道德增强：它会系统性地将道德上不正当的不利影响施加给他人。

我将会论证，实际上，对于在某些特定条件下所实施的生物医学道德增强，并没有好的理由加以驳斥，无论是基于社会的考虑还是其他考虑。我将表明，与生物保守主义命题相反，人们接受这样的增强在道德上是允许的。但是，在着手我的论证之前，有必要对道德增强如何进行多说几句。

## 三 道德增强的本质

很显然，大多数人都具有在道德上增强自己的空间。每一种合理的道德理论都认为，人们经常都有不良或次优的动机。而且，许多合理的理论也认为，世界上有些最为重大的问题（例如日益严重的世界贫困、气候变化以及战争）都可以归因于这些道德缺陷。

然而，目前尚不明确什么样的心理变化可以算作道德增强，这至少有两个原因。

第一，对于哪些动机在道德上是好的，以及在多大程度上是好的，几乎还没有达成共识。尽管有的人认为，最好是由形成于正确推理过程的规范性信念所驱动，[①] 但也有人强调同情这样的道德情感的重要性。[②] 还有人则赞成将这两种观点融合起来。[③] 而且，诉诸在何种考虑决定了一种动机在道德上是好的这个问题上的某种观点，仍然不能解决这种分歧，因为这

① 伊曼努尔·康德当然是这一观点的经典倡导者，他声称，唯一“本身即善”的东西是善良意志，而善良意志则被理解为在道德律的正确指导下运用实践理性的能力。尤其可以参阅 Kant（1993）。

② 比如，见 Mill（1979：27－28）。

③ 这一观点的经典阐述来自亚里士多德（1985）。

个问题上的共识甚至更少。例如，有些人认为，一种动机之所以在道德上是好的，是因为它能够带来好的后果；而另一些人则认为，一些动机之所以是好的，是因为它们在某种程度上构成了某些美德。

第二，什么样的动机才算好的动机，以及什么才算动机的改善，这对不同的人或承担不同角色的人来说都是不同的。对于一个法官而言，某种类型的法律推理可能是最佳动机；而对于父母来说，爱可能是更为合适的动机。同样地，对于一个几乎没有同情心的人来说，同情心的增加可以算作一种道德上的改善。但对于一个同情心已经泛滥的人来说，任何这样的增加都不太可能算作一种改善。

尽管存在这些困难，我仍然认为可以找到几种心理变化，这些变化在某些情况下对某些人来说可以毫无争议地算作道德增强。而在此，我只集中关注一种可能。我的想法是，有一些情感（此后我将称之为反道德情感）的减弱有时候可以看作一种道德增强，不论人们认可的是哪一种合理的道德理论和心理学理论。我心里想到的是那些可能会干扰公认的良好动机（道德情感、推理过程及其组合）的情感和/或本身就毫无争议属于不良动机的情感。总体而言，减轻这样的情感将会使得一个人拥有更好的未来动机。

对某些种族群体的极度厌恶也许就是反道德情感的一个例子。我认为，这种厌恶是不良动机的一个毫无争议的例子。它还可能会干扰那些原本良好的动机。比如，当一个人试图在某种推理过程中权衡相互竞争的个人的要求时，这种厌恶会在这个人身上导致一种无意识的偏见。此外，它还可能使得一个人不太能够对某一种族群体成员产生同情心。

反道德情感的第二个例子是暴力侵犯的冲动。这种冲动有时可以看作一种好的动机。当我看到一个人在街上攻击另一个人时，动手的冲动也许恰恰是我应该有的。然而，在很多情况下，动手的冲动似乎都是一种道德上不好的动机，比如，当我们只面临极度轻微的挑衅时就是这样。此外，与种族厌恶一样，它也可能干扰好的动机。比如，它可能会使得一个人丧失理智，导致推理变得困难，而且也不太可能体验到道德情感。

由此，我认为对于很多人来说，减轻对某些种族的厌恶，或减少暴力侵犯的冲动，都可以算作是一种道德增强。换句话说，这将使得我们可以预期这些人总体上会有比原来更好的动机。但是，我不想或不需要在这里接受这一主张。相反，我要提出一个更弱的主张：对于有些情感来说，减轻一个人对它们的感受程度在某些情况下是一种道德增强。

对这一主张，可以提出两条大致属于康德主义的驳斥。首先，可以驳斥说，当一个人在自己身上产生某种动机时，这种动机在道德上好不好完全取决于之前促使这个动机产生的动机。道德评价的对象从产生出来的（之后的）动机转移到了促使这个动机产生的（之前的）动机。这样，尽管通常情况下减轻某种情感确实会改善一个人的动机，但是当减轻这种情感本身就是一个被驱动的行为时，就未必是这样了。比如，如果一个人是受某种不良动机的驱使而去改变自己的情感，那么之前这个不良动机就可能影响到随后的动机。

然而，一个人在某个时候的动机好不好完全取决于之前促使这些动机产生的动机，这很不合理。假设一位新纳粹分子为了抗议犹太人涌入他的城市而去参加了一次反犹太集会，但出乎意料的是，他在这个过程中对其他抗议者的行为深感不适，并为那些恐惧的犹太旁观者的举止所动容。结果，他对犹太人的厌恶极大地减轻了。从直觉上说，这个人在集会之后的动机比之前的动机更好，但是，我们却很难看出，其动机上的这种改善如何能参照导致这种改善的那个动机来解释。之前那些动机毕竟都是种族主义的动机。

对我关于道德增强的论述的第二个驳斥会坚持认为，仅仅改变情感的做法无法真正赋予行为者更好的动机。他们可能指出，道德评价的唯一对象是意志。因此，唯一能够作好坏评价的动机就是作为意志之运用的动机。一个人是否感受到了某种情感与他是否具有这样的动机完全无关，因为情感并不在意志的界线范围内。相反，意志是通过从事独立于情感状态的推理过程来行使的——这些推理过程是唯一可以做好坏评价的动机。在康德看来，当它们受到道德律的恰当指导时，或者当它们是**正确的**（此后我将这样说）时，它们就是好的动机①。

① 为了论证的目的，我假设推理过程本身并不涉及情感。对这一观点的否认，见 Damasio (2006)。

推理过程是唯一可做道德评价的动机这个观点在我看来没有道理。从直觉上讲，我们有时可以通过培养同情从而在道德上改善自己的动机。但根据刚才所勾勒的那种康德主义观点，这不能算作一种改善，因为受同情驱使确实不算是在从事推理。不仅如此，即使我们承认推理过程是唯一能做道德评价的动机，**减轻**一种情感仍然可以算作一种道德增强。尽管情感并不在意志的范围内，但它们可能会通过腐蚀推理过程而干扰意志的运用。可能对推理过程造成干扰。因此，当从事正确推理已经变得不可能时，减轻成问题的情感可以使得一个行动者从事正确的推理过程。

必须承认，这种康德主义立场还有一个更强的版本。可以说，只有当我们从事**不受情感干扰**的推理过程时，我们才是在运用自己的意志。根据这个观点，即便减轻反道德情感可以使得一个行动者从事正确的推理过程，但这些过程本身也不能算作好的（或不好的）动机，这恰恰是因为它们要受到情感的干扰。

在此，我无法对这一反对意见做出充分的回应。但是，由于我并不相信很多人会赞成这一反对意见所预设的那种关于意志之本质的很强的观点，所以我并不确定是否需要做出回应。我只是要指出，和那种更弱的康德主义观点一样，这种更强的康德主义观点意味着，培养某些情感并不能以任何方式在道德上改善一个人的动机。而与那个更弱的康德主义观点不同，它还意味着（在我看来违背直觉），无论是训练自己去压制种族厌恶这样的情感，还是逃避确知会触发这些情感的环境，对一个人的动机好不好都没有影响。

## 四　生物医学道德增强的可能性

我要尝试着论证，通过生物医学手段来减轻人们的反道德情感，有时候在道德上是允许的。但是我首先想简要考察一个可能更具优先性的问题，即这种生物医学道德增强在不久的将来是否可能？

对于生物医学道德增强在不久的将来是可能的这个观点，有两条显而易见的理由加以质疑。第一，根据心灵与大脑关系问题上的某些观点，我们道德心理的某些方面原则上是不能通过生物干预来改变的。[①] 本文将不考察这一主张。它并非主流的哲学立场，我希望仅仅指出这一点就足够了。第二条质疑理由是，我们的道德心理很可能极其复杂，可以说，太复杂了，以至于在不久的将来，我们并不会充分理解其神经科学基础，从而也就无法可靠地发展出恰当的生物医学干预措施。

诚然，我们的道德心理确实有许多方面十分复杂，从近期来看，我们也许不能正确理解对康德绝对命令的相信的神经科学基础。但是，我们的道德心理中还存在着其他一些更便于理解的要素，而且在这些要素中至少会包含一些反道德的情感。我们来考虑我之前提到的两种情感——对某些种族群体的厌恶与暴力侵犯的冲动。行为遗传学和神经科学方面的工作已经使我们对二者的生物学基础都有了初步的理解，而且这种理解也日益加深。早已经有来自收养和双胞胎研究的证据表明，侵犯性有基因方面的原因，[②] 现在有越来越有力的证据表明，单胺氧化酶 A 基因当中有一种多态性，[③] 在神经生理学层面，5 - 羟色胺能神经递质系统当中存在着紊乱。[④] 对于种族厌恶的研究相对较少，但是，近期一系列功能磁共振成像的研究表明，大脑杏仁核发挥着重要作用，它是大脑的一部分，负责调节情感。[⑤] 基于神经科学中的这些进展，我们似乎有理由相信，在不久的将来能够开发出作用于相对简单的情感性驱动的道德增强技术。

## 五　可以进行道德增强的情境

接下来，我将提出一些条件，我要论证，人们在这些条件下对自己进

① 最显而易见的是，相信心灵与大脑在因果上没有关联的身心平行论者会持这种观点。这种观点最著名的倡导者是莱布尼茨（Leibniz，1973）。

② Crowe（1974）；Cadoret（1978）；Grove，Eckert，Heston et al.（1990）.

③ H. G. Brunner，M. R. Nelen，X. O. Breakefield et al.（1993）；H. G. Brunner，M. R. Nelen，P. van Zandvoort *et al*.（1993）.

④ A. Caspi & J. McClay（2002）；R. M. M. de Almeida，P. F. Ferari，S. Parmigiani et al.（2005）.

⑤ A. J. Hart，P. J. Whalen，L. M. Shin et al.（2000）；E. A. Phelps，K. J. O'Connor，W. A. Cunningham et al.（2002）；W. A. Cunningham，M. K. Johnson，C. L. Raye et al.（2004）.

行道德增强在道德上是允许的。一种包含五个假定的情境就体现了这些条件。①

第一个假定只是指出，我们在处理一种符合我表述的道德增强的增强形式。

> 假定一：通过在时刻T经受某些生物医学干预（比如吃一片药），在时刻T之后的某个时刻，和他原本可能有的动机相比，行动者史密斯将会如所意料地有更好的动机。

为了集中关注道德增强的理由在我看来是最有说服力的情况，我引入了第二个假定。

> 假定二：如果史密斯没有经受这种干预，那么他至少会如所意料地拥有一些不好的（而不仅仅是次优的）动机。

第三个假定涉及我之前在道德增强如何奏效这个心理学问题上的主张。

> 假定三：生物医学干预将通过减轻史密斯的某种或某些情感而奏效。

最后，第四个和第五个假定排除了一些对道德增强的无趣质疑。比如，道德增强可能会有副作用，可能被强迫实施，或出于其他不必要的不当理由而实施。

> 假定四：生物医学干预对于史密斯的影响仅仅在于（a）用且只

① 作为上述假定的背景，我还将假设史密斯是一个正常人，他所生活的世界类似于我们的世界——也就是说，他所生活的世界是一个受到科学原则与社会科学原则所支配的世界，而这些原则在我看来也支配着我们自己的世界。

用必要的方式改变史密斯的心理，以便使得他在 T 时刻之后的某个时刻将会如所意料地有更好的动机，以及（b）这些心理改变带来的结果。

假定五：在 T 时刻，史密斯能够自由地选择是否要对其自身进行道德增强，如果他选择这么做，他就会出于最好的理由（无论是何种理由）做此选择。[①]

史密斯在这些情形下对自身进行道德增强在道德上可以允许吗？我主张，也许是可以允许的。

## 六 支持增强的理由

史密斯很显然有某种理由对自己进行道德增强：若他真这样做了，那么和他原本可能有的动机相比，他将如所意料地有一系列更好的动机，而我认为毫无争议的是，他确实有某种道德理由促成该结果（在后文中，我将省略“道德理由”中的“道德”）。

他究竟为什么有这种理由，这是一个可以追问的问题。有一种解释是这样的：若史密斯使得自己如所意料地有了更好的动机，那么他至少就如所意料地促成了一个好的后果，即他有了更好的动机。[②] 我们所有人至少有某种道德理由如所意料地去促成某种好的后果，这一点似乎不无道理。

这种解释是一种温和的后果论，因为它依赖于这样一个前提，即我们有很好的理由如所意料地促成任何好的后果。但是，彻底的非后果论者却可以提供另一种解释。例如，他们可以坚持认为，史密斯的道德增强行为有某种内在属性，比如，这种行为是一种自我改善行为，这一内在属性使得他有理由去做这件事。

① 我认为假定五至少意味着，史密斯对自己进行道德增强不会面临任何物理或法律上的限制。

② 史密斯还可能带来许多其他可预料的良好后果，例如，他如所意料地有了好的动机后就会随之而来的那些后果。

但是，不论史密斯**为什么**有理由在我们设定的情境中对自己进行道德增强，我认为从直觉上看，他显然有这样的理由。而且，这种直觉还能够得到另外一些直觉的支持，那些直觉涉及的是与之密切相关的情况。让我们假设行动者琼斯与史密斯处于完全相同的情境之中，只不过就琼斯而言，道德增强不是通过生物医学来实现，而是通过某种形式的自我教育来实现，例如，反思和尽力减轻她的反道德情感。从直觉上说，琼斯有理由对自己进行道德增强，至少在我看来是这样。如果要问为什么她有这样的理由，那么很自然的做法就是指出她和史密斯所处的相似情境。例如，她对自己进行道德增强将会如所意料地产生好的后果，或是这体现了对他人利益的关心。①

## 七　拒绝增强的理由

当然，史密斯也有理由不对自己进行道德增强，接下来我将考虑这些理由是什么。②

### （一）令人反感的动机

有一种可能是，史密斯有理由不对自我进行道德增强，因为他只能基于某种不良动机来这样做。在确定史密斯可以进行道德增强的情境时，我假定，如果他要增强自己，他就会基于最好的动机这样做。但是最好的动机也有可能还不够好。

史密斯可能有各种各样的动机对自己进行道德增强。其中有些动机似乎是无可非议的：他可能认为他应该对自己进行道德增强，他可能希望将来道德地行动，或者他可能只是十分关心公众的利益。然而，在这个问题上，我们应该考虑一下迈克尔·桑德尔（Michael Sandel）提出的反对意见。桑德尔认为，增强体现的是一种想要改变自我的过度愿望，或者说体现出不完全接受“天赋”。由于我们有理由避免这种动机，因此他认为，

① 我并不认为史密斯进行道德增强的理由和琼斯的一样强。

② 该部分所考察的理由基于一系列不同的实质性道德观点。我并不认为有任何一种道德观点可以包含所要讨论的所有理由。

我们有理由不要对自己进行增强。[①]

就像任何自愿的增强一样，我们很难否认史密斯的道德增强在某种程度上是由于不愿接受天赋这一想法所驱动（尽管这未必是其有意识的动机）。这里，我们不得不同意桑德尔的观点。但是有一点就不是那么显而易见了，即为什么这就使得史密斯有理由不要进行增强。撇开桑德尔的建议所存在的一般性问题不谈，当运用于史密斯的情况时，它还面临一个具体的问题。如果运用于史密斯的情况，那么桑德尔的主张就意味着，史密斯有理由接受他的不良动机，也有理由接受妨碍着他的良好动机的那种动机。但这是不合理的。毫无疑问，如果存在一些他不应该接受的特征，那么他的不良动机以及阻碍其良好动机的因素就属于这些特征之列。对于这些属性，应采取的恰当态度恰恰就是不接受并**想要自我改变**。

**（二）令人反感的手段**

史密斯不对自己进行道德增强的第二个理由可能是，用来进行道德增强的生物医学手段令人反感。

对于所建议的手段令人反感这个观点，我们可以区分出一个弱版本和一个强版本。根据弱版本，说这种手段令人反感，就是说，如果他通过非生物医学的手段对自己进行道德增强，那就**更好了**。这个观点当然具有某种直觉上的吸引力。对史密斯来说，通过某种道德训练或自我教育来增强自身似乎更可取。与自我教育相比，服用药物似乎“太容易了”，或者说，与普通人的理解太脱节了。[②] 可以说，如果让史密斯在生物医学道德增强与通过自我教育来实现道德增强之间做选择，史密斯有充分的理由选择后者。

然而，需要注意的是，史密斯在此时面临的选择并不是不同的增强手段，而是要不要进行生物医学道德增强。只有当史密斯是否进行生物医学道德增强将影响到他会在多大程度上通过其他手段进行道德增强时，史密斯不得不通过其他手段进行道德增强的理由才与史密斯做何选择有关。若史密斯通过生物医学手段来对自己进行道德增强会使得他**更少地**通过其他

① Sandel（2004；2007）.

② 此处可参见 Kass（2003：21－24）；President's Council on Bioethics（2003：290－293）。

更好的手段（比如，通过自我教育）来对自己进行道德增强，那么史密斯就有理由不进行生物医学道德增强。但是我们却很难理解为什么史密斯会以这种方式将生物医学增强和自我教育视为相互替代的关系。他似乎至少可以将它们视作互补关系；以一种方式对自己进行了道德增强后，他可能更愿意以另一种方式对自己进行道德增强（比如说，因为他很享受基于良好的动机而行事的体验）。

讲到这里，我们可以转向“令人反感的手段”这一主张的一个更强的版本了，那个版本认为，采用生物医学手段来进行道德增强不仅仅相对于其他替代性手段而言是令人反感的，而且在一种**绝对的**意义上就是令人反感的。事实上，它是如此绝对地令人反感，以至于史密斯的道德增强带来的道德利益会被作为一种手段的生物医学干预引起的道德代价所压倒。

有人主张，用生物医学手段来实现道德增强绝对是令人反感的。这一主张的依据可能是这种手段不自然。的确，这是一个基于手段层面对生物医学增强的常见批评。[①] 但问题是，我们必须先对自然（或不自然）本身做出一些解释，以便使得下述两个说法都是正确的：（1）使用生物医学手段对某人进行道德增强是不自然的；（2）这种不自然使得一个人有理由不进行这种增强。能不能找到这样的解释呢？

大卫·休谟区分了三种不同的自然概念：一种可能与“奇迹”（miracles）相对应，另一种与“罕见和不寻常”（the rare and unusual）相对应，还有一种则指“人工产物”（artifice）。[②] 这种分类法向我们暗示了一种处理不自然概念的类似方法。我们可以把不自然等同于奇迹（或超自然）、罕见和不寻常或者人为（artificiality）。在下文中，我将思考这些自然概念中是否有任何一个能够成功地使得（1）和（2）都站得住脚。

**1. 作为超自然的不自然概念**

首先让我们来思考一下作为超自然的不自然概念。根据对这一概念的一种流行解释，某种与下述说法类似的说法是正确的：如果（或者在某种

---

① 见 Kass（2003：17，20－24）；President's Council on Bioethics（2003：290－293）。

② Hume（1888：473－475）.

程度上）某种事物在科学可以研究的世界之外，它就是不自然的。[①] 从这一观点来看，生物医学干预似乎根本不是不自然的，因为这种干预正是科学可以研究的。因此，作为超自然的不自然概念使得（1）显然是错误的。

**2. 作为不寻常的不自然概念**

休谟的分析所暗示的第二种不自然概念可以等同于不寻常或不熟悉（unfamiliarity）。利昂·卡斯（Leon Kass）认为，不自然即与日常的人类理解相脱节。这种看法可能也是这种不自然概念的一个变体。[②]

不寻常和不熟悉在下述意义上是相对的：某种东西必然对某个人来说是不寻常或不熟悉的。因此，对史密斯的生物医学干预是否可以算作不自然，就要看对谁而言是不寻常和不熟悉的。对于生活在今天的我们来说，为了道德增强而使用生物医学技术确实可以算作不寻常和不熟悉的，由此，也许就算得上不自然的。但是对于未来的人们而言，情况可能并非如此。因此，如果不准确说明不寻常或不熟悉是相对谁而言，那么（1）是否正确就不确定了。

然而，我们不必去追究这些复杂的问题，因为不管（1）根据当前的不自然概念是否正确，（2）似乎都是错误的。仅仅由于所用手段不寻常或不熟悉，或与日常的人类理解脱节，我们是否就有理由拒绝这种手段呢？这是令人怀疑的。我们通常可能更偏好熟悉的而非不熟悉的手段，理由是，因为有证据的支持，我们可以在信息更充分的基础上预测其效果，因此这种预测也更为确定。这样，如果有人让我在两种不同的药物中选择一种以治疗某种疾病，而这两种药物被认为同等安全和有效，我可能也会选择更为熟悉的一种，因为它可能得到了更充分的研究，因而也就具有更为确定的效果。但这里我们最终关注的却并非手段本身是否自然，或是否具有任何其他令人反感的特征，而是使用该手段所导致的效果。在下文我将回到史密斯的增强行为可能产生的不利影响。我在这里更感兴趣的是，我们对某种手段不熟悉，是否就有理由不采用它，而不管其效果怎样。对此做肯定回答在我看来就等于采取一种莫名其妙厌恶新事物的立场。

---

① 见 Moore（1903：92）。

② Kass（2003：22－24）.

### 3. 作为人为的不自然概念

最后来考虑一下作为人为的不自然概念。可以说，这是现代哲学中最为普遍的自然概念。[①] 可以将其粗略地描述如下：若某种东西涉及人类行为，或某些类型的人类行为（如有意行为），那么它就是不自然的。

根据这个不自然概念，主张（1）是相当合理的。生物医学干预显然涉及人类行为——而且它几乎总是有意的行为。然而，主张（2）此时看起来就不太合理了。**每当**我们有意地采用某种手段去达到某种目的，这种手段都涉及有意的人类行为。但这并不意味着我们有理由不采用这种手段。因为若是如此，我们就有理由不要有意地采用任何手段去达成任何目的。而这当然不可能是对的。

重新审视一下通过自我教育而不是生物医学干预来实现道德增强，也可以说明根据当前的不自然概念，主张（2）是不合理的。这种增强似乎没有什么问题，但如果我们将不自然理解为涉及（有意的）人类行为或是（有意的）人类行为的产物，那么它显然包含了不自然的手段。

在这里，我们应该考虑一种对作为人为的不自然概念的更为有限的解释，这种解释主张，某种东西要想被看作不自然的，它就必须不仅涉及（有意的）人类行为，还必须涉及**技术**——科学和工业这样的高度精细和复杂的社会实践的产物。转向这种解释也许就不必将训练和教育这样的实践归入不自然之列。但这种解释仍然会使得许多实践被说成是不自然的，尽管从直觉上看我们可能并没有基于手段的理由拒绝那些实践。比如，我们来考虑一下疾病的治疗。这往往涉及生物医学技术，然而我们并非显而易见有任何基于手段的理由不要进行疾病治疗。为了避免这个问题，作为人为的不自然概念仍需进一步加以限制，以便使得涉及技术的手段只有在不以治疗疾病为目的时才能看作不自然的。根据这个观点，史密斯所采取的手段本身并不是不自然的。相反，他所采取的手段是由于带有某些意图或目的才成为不自然的。也许通过这种方式限制不自然概念，我们就能够避免将一些似乎显然无可非议的做法（如自我教育或治疗疾病）归入不自

---

① Heyd（2003：156 - 157）.

然之列。然而，根据对不自然所作的这种解释，我们仍然不清楚为什么我们有理由避免不自然的做法。若要证明史密斯有理由不进行生物医学道德增强，仅仅提出某种不自然概念——根据那种概念，史密斯进行道德增强是不自然的，而看上去没太大问题的做法则是自然的——是不够的。必须证明，一种做法不自然使得它有问题，或至少构成了证据证明它有问题。如果没有这样的证明，那么说它不自然并不是在从事哲学工作，而仅仅是在断言我们有理由不要进行生物医学道德增强。我已经论证，休谟的分析所暗示的那三种不自然概念都不能使得（1）和（2）同时成立。如果我的结论是正确的，那就意味着，这些不自然概念都不能构成任何基于手段的理由来要求史密斯不要进行道德增强。也许基于其他某种不自然概念，我们可以更有说服力地论证主张（1）和主张（2）。或者，还有其他办法可以表明，生物医学道德增强涉及一些出于别的原因（而不是由于不自然）而令人反感的手段。但我并不确定这些概念和观点的内容是什么。

**（三）令人反感的后果**

史密斯对自己进行增强的后果又是否能够成为他不要进行增强的理由呢？关于这种可能性，有两点需要提前注意。第一，由于我们假定史密斯的道德增强不会产生任何副作用（假定四），那么他的行为将产生的仅有的后果就是：

（a）在时刻 T 之后的某个时刻，和他原本可能有的动机相比，他将会如所意料地有更好的动机；

（b）对于导致（a）来说是必要的那些心理改变，且只有那些心理改变；

（c）所有来自（a）与（b）的后果。

因此，若史密斯有基于后果的理由不进行道德增强，那么这些理由必须基于（a），（b）或（c）的特征，也许这三种后果就其内在而言就不好。

第二，有些道德理论限定了（a）和（c）是不是或在多大程度上是不好的后果。我们来考虑一下这样一些理论，根据这些理论，唯有快乐或痛苦的状态才是就其内在而言好或不好。在这些理论看来，（a）不可能就其内在而言就不好，因为动机并不是一种快乐或痛苦的状态。或者，我们再思考一种后果主义的道德理论，根据这种理论，一种动机在道德上好不好取决于一个人有这种动机的后果好不好。根据这个理论，如果史密斯在 T 之后的某个时刻有更好的动机，那么他有这些动机的后果——这些后果属于（c）——必定好过他有更坏动机的后果。史密斯有更好的动机，和他有更坏的动机相比，肯定会有更好的后果，因为正是有好的后果使得一种动机成为良好的动机。为了论证的目的，在下文中我将假设，以这些方式限制（a）和（c）好还是不好的道德理论是错误的。

1. **身份（identity）改变**

史密斯对自身进行道德增强的一个不良影响可能是，他将失去其同一性（identity）。对同一性丧失的担忧已经作为针对人类增强的一般性驳斥而提出，没有明显的理由能够说明为什么这些驳斥不应当运用于道德增强的情况。①

显然，我们考虑的那种道德增强未必会在一种很强的意义上改变身份，就是说，已经使得史密斯在接受增强后成为一个不同于以往的人。我们的道德心理状态无时无刻不在发生着变化，有时这种变化还是惊人的，例如在某种特别痛苦的经历之后。当这些变化发生时，我们并不会认为一个人已经被另一个人所取代。然而，也许史密斯所经历的道德增强会在更弱的意义上改变他的身份，就是说，它将改变他最根本的心理特征，例如，某些对于他如何看待自身及自己与他人关系来说至关重要的心理特征，或某些贯穿其人格的心理特征。②

假设我们承认，史密斯所经历的道德增强会在这种较弱意义上改变其身份。这并不能使得史密斯有理由不经历这种改变。只有当我们根本性的心理特征具有某种积极价值时，我们才有理由维系它们，这看起来是有道理的。但是，即使史密斯的反道德情感**可能**具有某种价值（例如，史密斯可能发现这些情感体验令人愉悦），它们却未必有价值。

2. **受到限制的自由**

通过对自己进行道德增强，和他原本可能有的动机相比，史密斯将会

① 见 Wolpe（2002：393 - 394）；President's Council on Bioethics（2003：294）。

② 对这种较弱意义上的“身份”的讨论，见 Schechtman（1996：74 - 76）。

使得自己在时刻 T 之后的某个时刻拥有总体而言更好的动机。然而，有人可能会认为，这一结果是以牺牲其自由为代价带来的，就是说，在时刻 T 之后，他将失去拥有某些不良动机并根据它们而行动的自由。即使拥有不良动机并根据它们而行动本身可能没有什么价值，仍然可以认为，拥有这些动机并根据它们而行动的**自由**是很宝贵的。事实上，这种自由似乎是人类理性能动性的核心要素。可以说，史密斯有理由不要限制这种自由。

我在这里所考虑的反对意见体现在以下两个主张之中：

（1）史密斯对自己进行道德增强将会使得他拥有不良动机并根据它们而行动的自由减少。

（2）史密斯有理由不要去限制他拥有不良动机并根据它们而行动的自由。

我认为主张（2）有问题。那里提到的那种自由并不是显而易见有价值。此外，即使这种自由确实有价值，限制它可能也没有问题，只要这种限制是自己选择的，就像史密斯所处的情形中一样。然而，我将在此集中关注主张（1）。主张（1）的支持者承诺了某种对自由的理解。他必须坚持认为，自由不仅在于没有外在的约束，而且在于没有内在的心理约束，因为只有史密斯的内在特征才会被道德增强所改变。这个观点可以通过下述方式得到支持：认为自我可以分为两个部分，一部分是真实的或本真的自我；另一部分是存在于真实自我之外的野蛮自我。这样，我们就可以将约束着真实自我的野蛮自我的任何方面都看作一种对自由的约束。[①] 因此，我们就可以这样来捍卫主张（1）：史密斯的道德增强会以某种方式改变其野蛮自我，以至于它会限制其自主的自我。

有正当理由认为史密斯的道德增强会改变的是其野蛮自我而非其真实自我。我们所假定的是，史密斯的道德增强将会减轻某些情感，所以这大概是通过改变大脑的情感产生机制来起作用的，而这些机制最好被看作野蛮自我的一部分。确实，如果认为那些往往会引发种族厌恶或侵犯冲动的机制（那些机制主要是潜意识的机制）是真实而自主的自我的一部分，那

① 这种进路的一个例子，见 Taylor（1979：175－195）。

就很奇怪了。

然而，道德增强会改变史密斯的野蛮自我以至于会**干预**其真正自我，这个观点似乎与我关于增强机制的假定（假定三）不符。由于史密斯的道德增强被认为会减轻某些情感，它大概是通过**抑制**那些产生相关情感的野蛮机制来起作用的。这种增强似乎是通过**减少**史密斯的野蛮自我的影响从而使得其真实自我有更大自由来起作用的。更为准确的说法是，这种增强增加了史密斯拥有良好动机并根据它们而行动的自由，而不是减少了其拥有不良动机并根据它们而行动的自由。

3. **诱发搭便车**

我想考虑的最后一种可能的批评是，史密斯可能有理由不进行道德增强，因为他拥有更好的动机会诱发他人搭便车。

为何会发生这种情况？我们可以通过以下情形来说明。假设在某个海湾工作的渔民只有杰克和吉姆。海湾里的鱼类资源即将枯竭，而两人都希望鱼群数量能够增加，却又不想限制自己的捕鱼量。尽管如此，他们还是制定了一个计划：下个月，他们每个人每天的捕鱼量限定为二十条——大大低于任何一方在鱼群数量即将枯竭的情况下的预期捕获量。

每个渔民要么坚持计划（“尊重配额”），要么不坚持计划（“过度捕捞”）。那么，就将有四种可能的行为组合（杰克尊重配额，吉姆过度捕捞；吉姆尊重配额，杰克过度捕捞；等等）。下面的图表 1 描述了每个渔民从这些行动组合中获得的收益（用利益来表示）。我们用它们用来反映一个事实，即每个渔民的收益与未来鱼类资源的枯竭程度呈负相关，但与自己目前的捕鱼数量呈正相关。①

假设两个渔民虽都不能观察到对方的捕鱼数量，但都能够察觉到对方

① 这些收益源于以下假设：假设每个渔民都尊重配额，那么到月底时鱼的数量将会较高；而如果只有一个渔民尊重配额，那么鱼的数量就会较低；如果两个渔民都不尊重配额，那么鱼的数量就会非常低。较高的鱼群数量对每个人来说价值为 16，较低的鱼群数量对每个人来说价值为 11，极低的鱼群数量对每个人来说价值为 1。此外，假设尊重配额对每个人来说短期价值为 -6，而不尊重配额则为 0。因此，一方尊重配额另一方也尊重配额，则另一方获得的价值为 16 - 6 = 10；一方过度捕捞而另一方尊重配额，则另一方所获得的价值为 11 - 6 = 5；一方尊重配额而另一方过度捕捞，则另一方获得的价值为 11 - 0 = 11；一方过度捕捞另一方也过度捕捞，则另一方获得的价值为 1 - 0 = 1。

| | | 吉姆 尊重配额 | 吉姆 过度捕捞 |
|---|---|---|---|
| 杰克 | 尊重配额 | (10，10) | (5，11) |
| 杰克 | 过度捕捞 | (11，5) | (1，1) |

**图表 1　杰克 & 吉姆**

的动机。且进一步假设吉姆的动机是**自利的**，也就是说他总是做一切能够使得其自身收益最大化的事，而杰克的动机要么**在道德上是好的**，也就是说他总是坚持计划，尊重配额，要么**在道德上是不好的**，也就是说他总是违背计划，过度捕捞。

若杰克的动机**在道德上是不好的**，那么吉姆就知道杰克会过度捕捞。由此，他将面临一个选择，要么尊重配额并获得数量为 5 的收益，要么过度捕捞并获得数量为 1 的收益。因为他的动机是自利的，故而吉姆将会尊重配额。

但是，现在假设杰克的动机**在道德上是好的**。这样，吉姆就知道杰克将会过度捕捞。[①] 由此，他面临着一个选择，要么尊重配额并获得数量为 10 的收益，要么过度捕捞并获得数量为 11 的收益。由于吉姆有着**自利的**动机，他将会过度捕捞。由于拥有在道德上好的而不是不好的动机，杰克诱发吉姆过度捕捞，而不是尊重配额。也就是说，杰克使得吉姆利用了他的良好动机，结果损害了杰克的利益，减少了他们共同的收益，且违背了他们之前的协议。

这是一个不太符合现实的情境。但它说明，一个人拥有更好的动机，可能会通过改变他人面临的收益结构，从而诱发他人以种种很可能被认为道德上不好的方式搭便车。

然而，正如我们可以构建出一个人的良好动机导致另一个人的不良行为的情境一样，我们也可以构建出一种结果相反的情境。让我们思考一下杰克和吉姆所面临情境的一种变化形式，其中的萨利和山姆面临一个类似

---

① 此处原文似乎有误，应为“吉姆就知道杰克不会过度捕捞”。——译者注

的问题，但这次的收益情况如下：

| | | 山姆 | |
|---|---|---|---|
| | | 尊重配额 | 过度捕捞 |
| 萨利 | 尊重配额 | (10，12) | (5，9) |
| | 过度捕捞 | (11，3) | (1，5) |

**图表2　萨利 & 山姆**

萨利的四种收益情况与杰克和吉姆的收益情况是一样的，但是山姆的收益情况则发生了变化，以此来反映他在未来鱼群数量上的价值函数略有不同。[①] 让我们再次假设渔民们不能观察到彼此的捕鱼数量，但却能够察觉彼此的动机，且山姆有**自利的**动机。这样，若萨利有**道德上不好的**动机，所以总是过度捕捞，那么山姆则面临着一个选择，他要么尊重配额并获得数量为1的收益，要么过度捕捞并获得数量为5的收益。山姆**有自利的**动机，因此他将会过度捕捞。另一方面，若萨利有道德上良好的动机因而始终尊重配额，那么山姆就将面临一个选择，要么尊重配额并获得数量为10的收益，要么过度捕捞并获得数量为9的收益。他会尊重配额。[②]

由此，我们就有了另一种互动关系，在这里，一个人具有更好的动机，则诱发他人**不**去搭便车。这个结果与我们在杰克和吉姆的情境中看到的相反。当然，还有许多集体行动问题，在这些问题中，一个人动机的变化可能对他人是否搭便车没有任何影响（标准的囚徒困境就是一个例子，在这种情况下，一个自利的行动者总是会搭便车）。

在许多情况下，史密斯的道德增强可能会减弱他自己的“搭便车”倾

① 对于杰克、吉姆和萨利来说，较低的未来鱼群数量的价值要远高于极低的鱼群数量，但是较高的未来鱼群数量而非较低的未来鱼群数量还是可以带来一点收益的。对于山姆来说，拥有较高的未来鱼群数量的价值远远高于拥有较低的未来鱼群数量，而较低和极低未来鱼群数量在价值上的差异则相对较小。表中所列的山姆的收益反映了下述基本价值：较高鱼群数量的价值为18；较低鱼群数量的价值为9；极低鱼群数量的价值为5；尊重配额的短期价值为 -6，过度捕捞的短期价值为0。

② 在收益表中，每组数字中左边的数字代表萨利的收益，右边的数字代表山姆的收益。由此看来，作者这里的表述似乎有误。作者先后提到的收益数1、5、10、9似乎应为3、5、12、9。不过这并不影响作者的结论。——译者注

向。而上述讨论表明，仅仅在这些情况当中的某些情况下，这才会增加其他人搭便车的倾向。因此，他的道德增强似乎不太可能导致搭便车的净增加。

## 八 结语

我已经论证，史密斯有理由通过生物医学手段对自己进行道德增强。我也已经拒斥了一些论证，那些论证主张存在着很好的相反理由。因此，我希望我已经为下述主张提供了某种支持：史密斯进行生物医学道德增强在道德上是允许的。但是，如果允许史密斯对自己进行道德增强，那么生物保守主义命题几乎确定无疑是错误的。因为正如我之前提到的，生物医学道德增强技术在不久的将来很可能会变得可行。几乎可以肯定的是，如果它们真的变得可行，那么一些（也可能是很多）未来的人们将会发现自己的情境与史密斯非常相似，以至于我们关于史密斯的结论也同样适用于他们：与生物保守主义命题相反，对有的人来说，进行生物医学增强在道德上是允许的。

然而，我最后要指出的是，生物保守主义命题并非增强的反对者唯一的主张。除了主张人们对自己进行增强是道德上不允许的以外，许多生物保守主义者还会断言，我们不可以**开发**以增强为目的的技术，我们也不可以**允许**增强。尽管我已经说了这么多，这些主张也可能是对的。鉴于必要技术已经出现而法律障碍还不存在，从未来有的人对自己进行道德增强将是可以允许的这一事实并不能直接推出，他们会被允许这样做，或我们会被允许开发人人可用的技术。这里，还有诸多其他因素需要考虑。例如，如果我们要开发道德增强技术，那么我们将无法防止有人以不合宜的方式使用这些技术，比如说，用来增强自利倾向或不道德性。因此，我们能否被允许开发或使用道德增强技术，可能取决于对正当使用和不当使用这些技术的可能性进行的权衡。

**参考文献**


Annas, G. A., 2002, "Cell division", *Boston Globe*, 21 April.

Aristotle, 1985, *Nicomachean Ethics*, T. Irwin, trans., Indianapolis: Hackett.

Brunner, H. G., Nelen, P. M. R., Breakefield X. O., et al., 1993, "Abnormal behaviour associated with a point mutation in the structural gene for Monoamine Oxidase A", *Science* 262, 5133, 578 - 580.

Brunner, H. G., Nelen, P. M. R., van Zandvoort et al., 1993, "X - linked borderline mental retardation with prominent behavioural disturbance: phenotype, genetic localization, and evidence for disturbed monoamine metabolism", *American Journal of Human Genetics* 52 (6), 1032 - 1039.

Buchanan, A., Brock, D., Daniels N., & Wikler, D., From Chance to Choice: Genetics and Justice (Cambridge: Cambridge University Press, 2000).

Caldwell, J. A., Caldwell, J. L., & Smythe, N. K., 2000, "A double - blind, placebo - controlled investigation of the efficacy of modafinil for sustaining the alertness and performance of aviators: a helicopter simulator study", *Psychopharmacology* 150, 272 - 282.

Cadoret, R. J., 1978, "Psychopathology in adopted - away offspring of biologic parents with antisocial behavior", *Archives of General Psychiatry* 35, 176 - 184.

Caspi, A., & McClay, J., 2002, "Evidence that the cycle of violence in maltreated children depends on genotype", *Science* 297, 851 - 854.

Crowe, R. R., 1974, "An adoption study of antisocial personality", *Archives of General Psychiatry* 31, 785 - 791.

Cunningham, W. A., Johnson, M. K., Raye, C. L., et al., 2004, "Separable neural components in the processing of black and white faces", *Psychological Science* 15, 806 - 813.

Damasio, Antonio, 2006, *Descartes' Error: Emotion, Reason and the Human Brain*, London, Vintage.

De Almeida, R. M. M., Ferari, P. F., Parmigiani S., et al., 2005, "Escalated aggressive behavior: Dopamine, serotonin and GABA", *European Journal of Pharmacology* 526, 51 - 64.

Farah, M. J., Illes, J., Cook - Deegan R., et al., 2004, "Neurocognitive enhancement: what can we do and what should we do?" *Nature Reviews Neuroscience* 5, 421 - 425.

Fukuyama, F., 2002, *Our Posthuman Future: Consequences of the Biotechnology Revolution*, New York: Farrar, Straus, and Giroux.

Grove, W. M., Eckert, E. D., Heston, L., et al., 1990, "Heritability of substance abuse and antisocial behavior: a study of monozygotic twins reared apart", *Biological Psychiatry* 27, 1293 - 1304.

Hart, A. J., Whalen, P. J., Shin L. M., et al., 2000, "Differential response in the human amygdala to racial outgroup vs. ingroup face stimuli", *Neuroreport: For Rapid Communication of Neuroscience Re-*

search 11, 2351 -2355.

Heyd, D. , 2003, "Human nature: an oxymoron?" *Journal of Medicine and Philosophy* 28 (2), 151 -169.

Hume, D. , *A Treatise of Human Nature*, ed. , by L. A. Selby - Bigge, Oxford: Clarendon.

J. A. , Caldwell, J. L. , & Smythe, N. K. , 2000, "A double - blind, placebo - controlled investigation of the efficacy of modafinil for sustaining the alertness and performance of aviators: a helicopter simulator study", *Psychopharmacology* 150, 272 -282.

Johnston, L. D. , O'Malley P. M. , & Bachman, J. G. , 2003, *Monitoring the Future National Survey Results on Drug Use, 1975 -2002: II. College Students and Adults Ages 19 -40*, Washington DC: US Department of Health and Human Services.

Kass, L. R. , 2003, "Ageless bodies, happy souls: biotechnology and the pursuit of perfection", *The New Atlantis* 1, 9 -28.

Kant, I. , 1993, *Critique of Practical Reason*, 3rd edn. , L. W. Beck, trans. New York: Macmillan, 1993.

Leibniz, G. W. , 1973, *Philosophical Writings*, ed. , by Parkinson, G. H. R. , Morris, M. , trans. , London: Dent.

Lynch, G. , 2002, "Memory enhancement: the search for mechanism - based drugs", *Nature Neuroscience* 5, 1035 -1038.

Mill, J. S. , 1979, *Utilitarianism*, ed. , by G. Sher, Indianapolis: Hackett.

McKibben, B. , 2003, "Designer genes", *Orion*, 30 April.

Mehlman, M. J. , 2005, "Genetic enhancement: plan now to act later", *Kennedy Institute of Ethics Journal* 15 (1), 77 -82.

Moore, G. E. , 1903, *Principia Ethica*, Cambridge: Cambridge University Press.

Phelps, E. A. , O'Connor, K. J. , Cunningham W. A. , et al. , 2000, "Performance on indirect measures of race evaluation predicts amygdala activation", *Journal of Cognitive Neuroscience* 12, 729 -738.

President's Council on Bioethics, 2003, *Beyond Therapy: Biotechnology and the Pursuit of Happiness*, Washington DC: President's Council on Bioethics.

Sandel, M. J. , 2004, "The case against perfection", *The Atlantic Monthly* 293 (3), 50 -65;

——, 2007, *The Case Against Perfection: Ethics in the Age of Genetic Engineering*, Cambridge, MA: Harvard University Press.

Schechtman, M. , 1996, *The Constitution of Selves*, Ithaca, NY: Cornell University Press.

Scott, R. , Bourtchouladze, R. , Gossweiler S. , et al. , 2002, "CREB and the discovery of cognitive enhancers", *Journal of Molecular Neuroscience* 19, 171 -177.

Taylor, C. , 1979, "What's wrong with negative liberty", ed. , by A. Ryan, *The Idea of Freedom*,

London, Oxford University Press, 175 - 193.

Teter, C. J. , McCabe, S. E. , LaGrange, K. , et al. , 2006, "Illicit use of specific stimulants among college students: prevalence, motives, and routes of administration", *Pharmacotherapy* 26 (10), 1501 - 1510.

Tindall, B. , 2004, "Better playing through chemistry", *New York Times*.

Tully, T. , Bourtchouladze, R. , Scott, R. , et al. , 2003, "Targeting the CREB pathway for memory enhancers", *Nature Reviews Drug Discovery* 2, 267 - 277.

Turner, D. C. , Robbins, T. W. , Clark, L. , Aron, A. R. , Dowson, J. , & Sahakian, B. J. , 2003, "Cognitive enhancing effects of modafinil in healthy volunteers", *Psychopharmacology* 165, 260 - 269.

Verroken, M. , 2005, "Drug use and abuse in sport", *Drugs in Sport* (ed.) by in D. R. Mottram, London: Routledge, 29 - 63.

Wolpe, P. R. , 2002, "Treatment, enhancement, and the ethics of neurotherapeutics", *Brain and Cognition* 50, 387 - 395.

Yesavage, J. , Mumenthaler, M. , Taylor, J. , et al. , 2001, "Donezepil and flight simulator performance: effects on retention of complex skills", *Neurology* 59, 123 - 125.

# 新书研讨专栏
# New Monography Symposium

## “思想与时代”新书研讨会专栏导言

**Editorial Foreword to the Special Issue: “Thinking Between Times” New Monography Symposium**

# 黄裕生:《摆渡在有—无之间的哲学:第一哲学问题研究》*

瞿旭彤(Xutong Qu)**

Huang Yusheng: *A Philosophy Ferrying Between Being and Non-Being: A First Philosophical Investigation*

为了以思想把握和回应时代,践行彼此欣赏和共同求真的学术批判,促进立足现在、兼顾过去和将来的思想创新,推动和参与求真学术共同体的建设,清华大学人文学院哲学系决定不定期主办“思想与时代”新书研讨会。研讨会形式为:邀请一位近期出版新书的学者作45分钟左右的书面主题报告,邀请3—5位学者分别发表20分钟左右的书面评议报告,其他受邀学者自由发言和评议。研讨会第一期于2021年6月12日举行,专门研讨清华大学人文学院哲学系黄裕生近期出版的著作:《摆渡在有—无之间的哲学:第一哲学问题研究》(清华大学出版社2019年版)。

在书面报告环节,黄裕生发表主旨报告,介绍全书写作缘由、主要思路和主要观点。黄老师特别强调,他的研究和思考并没有转向到政治哲学

---

* 黄裕生(2019)。

** 清华大学人文学院哲学系。

领域。

他关注的始终还是第一哲学，而且，政治哲学也不能独立于第一哲学；有第一哲学作为基础的政治哲学才是审慎的政治哲学。黄老师坦言，他的这部作品是多年以来困惑、挣扎、研究与思考的结晶，不仅是一部以技术化的专业研究为基础的研究型作品，更是一部以哲学问题本身为旨趣的思想型作品。在笔者看来，黄老师带有中国知识分子惯有的强烈使命感，立足于中国和世界当下的现代性处境和时代问题，[①] 以"摆渡"于康德和海德格尔之间的思想立场，[②] 试图从形而上学的高度把握和回应虚无主义时代的根本困境。诚如他自己在新书导论中所期许的："作为追寻世界本原的努力，哲学不只是一种返乡之旅，同时也是一种'未来之旅'"(9)。在这样的哲学旅程中，"穷通古今未来之变，追寻天下普遍之理"(12)，"以会通了中西普世之理的哲学参与开辟新的世界史。这也是我们作为中国人在今天的哲学研究中能够打开和应当打开的一个希望"(13)。

之后，中国人民大学哲学院张志伟（代读人：武汉大学哲学学院杨云飞）、山东社会科学院哲学研究所尚文华、天津社会科学院伦理学研究所李科政三位学者分别作评论发言。在自由发言环节，多位与会学者与主旨发言人进行了对话和互动。[③] 组成此次专栏的三篇文章即是上述三位学者在研讨会后再加修订和增补的作品。

在《我们为什么必须重建"第一哲学"》一文中，张志伟进行着与黄裕生类似的思想努力，不仅在分享自己的哲学史研究心得，而且也试图接着海德格尔从事哲学思考，"以思想行走于历史与未来之间"。面对哲学自身的根本性危机、伴随着现实物理世界与主观精神世界分离而来的"古今之争"乃至"古今断裂"，以及由此产生的人类文明不得不"重新"面对的虚无主义威胁，张志伟认为，"我们需要构建'第二轴心时代'或者'新的轴心时代'的文明理念"，"重新激发本原文化的潜力，发挥历史的

① 黄裕生（2014）。

② 黄裕生（1997/2012；2002；2008/2018）。

③ 具体详情参见胡嘉乐关于此次研讨会的综述长文，载于《现代哲学》2022 年上半年即将刊发的最新一期。

可能性，让历史走向未来”。在此过程中，哲学在方法论的意义上，“因为其问题意识、批判精神和理论思维，可以构成新的轴心时代的全球性价值理念的基础”，“融合不同的文化”。这样的哲学，在张志伟看来，不是“地方性的”东方哲学或西方哲学，而是“作为哲学的哲学——第一哲学”。

在《同一性、差异性与生存：有关“第一哲学”基础原理的争论》一文中，尚文华接续之前与黄裕生的持续思想交流与争鸣，试图就“同一”与“差异”这一形而上学的根本问题，展示他与黄裕生在原理层面上所作相关思考的“差异性”。在尚文华看来，黄裕生的思想进路“可能更接受康德式的原理”，“把思想关于存在的经验视为同一性的展示”，而以黑格尔、马克思和克尔凯郭尔为代表的思想进路则不接受“康德式把同一视为思之经验之起点的命题”，而是以差异作为思之经验的起点。

如题所示，在《康德哲学中存在与自由的限度：以黄裕生的第一哲学思考为视阈》一文中，李科政试图从黄裕生所谓的“哲学的摆渡”和康德意义上的“辩证法”出发，探讨和阐明康德批判哲学的存在观念和自由观念的内涵及其限度。对李科政来说，“在康德批判哲学中，存在与自由只能间接地关联起来”，而并非黄裕生接着海德格尔思想而阐发的“自由与物自身在（显现）是同一件事（Ereignis），是同一性存在”。

**参考文献**

黄裕生，1997/2012，《时间与永恒：论海德格尔哲学中的时间问题》，江苏人民出版社。

——，2002，《真理与自由：康德哲学的存在论阐释》，江苏人民出版社。

——，2008/2018，《宗教与哲学的相遇：奥古斯丁与托马斯·阿奎纳的基督教哲学研究》，江苏人民出版社。

——，2014，《站在未来的立场上》，生活·读书·新知三联书店。

——，2019，《权利的形而上学》，商务印书馆。

# 我们为什么必须重建“第一哲学”？

张志伟（ZHANG Zhiwei）*

我和裕生君子之交，多年的朋友。我一向以为裕生有乃师风范，他摆渡于“有—无”之间的沉思，不仅仅是哲学史的研究心得，更是在从事哲学思考，所以他的思考是开放的和指向未来的——以思想行走于历史与未来之间。讨论《摆渡在有—无之间的哲学——第一哲学问题研究》乃心之所愿，因为我也对第一哲学或形而上学的问题十分关心。不巧的是先有了其他的安排，所以乃以此文就教于裕生和诸位方家。本文的主要思路是海德格尔式的，在形而上学问题上，我受海德格尔影响比较深。

在历史与未来之间思考，那是一种什么样的思考？

哲学是历史性的思想（叶秀山先生语），因而哲学并非仅仅停留在已经发生的过去，而且蕴涵着未来。历史标志着过去，人们要回到源头，然而如果这源头是自由的、开放的，从而体现为可能性，那么回到源头也可以说是走向未来。这里所说的并不是黑格尔“前进—回溯”式的辩证法，从潜在、展开到现实的目的论式的辩证运动意味着逻辑展开在历史之中，未来本已在过去决定了，所以实际上并没有未来。我要说的是源头之无限开放的可能性，这种可能性呈现在我们与历史的“视域融合”之中。历史虽然已经发生，貌似是发生了的事实，但是作为“生存实情”（Faktizität），人类历史却是渗透着可能性的存在，故而哲学的功能（之

* 张志伟，中国人民大学哲学院教授。

一）就是激发历史的可能性。套用"平行宇宙"的说法，历史意味着无穷无尽的可能性，其中任何一种可能性都是一个宇宙，所以打开历史不仅仅是打开了过去的传统，也可以说是打开了未来，此即行走于历史与未来之间，就此而论，哲学思考亦意味着"创生"。作为"向死而在"的人，阅读和写作哲学作品，就像阅读和写作文学作品一样，相当于在历史或现实中经历或者演历未来，以有限的人生开展出无限的可能性。因此，哲学本身就是可能性，就是未来，就是自由。哲学家们原本也想像宗教先知或者科学家那样"一统天下"，提供出一套绝对真理的规律、法则或教条，但是因哲学之本性的驱使，留给后人的却是一条条通往不同世界或可能宇宙的思想之路。然而，曾几何时，我们的哲学沉溺于"学科建设"，或者仅仅解释历史，或者仅仅分析语言，或者迷失在了历史之中，或者迷失在了逻辑之中，最终迷失了未来。究其原因，是因为第一哲学的缺失。

对于我们这个时代，第一哲学的"缺席"构成了重大的理论问题和现实问题。不过我们也应该反思的是，"第一哲学"本身也是可能性，所以在变化之中。

## 一　哲学的危机

第一哲学在古典哲学中体现为"形而上学"，哲学的根本性的危机发生在古典形而上学的终结。通常我们以黑格尔哲学作为古典形而上学的终结，然而实际上危机早就蕴涵在近代哲学的开端，若按照海德格尔，甚至可以追溯到哲学的开端。

17 世纪的科学革命将科学乃至哲学分成了两个阶段。此前的哲学或科学是自上而下地解释宇宙之合理性的理论体系，此后科学与哲学分道扬镳，最终形成了我们今天这个科学技术的时代，而哲学为了适应这一变化，试图重建形而上学以便重新为科学奠基。然而事与愿违，一方面以笛卡尔为代表的近代哲学发展到康德，形成了"知性为自然立法"的先验哲学，世界自身（物自体）失去了意义。另一方面随着实证科学的发展，科学家们最终放弃了形而上学所构建的超感性的本质世界，认现实的物理世界为唯一的世界。前者失去了客观世界，后者摒弃了主观世界（精神世界），两者的“合力”造成了古典形而上学的终结。在此之后，虽然有数理逻辑和现象学方法使哲学“满血复活”，但是并没有找到（或者没有想去找）形而上学的替代之物，以至于我们这个时代是一个没有“第一哲学”的时代。这就使得我们今天面临着一个撕裂的知识世界：科学技术的世界看起来秩序井然，向着未来高歌猛进，而人文的世界则是莫衷一是，心心所念的是过去的传统，正所谓肉身“向前”而灵魂“滞后”。这其中一个重要原因是，科学技术作为工具理性无法产生新的价值观念，而人文领域的传统观念却落后于时代，难以适应现代社会。这种“古今之争”乃至“古今断裂”既揭示了哲学的危机，也昭示了哲学尤其是第一哲学的必要性。

按照社会学家艾森斯塔特的理论，现代性文明（他不认为有一种统一的现代性文明，而是主张多元现代性）区别于传统文明的地方在于，它是一个向未来无限开放的文明，发展、进步和创新构成了它永不衰竭的生命力，而传统文明则难逃生老病死的结局。不恰当的类比：传统文明的灵魂不朽（天不变道亦不变），只是在不断地更换“身体”（例如中国的朝代更替），而现代文明已经可以做到“肉身不死”，但是灵魂却“过时”了。这意味着人文学科固执于历史，自然科学和技术则开辟着未来，所以历史与未来是“分裂”的。人们或者固执于传统而批评现代，或者固执于现代而批评传统，而哲学则因为成为一个技术性的学科而繁荣，但却在精致分工创新发展中迷失了哲学的根本问题。

在某种意义上说，哲学的危机根源于在哲学中形成的科学思维方式。

## 二　形而上学

历史上的第一哲学即“形而上学”。苏格拉底—柏拉图和亚里士多德奠定了西方哲学的基础，也决定了西方文明看待世界的基本方式，这种思维方式和印欧语系有关，是围绕“是什么”的问题而展开的。仅就亚里士多德而论，各门科学“分门别类”地研究存在物，试图认识的是存在物

“是什么”的“什么”，而哲学——第一哲学——形而上学，探索的则是使所有存在物“是什么”的那个“是”本身，即使一切存在物存在的前提条件。就此而论，我们面前的世界是一个意义的世界，如果说哲学与科学有什么分工，那么可以说，科学“分门别类”地在世界中“发现”事物的不同意义（不同的事物“是什么”的“什么”），哲学则要给意义世界的意义奠基，其对象是所有存在物之整体的存在。具体说来，按照亚里士多德的传统，就是以存在的范畴体系给所有存在物“是什么”的那个“是”（存在）“分类”，因为存在有多种意义，存在的意义构成了所有不同类的事物的共同的也是最普遍的意义。所以，王路教授强调 Being 不应该翻译为“存在”，而应该翻译为“是”，形而上学即是逻辑，是有一定道理的。

然而，虽然亚里士多德区别了哲学与科学的工作，强调“存在”不是种，“存在”是不可定义的，因而存在的普遍性不同于种属意义上的普遍性，而是类比的普遍性，但是当他以一套范畴体系来规定存在的意义的时候，它们仍然类似描述存在物“是什么”的“什么”的确定性的概念，按照海德格尔，这相当于把存在当作了可以用概念来规定和把握的“对象”，由此而忽略了存在与存在物的存在论差异，导致了“存在的遗忘”。所以，哲学在此实施的正是由哲学而产生，后来在自然科学中卓有成效的科学思维方式。

哲学的“初心”是提供一套解释宇宙之合理性的理论体系，为纷繁杂乱变动不居的现实世界奠基，这应该就是“第一哲学”。如前所述，科学为自然万物分门别类，哲学——第一哲学则是给存在物的存在“分类”。所以，科学描述或者揭示世界的意义，哲学——第一哲学则是解释世界的意义的意义——意义世界的基础和根据。问题是，随着以黑格尔哲学为标志的古典形而上学的终结，对于已经与哲学分道扬镳的科学来说，存在着的只是由科学发现和描述的意义世界，尼采则强调看上去是存在的意义的东西，实际上不过是对存在物的抽象，因而存在的意义原本就是存在物的意义，所以存在没有意义，故而形而上学是本真的虚无主义。而对于另一些哲学家来说，以前哲学的工作实际上归根结底应该是科学的工作，哲学并不因为它的工作现在都转交给了科学而退休离场，它要探究的是意义世界的意义的源泉，这个意义的源泉不是范畴可以规定和描述的。按照前期的海德格尔，“是什么”的范畴体系属于描述存在物的科学，而存在的意义必须通过人这种存在者即此在（Dasein）来呈现，而此在的存在不是由“是什么”的“什么”来规定的，而是通过“去存在”（to be）的生存活动而显现的，所以 Being 在此不再是“是”，而是“去是”，存在于此在的生存（Existenz）中“现身”。因此，不是主体的理论活动，而是此在的生存活动，才是意义生成的源始境域。所以，王路教授的“一是到底”论是有条件的，那对于已成过去的形而上学是成立的，但对于形而上学之后的“第一哲学”则未必如是。

我们不一定认同海德格尔的理论，但是他的思想对于重建第一哲学具有深刻的启发意义。

哲学家们原本认为世界的意义存在于世界自身之中，哲学以及科学试图在世界中发现客观存在的意义。从 17 世纪近代哲学开始，尤其是在康德的“哥白尼式的革命”中，世界本身是不可知的，我们面前的世界的意义源自先验主体，这显然是主客二元论的必然结果。胡塞尔试图克服二元论，以意识的意向性结构作为世界显现的条件，而海德格尔则更深入一步，是此在的生存活动形成了世界（Umwelt）。如果仅仅到此为止，海德格尔不过是把认识论的主体中心论转换成了生存论的主体中心论而已，而实际上他并没有停留于此，或者说他从一开始便志不在此，他要进一步通过此在的存在追问存在的意义，把存在问题从形而上学中拯救出来。按照裕生的“有—无”、“显—隐”之喻，海德格尔是要“知其白，守其黑”，对他来说，那个作为无的存在，始终隐而不显的存在，才是第一哲学的“对象”。

仅就《存在与时间》而论，此在乃居于存在与存在物“之间”，如果说存在物是“有”，那么存在就是“无”，所以此在居于“有—无”之间。进一步“发挥”，也可以说此在居于“历史与未来”之间。此在的存在结构是“时间性”，而时间性在海德格尔那里是以“将来”（Zukunft）为核心的，按照海德格尔之理想的此在，它之“去存在”乃是将所有的可能性“收回”到自身，此在由此而是一个自由的“能在”，亦即纯然的可能性。

海德格尔哲学深刻的启发还在于，他揭示了此在之能在、自由乃至存在之“无”令人恐怖的地方，任何试图重构第一哲学的人不可不察。

## 三　第一哲学

海德格尔之后，有很多哲学家讨论第一哲学，例如把伦理学作为第一哲学，把政治哲学作为第一哲学，等等。然而，迄今为止，伦理学和政治哲学等等都没有能够取代此前形而上学的地位。那么，我们以什么作为第一哲学？

我仍然相信哲学的“初心”，即为现实世界提供合理性的基础和根据。只不过这个“初心”不再能够按照自然科学的方式实现了。正如霍金所说，哲学已死；海德格尔也说哲学终结于科学技术，换言之，描述世界的意义这项工作已经转交给科学技术了，或者说，科学技术完美地实现了哲学描述世界的理想，但是这并不意味着世界的意义不再是问题。我们是不是心甘情愿地接受科学技术对世界的意义的描述和解释？关于流俗的三个问题：“我是谁”，“我从哪里来”，“我到哪里去”，或许科学已经有了答案：“我”不过是大脑数以亿计的神经元相互关联相互作用的结果。人类“走出非洲”，“我”从非洲而来。“我”死之后归于虚无，从来没有所谓“死后生命”那样的事……但我相信没有人心甘情愿地接受这样的答案。然而，当哲学同样出于科学思维方式而对世界之意义的解释完全被自然科学所覆盖乃至代替，不同于哲学的文明理念赋予世界的意义经过“祛魅”而变成了历史，失去了现实意义，而人文主义试图对世界的意义做不同于自然科学的人文解释显然与我们这个科学技术的时代格格不入，自然科学（和技术）作为描述物理世界之意义的一种方式终于变成了唯一的方式，其结果就是：科学成了第一哲学，而作为哲学的第一哲学缺席。

第一哲学之缺席不仅仅是因为科学技术的强势，更因为其自身的困境。

正如裕生所说，亚里士多德的第一哲学追问存在者之为存在者（的存在），而存在者的存在却不能像存在者那样通过“是什么”得到答案，这意味着存在不是“什么”，换一个东方思想表达，存在竟然可以是“无”，那绝对者不在别处，而在“有—无之间”，“显—隐之际”。[①] 沿着海德格尔的思路，首先需要追问的就是，为什么形而上学遗忘了存在？他的回答是：“科学不愿与闻无”（教授就职演讲《形而上学是什么》）。一是形而上学对于“无”是无能为力的，二是形而上学对于“无”实乃避之不及。按照《存在与时间》，此在之所以作为常人而沉沦于世，是因为它在逃避自己的能在，其存在乃是在“畏”所启示的“无”中“现身”的，此在与自己的存在最为亲熟，但却是它千方百计要掩盖、遮蔽的东西，形而上对存在的遗忘在此有其根源。思想“转向”之后，海德格尔更是强调，存在作为存在者的源始基础（Urgrund），乃为“无”基础（Ungrund），所以是“深渊”（Abgrund）。在形而上学那里，存在是思想的对象，并且是明亮的、高大上的以至于包含着“至善”意味的神圣的东西，而东方思想中的“无”貌似也没有什么可怕之处，体现的是某种带有神秘色彩的体悟和直观，只是难以企及罢了，即便是中国佛教的“空”也往往被视为“真空妙有”。而现在海德格尔所说的存在之为“无”却恰恰揭示了存在的另一面，就此而论，面对存在的感受是：茫茫然失其所在（unheimlich），那是阴森惊人的（ungeheuer）深渊（Abgrund）。因此，我们不仅要看到形而上学作为第一哲学所体现的存在的神圣性，也要看到海德格尔称之为“另一开端”作为第一哲学所体会到的“惊恐”。即便从信仰的角度看，我们也面临着克尔凯戈尔所说的成为基督徒所面临的恐惧与战栗。

就此而论，人类文明重新面临着虚无主义的威胁。

## 四 虚无主义

我之所以说人类文明“重新”面临虚无主义的威胁，是因为所谓轴心时代各大文明理念均可看作面对虚无构建起来的“堤坝”。按照雅斯贝尔斯，轴心时代标志着人类文明的“觉醒”。当人类从自然母体中分娩而出，

① 黄裕生（2019）。

切断了联结大地母亲的“脐带”，只能依靠自己而生存于世，或者说，要求它自己去寻求安身立命的基础和根据，这使它意识到整体，意识到自身乃至自身的限度，面对空无，他力求解放和拯救。由此，各大文明的古代先贤们构建起了抵御虚无的哲学理念或者宗教信条，这相当于构建起一个个意义世界以作为我们的家园，我们可以把这些哲学理念或者宗教信条称为各大文明的“第一哲学”。不过，套用文化人类学的概念，它们最初都是“地方性知识”，希腊哲学也不例外。然而，随着 17 世纪科学革命，18 世纪启蒙运动和工业革命，西方在少数国家带领下走上了现代化道路，从而由传统社会转型为现代社会，由此而产生了两个相关的后果。其一是从哲学之科学思维方式产生的自然科学理论与技术相结合，逐渐成为遍及世界的带有普遍性的现象，而哲学学科则因为与自然科学的“血缘关系”而成为任何一所研究型大学的“标准配置”，渗透到了各种文化之中。其二是伴随着社会的转型，原本适应传统社会的传统观念对于现代社会失去了原本决定性的影响力，我称之为轴心时代的没落，在基督教表现为尼采的那句话：“上帝死了”，在中华文明表现为“三千年未有之大变局”，而在哲学上则表现为古典形而上学的终结。我们遭遇的挑战是，再也不能像过去那样信仰上帝了，再也不能像过去那样相信天道不爽了，再也不能像过去那样相信宇宙是一个合乎理性的存在了……由此而产生了第三个后果：我们重新面对虚无主义的威胁。

在我们这个时代，虚无主义无处不在。在一个虚无主义的时代，如何重建第一哲学？虽然我把轴心时代各大文明的理念都称之为不同文明的第一哲学，但是真正意义上的第一哲学还是属于哲学，于是我们面临的问题就是——我们如何在哲学中重建第一哲学？

如前所述，哲学与其他轴心时代的文明理念一样最初都是“地方性知识”，但是哲学与众不同之处在于，它的问题意识、批判精神和理论思维具有自我否定的“自反性”，使得哲学始终在探索之中，从来没有建立起某种终极的理论、信条或者教条，而其他文明理念虽然都具有普遍化的倾向，但都因为自身的信条或者教条而相互隔绝或者相互抵触，未能超越“地方性知识”。了解这一点对于我们这个全球化的时代来说具有非常重要的意义。

## 五　历史与未来

如前所述，我们的世界被撕裂为二：现代性文明指向未来，传统观念则心念过去，现代性文明自身难以形成适应于现代社会的价值理性，而传统观念则自说自话，难以适应现代社会的发展和进步。如何使得两者相互适应？在某种意义上说，人类各大文明都面临着“内外交困”的难题：一方面每一个文明自身都面临着“古今之争”；另一方面在这个全球化的时代，文明与文明之间面临着碰撞与融合的问题。全球化的时代，我们的地球变成了“地球村”，形成了“人类命运共同体”，但是我们的思维方式仍然停留在由“丛林法则”主导的动物性思维。这就是当今时代面临的困境。

威廉斯在《伦理学与哲学的限度》这本书的序言里说了一句话很有意思，他说：“我的结论是，现代世界对伦理思想的需求是没有前例的，而大一半当代道德哲学所体现的那些理性观念无法满足这些需求；然而，古代思想的某些方面，若加以适当的改造，却有可能满足这些需求。”① 我个人的看法，最好不要把现代世界对伦理思想的需要仅仅局限在伦理学的领域，虽然形而上学衰落了，但是当伦理学从神圣回归世俗之时，植根于不同文明的伦理思想显然不能复归“原型”，退回到“地方性知识”，而是需要相互之间的协调与融合，因而面临着如何为之重建基础的难题。换言之，形而上学虽然过时了，但是伦理学仍然需要第一哲学的奠基。

各大文明的文明理念原本都是某种“地方性的知识”，我们弘扬传统文化，力图使之返本开新，但是如何让它成为全球性的普遍共识，需要跨越文化之间的屏障，更需要经受哲学——第一哲学——的“洗礼”。在轴心时代没落，全球化成为事实的背景之下，我们需要构建“第二轴心时代”或者“新的轴心时代”的文明理念，然而，我们不可能以某一种文化

① 威廉斯（2018：1）。

或者某一种宗教作为全球化时代的主导思想，哲学很可能是不二之选。当然，或许不是作为理论学说的哲学，而是“以哲学作为方法”，权且称之为作为方法的第一哲学。

回到我们的主题——“在历史与未来之间”。如前所述，现代文明的“肉身”与“灵魂”并不“匹配”。如果要让我们重塑现代文明的灵魂，我们以什么为“原料”？“肉身”（工具理性）不能充当“灵魂”（价值理性），在此除了传统，我们一无所有。这意味着我们必须重新激发本原文化的潜力，发挥历史的可能性，让历史走向未来。

海德格尔在《存在与时间》中将现象学方法“改造”为现象学的诠释学，值得我们思考。就传统观念而论，上帝通过耶稣“道成肉身”，绝对通过人类精神而成为精神（黑格尔），存在通过此在之“去存在”而显现（海德格尔），天道不爽，需由人而弘道（中国哲学）……在古典时代或古典哲学中，那个至高无上的理想对象总有对象性的缺陷，海德格尔则试图将存在由思想的对象转变成为人之此在对自身存在的“言说”——通过让此在道说出自身而呈现存在的存在。尽管这条“此在之路”失败了，但是它的启示是：神圣的东西并不在我们之外，就如同托尔斯泰所言——“上帝在我们心中”。这至少让我们意识到，对象性的思维方式不适合第一哲学。

如果我们从海德格尔的现象学诠释学进一步去看伽达默尔的哲学诠释学，或许可以考虑通过“视域融合”来沟通历史与现在乃至历史与未来。如果说“意义”生成于历史性的视域融合之中，那么视域融合在两个方面可以有所作为：一方面在一种文化内部，我们可以与自身的历史进行视域融合，返本开新，激发传统的潜在可能性；另一方面在不同文化之间做“视域融合”，使它们在相互碰撞中相互融合，以形成人类命运共同体的普适性的价值观念。就此而论，哲学具有方法论的意义，我们甚至可以说，哲学因为其问题意识、批判精神和理论思维，可以构成新的轴心时代的全球性价值理念的基础。或者说，在哲学的基础上，融合不同的文化。这里所说的哲学不是西方哲学也不是东方哲学，而是作为哲学的哲学——第一哲学。

## 六 哲学何为

轴心时代各大文明的理念至少具有三重意义：首先，它是人类文明面对空无抵御虚无的“堤坝”，它呈现的是一个意义世界。其次，它是维系一个文明之整体的精神纽带；第三，它构成了个人安身立命的基础和根据。人类文明的诞生，起源于打破血缘氏族的界限，继而打破民族之间的界限，以某种文化精神（本原文化）而形成的文明共同体。而全球化发展至今天，人类文明的未来则寄托于如何打破不同文明之间的界限，以新的轴心时代理念，形成人类命运共同体的价值观念。这里所说的“新的轴心时代理念”需要跨越不同文明理念的屏障，超越迄今为止国与国之间，文明与文明之间的“丛林法则”。显然，造成当今时代之难题有很多原因，其中之一便是文明理念之间的碰撞与冲突，就此而论，我们不可能让任何一种文明理念或者宗教成为全球化时代统一的理念，那不会形成和谐，只会造成冲突。如果说我们还有希望，那么可以说希望在哲学。

哲学自希腊而诞生，原本也是一种“地方性知识”，但是它的科学思维方式催生了自然科学，由于与自然科学的“血缘关系”而跨越了文明之间的屏障，加之所有的文明原本亦具有哲学的思维方式特性，所以具有了普遍性的影响。哲学之所以超越了文明的屏障，恰恰是因为我们对哲学的批评：“众说纷纭，莫衷一是”，哲学没有形成统一的理论学说或者绝对真理看上去是它的缺陷，但现在变成了它的“优势”。我们可以考虑如何以哲学为方法，激发不同文明理念的潜能，融合而形成“地球村”的文明理念。这并不意味着我们必须形成统一的理论和教条，因为那将意味着专制，既不可能也不应该。第一哲学的理想性意味着哲学的自由和开放，理想可以不同，但一定得是理想。而理想的“理想状态”便是“万物并育而不相害，道并行而不相悖”（《中庸》）。

第一哲学的最高理想是开放的，而其最低原则需要有确定性，这就是形成一套国家与国家、民族与民族、文化与文化……之间和平共处相互共存的“底线”。显然这是我们这个时代的当务之急，不过要从根本上解决问题，还需要第一哲学的理想。如前所述，我们这个时代“灵魂”与“肉身”不相配，就像人的生物学意义上的基因仍然停留在几万年前，远远跟不上现代社会的发展，虽然文化的“进化”突破了自然进化的限制，使得人类社会进展神速，但是在近几百年来却跟不上科学技术的进步。“原始状态”的身体要适应现代的生活方式，形成于轴心时代的文明理念则要适应日新月异的科技时代。如果要从根本上解决问题，恐怕需要“以哲学为方法”，重塑灵魂，不仅要让“灵魂”跟上“身体”的“进步”，更应该让“灵魂”引领“身体”的未来。

哲学凭什么能够当此重任？因为哲学的问题意识、批判精神和理论思维，使得哲学可以在康德的意义上重建一个纯粹理性的“法庭”，实际上也可以看作是任何一种文明理念的自我反思，由自我反思而返本开新，在第一哲学的基础上融合而形成“万物并育而不相害，道并行而不相悖”的新的轴心时代理念。

这就是我所理解的“第一哲学”，当然这样的“第一哲学”还不存在。

裕生的大作对我很有启发，以上就是我关于第一哲学的思考，这些个人意见极不成熟，无法给出建设性的意见，更多的是提出问题，敬请方家批评指正。

修改于 2021 年 7 月 25 日

**参考文献**

黄裕生，2019，《摆渡在有无之间的哲学——第一哲学问题研究》，清华大学出版社。

威廉斯，2018，《伦理学与哲学的限度》，陈嘉映译，商务印书馆。

# 同一性、差异性与生存
## ——有关“第一哲学”基础原理的争论*

尚文华（SHANG Wenhua）**

**摘要：**哲学家之间最深层也是最深刻的差异乃是基础原理上的差异，而其最深刻也最有意义的对话亦是基础原理层面的对话。本文把黄裕生教授的“第一哲学”原理视为康德哲学基础原理的汉语表达：以同一性作为思想之经验的起点；并在分析的基础上引导出差异性对于思之经验的重要性。黑格尔、马克思和克尔凯郭尔分别以不同的方式将差异性作为思想之经验的起点，而给出各自不同的哲学原理。其中，是否存在以及已经如何言说一种绝对的差异经验是检验思想家之间，以及思想与存在之深度关系的关键点。在此基础上，本文提出返回的道路与前行的道路的深度纠缠，这把哲学性的原理之争引入生存和思想如何相契的实际方向上。

**关键词：**哲学原理；同一性；差异性；绝对差异性；生存

---

* 本文系山东省泰山学者专项资助计划“生存与思想的张力：现代性与儒学传统的交汇及其可能”的阶段性成果。

** 尚文华，哲学博士，山东社会科学院哲学研究所研究员，研究方向为西方哲学、基督教神学、中西哲学比较。

# Identity, Difference and Existence —Controversy over the Basic Principles of "First Philosophy"

**Abstract**: The deepest and most profound difference between philosophers is the difference in fundamental principles, and the deepest and most meaningful dialogue is also the dialogue on fundamental principles. This article regards Professor Huang Yusheng's "First Philosophy" Principle as the Chinese expression of the basic principles of Kant's philosophy: taking Identity as the starting point of the experience of thought; and on the basis of analysis, it leads to the importance of Difference for the experience of thinking. Hegel, Marx, and Kierkegaard each took Difference as the starting point of the experience of thought in different ways, and gave their different philosophical principles. Among them, whether there is and how to say an Absolute Difference experience is the key point to test the deep relationship between thinkers and between Thought and Existence. Finally, this article proposes the deep entanglement between the path of Return and the path of Forward, which introduces the dispute of philosophical principles into the actual direction of how Existence and Thought fit together.

**Keywords**: Philosophical Principles; Identity; Difference; Absolute Difference; Existence

在为黄裕生教授2019年出版的著作《摆渡在有—无之间的哲学——第一哲学问题研究》所作的评论《从"自身同一物"与"自在物"谈起——评黄裕生教授〈摆渡在有—无之间的哲学——第一哲学问题研究〉》[①] 中，笔者从对"自身同一物"和"自在物"的相关"界定"及其

① 分别参阅黄裕生（2019）；尚文华（2020b）。

逻辑区分角度阐释了黄裕生教授的“第一哲学”的相关原理。在《思想本身与时代问题：“古 - 今—中 - 西”交口处的中国哲学——以黄裕生教授的相关思考为契机》① 中，笔者进一步在此原理性的界定和区分基础上阐释了黄教授在具体思想内容方面的研究及其之于中国思想界的推进作用。无论在对其“第一哲学”相关原理的阐释部分，还是对其具体内容的相关阐释部分，笔者都曾提纲挈领地指出我们之间的“相同”和“差异”。

在这篇文章中，笔者想就“同一”与“差异”问题——大致上对应于该著作标题所显示的“有—无之间”——具体地展开，努力展示黄教授与我在“第一哲学”原理层面上所作相关思考的“差异性”。首先，笔者会沿着“自身同一物”与“自在物”的区分在原理层面切入“同一”与“差异”问题；并在这个问题的指引下，切入黑格尔、马克思和克尔凯郭尔的一些分析，这些分析不得不把“生存”问题引导出来。正是在生存问题上，笔者与黄教授在原理层面的“差异”会被打开，打开的这个空间正是思想的对话空间。

## 一　“差异”问题的提出

一切有意义的思（想）都建立在思（想）的基本经验中，但思的经验又往往被已建立起来的“现实的”经验所遮蔽。故而，能否回到原始的思的经验就是检验思之深度的标尺，亦是检验哲学之“第一原理”的关键所在。在黄裕生教授成熟时期的思考中，“自在物”和“自身同一物”的区分刻画了思的经验与现实的经验的错综复杂的关系。简言之，思之最原始的经验乃是对“自在物”或存在的“思”，其逻辑表达式为“A 在”或“A 是”；思之现实的经验以“自身同一物”的建立为前提，其逻辑表达式为“A 是 A”和“A 是 P”，后者以前者为基础，即：“A 是 P”乃是“A 是 A”在具体时空经验中的展开。

康德知识学或逻辑学的核心目的在于给出自身同一物，亦即第一经验

① 参阅尚文华（2021）。

物（相关于现实经验或知识而言），由于是第一经验物，其与现实的经验或知识的差异就在于其本性乃是先验的，但又是经验由以可能的条件。如是的“界定”方式证明康德不承认我们拥有关于“自在物”，或关于“A在”“A是”的基本经验，这也便是康德得出“物自体不可知”这一论断的原因。既然“物自体”或“自在物”不可知，我们又怎么“知道”它“存在”呢？——康德的解决方案是论证，其要点是，我们的经验不是生产性，而是接受性的；既然是接受性的，它必然是有来源的；这个来源便是“物自体”。由此，我们只能说：“自在物存在，但不可知”；对于其如何，那就只能是信仰和实践空间的事情。

在笔者看来，黄教授完全接受了康德这一基本的原理性区分。如果把由“自身同一物”所引领的经验世界或知识世界称为“有”（的世界），那么“自在物”的“世界”则是“无”（的世界）；但无论如何，如果没有“无”（的世界），“有”（的世界）便是没有来源，没有根基的，或者说，正是“无”让“有”成了一个整体，一个整体世界。思想的任务乃是摆渡在“有”—“无”之间：“有”为“无”提供了一个经验的世界，“无”为“有”提供了来源和根据。或言之，“有”的世界乃是一个概念的世界，知识的世界，因而是以“同一性”为基础建立起来的世界；相关于这个同一性的世界，“无”（的世界）乃永远对其彰显为一个“非同一性”（的世界），或者说同一性的世界永远无法穷尽这个“无”“非同一性”（的世界），即：相对于同一性，无永远展示为一种差异。

一旦接受了康德的原理性区分，差异永远保持为差异，我们“知道”它存在，却永远无法认识它，无法将其占据为一种思的经验。尽管相关于实践领域，康德将“无”或“差异”论述为一个自由的世界，但这个自由的世界与现实的经验世界乃是截然二分的，在“批判哲学”体系中，康德也明确地提出了两个世界的问题。由于这种区分乃是原理性的，两个世界的区分便是无法弥合的。希腊以来的哲学传统中的“思”乃是“思—在一体”的思，康德对思的经验则根本性地背离了这个传统；尽管在“第三批判”中，康德意图通过对“审美”和“目的论”的反思重新弥合其根据思的经验而来的两个世界（存在与思想）的分裂，但其最终的落脚点只是

“主观性”或“反思的主观性”。其最终也是真实的依据乃是“有”与“无”、“同一”与“差异”、“存在”与“思想”，亦是“理论”（知识）与“实践”（道德和信仰）之间无法弥合的分裂。

也正是因着这种由原理性的区分而来的两元分裂，信仰和上帝只能根据实践的道德得以“确证”、道德也只能通过对现实世界的“否定”而“确证”自身、自由意志也只能是对出于现实世界的“任性”和“必然性”的“说不”而意志自身。换言之，“第一批判”所进行的知识学和逻辑学努力于人的实践而言，只能是“批判性”或“否定性”的；“第二批判”所致力的努力于知识和现实世界而言，根本性地不从属于思的经验，亦是思的经验永远无法触及的边界。①

这一切的根源在于两点：同一与差异之间的区分是绝对的；思之经验的起点在于同一性，而非差异性。这看起来非常吊诡：致力于对自由及自由意志作辩护的康德体系，其思的基点恰恰是同一性，以及建基于同一性的经验；由之而来乃是，自由和自由意志成为“虚无”和“空洞”。康德哲学的困境正是现代性和现代生活的基本困境。② 难道不能给出别样的原理吗？换言之，“第一哲学”的原理体系非如此不可吗？

## 二 差异可否成为思之经验的起点？——一种思想的尝试

思之经验的起点在于同一性，意味着思的对象只是由意识建立起来的对象，因而是由意识建立起来的对象的同一性存在，换言之，对象的同一性存在只是相关于意识的，而非其自身的（自在的）存在。因此，相对于对象的同一性存在方式，对象自身的存在永远保持在一种“不同于”或“差异性”。但实情如何呢？——正是在这个最原始、最关键的地方，黑格尔“领会”到一种有关于“差异的经验”：

① 费希特致力于在康德同一性原理的基础上重建形而上学的知识体系，其核心任务就是把实践上的“不”（其实就是差异度）纳入知识学中。但这种努力是不成功的，其关键就在于同一性原理无法含纳真正的“他者”或“差异性”维度。

② 笔者有文专门揭示这一点。参阅尚文华（2020a）。

> 意识之一般地具有关于一个对象的知识这一事实，恰恰就已经表明是有区别的：一个环节是某种自在于意识之外的东西，而另一个环节是知识……根据这个现成存在着的区别，就能进行比较考查。如果在这个比较中双方不相符合，那么意识就必须改变它的知识，以便使之符合于对象；但在知识的改变过程中，对象自身事实上也与之相应地发生变化；因为从本质上说现成存在着的知识本来是一种关于对象的知识：跟着知识的改变，对象也变成了另一个对象……意识因而就发现，它从前以为是自在之物的那种东西实际上并不是自在的……意识对它自身——既对它的知识又对它的对象——所实行的这种辩证的运动，就其替意识产生出新的真实对象这一点而言，恰恰就是人们称之为经验的那种东西。①

意识能够建立起对象的同一性存在，即意识拥有关于对象的知识，这是一种事实。但是，这一事实本身证明，对象的存在与意识对对象存在的同一性建构之间是有区别的；同时也正是这个区别引导着意识在对象的存在与对其的同一性建构（知识）之间作比较；也正是因着这种比较，知识能够更新改变，与之相关的对象的存在亦发生改变：因为知识是关于对象的知识，因着知识的改变，对象也就变成另一种相关性的存在。因此，如果把意识的关注点放在其同一性建构方面，则对象的存在似乎就是自在的，与知识无关的；但如果把意识的关注点放在现成地存在着的区别方面（即差异），则意识乃是相关于对象自身即其存在的。不同于“抽象”设定的自在物或与认识无关的存在，对象的存在在意识的认识过程中乃是不断地产生着的“新的”，也是“真实的”对象。换言之，尽管意识无法断定“存在即是如此”，但是，它能够产生新的真实对象则意味着，对象的存在是相关于意识的，即：意识或思的经验本身关乎对象的存在。

就此而言，尽管无法说意识拥有一种关于差异性（相关于同一性）的

---

① 黑格尔（1997：59－60）。

直接经验，但意识的经验关乎对象的存在至少能够证明，在形式上，存在乃是以同一和差异相统一的方式展示在意识中。或者说，思之经验的起点绝非同一性建构，相反地，它乃是关乎存在的，存在是在经验的辩证运动过程中的同一和差异的统一。也正是因着这种基本见识，这种本源性的经验领会，黑格尔能够给出一种不同于康德式的知识学和逻辑学，其对自由（意志）和历史的理解也本质性地不同于康德。从而，与康德的“批判哲学”体系相对，在《精神现象学》中，黑格尔依据对思之经验的这种原初性的领会，重新界定了感觉、知觉、理性、精神，等相关题材，它们都是存在展示自身的诸般方式。可以说，康德与黑格尔之间关于“第一哲学”的原理之争乃是自希腊以来对思（想）与存在之关系的现代展示：前者的思只是同一性之思，主体之思；后者的思则是“思—在”一体意义上的思，即广为人知的主体即是客体命题。

在黑格尔的基础上，马克思等思想家才可能实现“辩证法的颠倒”。尽管黑格尔看到意识（思）之经验乃是存在之同一和差异的辩证运动关系，但在黑格尔的体系中，这种运动关系以建造（绝对）知识为使命。在知识使命的完成之处——这种完成也只是形式性的，辩证运动的过程性决定了意识无法在内容上完成之——，存在之差异也便消解在绝对知识的体系之中。换言之，尽管黑格尔看到了差异可能正是思之经验的起点，但“求知识”的使命让他无法接受差异就是思之经验的起点。正是在这个问题上，马克思跨出了大胆而冒险的一步；这一步很关键，但却也可能问题无穷：

> 辩证法在黑格尔手中神秘化了，但这决没有妨碍他第一个全面地有意识地叙述了辩证法的一般运动形式。在他那里，辩证法是倒立着的。为了发现神秘外壳中的合理内核，必须把它倒过来。……（引者加）辩证法，在其合理形态上，引起资产阶级及其夸夸其谈的代理人的恼怒和恐惧，因为辩证法在对现存事物的肯定的理解中同时包含对现存事物的否定的理解，即对现存事物的必然灭亡的理解；辩证法对每一种既成的形式都是从不断的运动中，因而也是从

它的暂时性方面去理解；辩证法不崇拜任何东西，按其本质来说，它是批判的和革命的。①

马克思所谓黑格尔辩证法的倒立正在于他“设想”（形式上的）了知识的终极，因而在终点之处同一性取代了差异性。但在现实中，其对存在的肯定（同一性）必然包含对存在的否定（差异性），这种否定意味着一切现实必然会取消自己，即：差异和否定才是现实运动（包括一切知识）的动力和基础，是一切能够往前走的真实起点。② 如果纯从思想上看，不得不说，马克思的这种基本见识乃是一种真知灼见，其对后续思想史以及现实历史确也有着重大的影响。其根据正在于差异乃是现实历史和思想的真实起点，这个起点一旦被保持住，我们也便如同马克思那样获得了批判现实和历史，甚至知识和思想批判的根据——当然，这个根据究竟是出于纯粹否定性的“虚无”，还是出于自身运行着的“存在”（何种意义上的存在呢？——它在现代社会中检验“思—在”的一体性），才是真正检验思之经验的。

在这里，笔者不想，可能也无法评判黑格尔和马克思对差异何以能够作为思之经验的起点，也是相对于笔者所理解的黄裕生教授和康德之“第一哲学”原理的变更究竟意味着什么。但是，可以说的是，相关于思之经验的原初性和本源性，这种变更能够得到见证：在黑格尔这里，对象的存在与知识之间的差异是现成的，因而正是差异推动了知识的建构和存在的显现；在马克思这里，现存事物的肯定性和否定性是共存的，一切现实都将取消自己，因而差异才是事物进入存在而有存在的根据。于是，无论是在思想层面，还是现实层面，差异才是真正的动力和起点。但无论如何，差异都是存在所“彰显”的，都是对存在之同一性的差异；都是对现实的否定，都是对现实之进入存在的力量。换言之，与以同一性作为思之经验的“设定”相比，差异作为思之经验的起点都离不开同一（知识和现存事

① 马克思（1995：112）。

② 对相关问题的进一步处理，及其所可能带来的思想进展和现实困境，笔者有文作分析。请参阅尚文华（2019）。

物），即：差异乃是存在中的差异。不深刻知晓这一点，就会进入把一切（包括存在）全然虚无化的境地——这可能不仅是思想的灾难，也是历史和现实的灾难。

如是理解和领会的差异与同一之间的区别似乎就不再是绝对的，换言之，它不仅不接受康德式把同一视为思之经验之起点的命题，也把康德设定的同一与差异之间的绝对区分命题颠覆掉。也正是因此，黑格尔意义（可能也是传统意义上）的形而上学是可能的；非激进意义的马克思式的实践哲学是可能的。这是一种不同于黄裕生教授所接受的康德式“第一哲学”的基本原理。尽管不同，这些原理涉及的只是同一和差异的起点之争，但都以存在的同一性和差异性展示为基础，换言之，存在的展示及其不同层面的可认识性是其共同持守的原则。是否存在一种绝对的差异呢？或者说，存在本身是否就是可认识的呢？——这是更有深度的原理之争。

## 三 绝对差异与生存

无论是把思之经验领会为同一性，还是将其领会为差异性，对思之对象的存在的认识（知识化）都是主导性的——表面上看康德和马克思是例外，但意图分析审美和目的论、意图“制造”另一种合乎理想的存在，都证明他们并未严格地摆脱以往的形而上学传统。也正是因为把存在“论断”为可认识的，这个传统乃是一种理性的传统。——需要说明的是，这里的理性绝非简单的“根据什么作判断”，相反地，因为其关乎存在本身，超出于“根据什么”的存在的显现才是理性的真正依据。换言之，理性的根据只在自身，及其与存在的共同发生，即：其根据恰恰是无根据，因而其对象和内容乃是整体性的。前面对“无”和“差异”的分析已经表明这一点。

但无论如何，理性做出“存在是可认识的”这一命题的前提性恰恰是需要反思的。遵循这一前提意味着存在乃是以理性的方式展示自身，因而理性（思）与存在乃是共属一体的。但是，如同黑格尔看到的，意识拥有关于对象的知识证明两者的差异是现成的，存在以理性的方式展示自身恰恰也意味着存在与理性是有差异的。理性能够做出这一命题意味着存在是其不得不面对的，正因为存在的不断发生推动着理性不断地发生，不断地建构着其关于存在的知识。逻辑上可以做出这样的论断：相对于理性，存在是在先的；正是存在的在先性保证着理性的认识（知识）可以是“符合”存在（对象）的——这正是希腊以来关于知识之真理性的一般判断。[①]

如果“大胆地”把黑格尔关于经验中“现成存在着的差异”这一见识往前推进一步，则可能更加“合理”的说法是：相对于理性（意识等）的认识建构，存在自身永远保持在绝对的差异之中；那相关于同一性建构的差异只是为了认识的目的而“设定”的——这种设定本质上从属于“存在之可认识性”命题。马克思在相当程度上看到黑格尔的这种知识化的思辨形而上学倾向，否则颠倒辩证法就是无从谈起的，但其引起的“震动”主要是社会—历史性，而非思想性的。这一方面源于其不是以哲学的方式反思，另一方面在“弃绝”了宗教之后，这种基础经验得不到深入的检视。故而，从黑格尔到马克思，差异作为思之经验的起点已经得到充分的论证，绝对差异沿着这条思想线索也可以被充分地引导出来。可以说的是，到马克思，（德国）古典哲学已经在论证和思想上走到它的尽头，此尽头恰恰也开出一个全新的起点：绝对差异问题；但由于理性一开始就设定了存在的可认识性，如何“思考”作为绝对差异的存在就无法在理性的思路走下去。

我们是否拥有关于绝对差异的经验？——真正沿着这条路线走下去的是克尔凯郭尔，也只有沿着这条路线，我们才能真正看清克尔凯郭尔在启蒙背景下重提信仰问题的思想史意义。既然理性（哲学）无法真正面对绝对差异问题，若寻其根据，就只存在于（人之）生存的其他维度；而这正

① 能进入思想，或者熟悉思想史的人都知道，这里讨论的是“存在先于本质，还是本质先于存在”问题，这两个命题既是思想本身，也是在思想史上不断被提起的最核心的命题。但严格来讲，“本质先于存在”是不可能的，如果本质不关乎存在，那就是“瞎想”；至少需要说，本质与存在共同发生，或者说根据存在而发生。这便意味着，实情上，存在是在先的，因为本质（或知识）能够合乎存在，乃是以存在的发生为前提。近代以来，尤其黑格尔之后，对这个命题的回答检视了我们对待这个所谓启蒙了的时代的态度。克尔凯郭尔通过分析对神存在的证明阐释理性的本质建构与神（学）本身的关系，笔者在此不深入讨论这一点。可参阅克尔凯郭尔（2013：44－50）。

是受到德国哲学强烈影响的克尔凯郭尔突破理性哲学，重回基督信仰，并致力于就（人之）个体化生存展开思想性分析的原因。首先，理性设定存在之可认识性，意味着其关注的是生存之主动建构的倾向，因其如此，只能在被动中的、接受中的绝对差异无法被思想；故而，如果生存有关于绝对差异的“经验”，就只能在生存的被动性的接受性的维度中出现。其次，绝对差异不是相对差异，因而其能够被接受只在生存之纯然的被动性和接受性中，而这，只能出乎一种全然的信，即：对绝对者的信，而非任何相对意义的对象的信。换言之，对绝对差异的经验只可能是对绝对者（上帝存在）的信仰；耶稣的肉身化；等等，于现实的生存而然只是一种对绝对差异的经验（信仰）——这或许是克尔凯郭尔接受的唯一的基督教信条，[①]之所以如此，在于其思想的背景乃是德国古典哲学。

由于信仰只是对作为绝对差异的绝对者的信仰，其对（人之）生存的塑造只能建立在绝对差异的经验中，换言之，由理性建构起来的同一性生存都是有待“拆解”的、绝对有限的、罪性的。也正是因为生存建立在绝对差异的经验中，所有由理性建构起来的生存才可能保持为罪性的，即：罪性不止是一种类形而上学意义的宣称，它更是生存所保持着的一种存在状态。也正是因此，生存能够恒久地与绝对者的存在建立联系，进而与被接受的一切存在（可称为上帝的造物）建立联系，这种联系不再是与被同一性建构起来存在的联系，而是出于作为起点的存在本身的联系。如果把与存在自身同在视为真理状态或自由状态，那么由绝对差异经验建立起来的生存恰恰是有真理性的：只是这种真理性以全然地接受自己生存本有的罪性为前提。

这种由绝对差异经验组建起来的生存并不拒绝理性的同一性建构，亦不拒绝出于这种同一性建构而来的知识，等等；相反地，正是这些建构，让它看到生存之本有的有限性（罪性）的限度，只要这些限度得到充分的彰显，绝对差异就越能被生存经验到——克尔凯郭尔对生存各个维度的分析都是在展示这一点：所有的限度都指向那一跃。换言之，从生存本身来

① 克尔凯郭尔几乎不谈论三位一体、复活、审判等传统基督教思想，其对道成肉身、基督再来的复活主题、生命的更新等重生主题等的处理都是思想性的。

看，它接受康德、黑格尔、马克思等思想家和科学家的诸般知识性和建构性的贡献，但这些贡献的意义在于生存中的“那一跃”，那一跃让这些知识拥有建立在绝对者中的真理性。我想，这也是谢林之强调“肯定哲学”和“否定哲学”间的区分、海德格尔无时无刻不在区分“存在与存在者之绝对差异”的原因：“否定哲学”建构着“自认为”的完满体系，存在者的体系，但这些体系如果脱离了“肯定哲学”以及存在之绝对差异的领会，就是没根基的；思想的意义在于认识到这些建构的基本限度，并向着绝对差异（者）敞开。

笔者无意在此展开更详细的论述，需要指出的是，有关绝对差异及其经验的原理——在克尔凯郭尔这里是信仰问题，在谢林、海德格尔等人那里有些暧昧不清——是黑格尔和马克思的原理体系需要面对的，可能更是康德式的以同一为思之经验起点的原理体系需要面对的。黄裕生教授可能更接受康德式的原理，在此提出这种原理之争因而可能就更加切身。在最后的部分，笔者想在已经分析过的幅度里探讨下这种原理之争于生存和思想的一点儿基本意义。

## 四　返回，还是前行？

在《哲学片段》中，克尔凯郭尔提醒我们，思想的道路只有两条：一条以苏格拉底为代表，另一条则以耶稣为代表。前一条道路被苏格拉底表达为“自知无知”，在柏拉图那里，这条道路进一步被表达为“灵魂回忆”。既然生存之日常在于现实性，即：已经被思想所建构起来，甚或成为现实生活的那部分；那么回到本源，回到存在自身（柏拉图领会为理念）就依赖于“拆解”掉现实性，但拆解掉之后剩下生命呢？——这便是与存在“曾经”相契合的灵魂中的那部分。换言之，苏格拉底的理性道路乃是一条“返回”的道路：返回到本源、返回到存在。但无论如何，既然生存事实性地“已经”“沉沦于”现实性中，它又怎能有力量返回呢？能够返回能够回忆意味着什么呢？——无怪乎一种“差异意识”已经进入生存，否则返回是无从谈起的。

康德原理体系中的对自然和对必然性（现实性）“说不”、黑格尔原理体系中的“现成地存在着的区别”，以及马克思颠倒黑格尔的辩证法以把“否定”和“差异”设立为起点等，都从属于以苏格拉底和柏拉图代表的灵魂的回忆的思路。差别只在于随着时代的进展，思想家们需要把有关回忆或差异的“意识”贯穿在现实的思想和历史道路中。但问题是，思想有其自身的“执着”和“惰性”，即使它能够，也必然需要接受差异，它总也要把差异消化在其自身的建构中；这种执着和惰性甚至本就是思想的本性：思的道路本就是逻辑性的，寻求确定性和必然性是其本性所在——哪怕在哲学上，我们认为这些确定性和必然性只是对存在自身的指引；但把指引视为思想本身也是它无时无刻不在犯的“错误”。所以，一切真正伟大的思无不同时就是伟大的冒险；所以，返回的道路既是艰难的，也是冒险的，因而也是需要时刻警醒自己的：警醒的依据在于时刻知道存在有其自身的发生，知道差异永恒性地存在在那里。

与灵魂回忆或返回本源的道路相对，耶稣提供了另一条道路，这条道路以生存中发生一种没有任何缘由的嬗变为条件。内在地或从主观方面看，生存中这种嬗变被称为信仰；外在地或客观方面，绝对者因着信仰进入生存（恩典）。因着这种进驻，生存中的一切，包括与之相应的现实状况，亦随之发生一种完全意义上的变更。换言之，这种进驻意味着一种绝对的差异者进入生存，生存亦根据这种绝对的差异经验重新审视和建立自身；因而就是在进驻的当下，生存开始拥有一个全新的起点。因此，与返回的道路相比，这是一条以当下为基础的前行的道路。无论在一般的时间结构中理性建立起什么，亦无论这种建立以同一性为依据，还是以差异性和同一性共同作为根据，它们都不是限制以当下为基础的前行的力量——最多只是一种参照，或者是以绝对差异经验为基础的需要“更新”的力量。正是在这种更新中，已建构起生存的存在整体展示为别样的存在意义，即：不再是根据什么而建构起来的存在，而是与之相差异的存在。

就此而言，耶稣所提供的前行的道路以绝对的差异者（上帝以及一般的存在）进驻到生存中为起点，从而存在的意义不断地在绝对的差异经验中发生着变更和更新——《圣经》于生存和实际生活的意义需要在这个层面进行解释。与返回的道路可能会“错失”差异或存在相比，依据绝对差异者而前行的道路不会迷失——除非它出于自身的理解构造了一套关于绝对者的神学的或理论的知识，并据之为“应该”或“教条”。但是，历史上，这样的事情时常发生，这证明把绝对的差异视为与同一并立的差异，于生存和思想而言是多么的正常。但同时，这也证明，绝对的差异经验于生存而言是何等的重要，它把生存从自以为是的生存和存在建构中解放出来，从而能够让生存看到它能够随时从当下前行。

因此，无论是返回的道路，还是前行的道路，也无论它们在原理和生存方向上表现的何等殊异，它们可能都是生存在本性中拥有的方向。“第一哲学”的原理无论如何设定，它都不得不面对具体的生存问题；信仰的原理无论如何迥异于哲学的原理，生存永远有一种建构一般性和普遍性思想的冲动。同样地，无论如何，如果只根据一种原理思想，把思之经验只限制在一个维度，那就很容易错失其他原理体系和生存方向。所以，本文所提到的这些原理之争，都需要在生存的两个基本方向（返回，还是前行）上得到彼此的检验和见证；如是，思想的任务也便开始清晰起来。

论述至此，可以说，这些原理之争本质上是希腊哲学对思想与存在之争的现代展示：思想或思之经验的依据是否是“思—在”共属一体性的？如果是，回到原始的经验就是一条返回的道路；但同时需要问的问题是，基督信仰究竟是何种意义上的经验，它可否成为思之主题？或者说，如果“思—在”一体是有效的，那么信仰所指向的存在（或上帝）的自行发生究竟意味着什么？这条以当下为根据的前行的道路于哲学而言究竟意味着什么？——毫无疑问的是，正因为两条道路都如此切身和本己，这种对思之经验的追问、对原理的不息的争论才是思想和生存的动力所在。思想家之间在原理上的同一和差异才真正在真理意义上是能够彼此见证的。

无论如何，我想可以分别用一句话概括已经分析过的康德、黑格尔、马克思和克尔凯郭尔在原理上的差异：黄裕生教授接受的康德体系把思想关于存在的经验视为同一性的展示（因为不存在关于存在自身的经验）；黑格尔以求知识为归旨把存在视为差异性和同一性的统一展示，同一性是其终点；马克思以实践为归旨把存在视为差异性和同一性的统一展示，视差异性为起点；克尔凯郭尔则把存在视为绝对的差异性展示。在笔者所看到的范围内，这些经典作家的所有写作都内在地建立在各自的基础原理基础上。

**参考文献**

黑格尔，1997，《精神现象学》上卷，贺麟、王玖兴译，商务印书馆。

黄裕生，2019，《摆渡在有—无之间的哲学——第一哲学问题研究》，清华大学出版社。

克尔凯郭尔，2013，《哲学片段》，王齐译，中国社会科学出版社。

马克思，1995，《〈资本论〉1872 年第二版跋》，《马克思恩格斯选集》第 2 卷，人民出版社。

尚文华，2019，《差异意识：形而上学与实践哲学的分野之处——论从黑格尔到马克思的转变》，《求是学刊》2019 年第 4 期。

——，2020a，《在崇高与虚无之间的自由意志——兼论现代自由原则及其可能出路》，《哲学动态》2020 年第 1 期。

——，2020b，《从“自身同一物”与“自在物”谈起——评黄裕生教授〈摆渡在有—无之间的哲学——第一哲学问题研究〉》，《伦理学术》第 9 卷，2020 年秋季卷，第 289—296 页。

——，2021，《思想本身与时代问题：“古 - 今—中 - 西”交口处的中国哲学——以黄裕生教授的相关思考为契机》，《关东学刊》2021 年第 1 期。

# 康德哲学中存在与自由的限度

## ——以黄裕生的第一哲学思考为视阈*

李科政（LI Kezheng）**

**摘要**：哲学是由“本原意识”所引发的在“有”与“无”之间摆渡的人类思想的“返乡之旅”和“未来之旅”，对存在问题和自由问题的思考与回答是推动这一历史进程的根本动力，康德的批判哲学及其存在观念与自由观念则是该进程中一个重要环节和典型案例。在某种意义上，批判哲学的提出是为了解决哲学领域各个层面上的“辩证法”，其基本方法是退回到冲突的“本原”，通过对人类认识能力、欲求能力和判断力的批判来加以解决。但康德的努力并未如其所愿地终结哲学，而是存在种种局限性，必须面对新的对立面。在存在问题上，康德揭示出了“存在/是本身”作为“显现”的意义，但却始终在概念与客体的关系中理解存在，使之成为一个与“无”或“不存在”绝对对立的概念，也难以揭示出“存在”与“自由”之间直接的、而非间接的关联。在自由问题上，康德通过道德法则的普遍有效性论证了作为其可能性条件的自由的客观实在性，但也因此将自由解释为一种独立于自然法则的必然性。这种本质主义的自由观念很难让当代学者满意，但却为自由问题的深化开辟了道路。

**关键词**：康德；辩证法；存在；自由；第一哲学

---

* 本文系国家社会科学基金青年项目（20CZX037）的阶段性成果。

** 李科政，中国人民大学哲学院讲师，电子邮箱：paulus 0928@163. com。

# The Limits of Being and Freedom in Kant's Philosophy: From the Perspective of Huang Yusheng's Thinking of the First Philosophy

**Abstract**: Philosophy is the "return journey" and "future journey" of human thought between "Dasein" and "Nichts" triggered by the original consciousness. Thinking and answering questions of "being" and "freedom" constitutes the fundamental driving force to propel this historical process. Kant's critical philosophy, especially his conceptions of being and freedom, is a crucial moment and a typical example of this process. In a sense, the proposal of critical philosophy is to address the "dialectics" at all levels in the field of philosophy. Its basic method is to return to the "origin" of the conflict and address it through the critiques of human's faculties of cognition and desire, and the power of judgment. However, Kant's endeavors did not terminate philosophy as expected. Instead, Kant had to face the new opposites due to various limitations of his philosophy. On the question of "being", Kant revealed the meaning of "das Sein selbst" as "erscheinen" while he tended to explain "being" in the relationship between concepts and objects, thus making it an absolute opposite concept to "Nichts", and this added to the difficulty of revealing a direct relationship between "being" and "freedom". On the question of "freedom", Kant revealed the objective reality of freedom as the condition of moral law's possibility through its universal validity. However, this also explained freedom into a necessity independent from natural laws. The essentialist conception of freedom hardly satisfies contemporary scholars, but it paves a way for the deepening of question of freedom.

**Key words**: Kant; dialectics; being; freedom; the First Philosophy

黄裕生在《摆渡在有—无之间的哲学——第一哲学问题研究》中提出了两个重要的观点。首先，关于“哲学是什么”的问题，他拒绝一种定义式的回答，将哲学描述为一场由“本原意识”所引发的在“有”与“无”之间摆渡的人类思想的“返乡之旅”和“未来之旅”。在某种意义上，这个颇具浪漫色彩的描述还原了哲学作为“爱智慧”（φῐλόσοφος；philosophos），而非“智慧”（σοφίᾱ；sophia）的本来面目，将哲学史呈现为人类思想作为一个整体永不停歇地在曲折中前进的过程。其次，在黄裕生看来，哲学史的整个进程都是在对存在问题和自由问题的追问中被推动的。他把这两个问题称作“第一哲学问题”，并认为哲学史上每一个重要时刻都伴随着对这两个问题的某种突破。在这个进程中，冲突构成了环节，辩证法构成了深入本原的契机。在本文中，我们将尝试以此种哲学视阈来考察康德的批判哲学，将其视为“哲学摆渡”中的一个重要环节和典型案例。这意味着，我们将重点讨论康德的方法以及他对存在问题与自由问题的具体看法，但却并不满足于说明和解释他的观点，而是要尝试揭示出其存在观念与自由观念的限度。但是，本文无意于仅仅将其当作批判的靶子。相反，我们将关注的是康德如何以各种层面上的辩证法为契机开启了他的“返乡之旅”和“未来之旅”，并且尝试从其种种局限性中看到他如何为当代哲学思考打开了局面。为此，我们将首先从黄裕生所谓的“哲学的摆渡”和康德意义上的“辩证法”谈起。

## 一　哲学的摆渡与康德的辩证法

在《形而上学》的开头，亚里士多德曾以同情的态度批判过古希腊先贤们追问本原的努力。亚里士多德没有把他们相互冲突的观点见解看作平行的，而是将其看作人类思想的一个曲折前进的整体进程。起初，人们想从质料中寻找本原（质料因）；后来，人们发现质料的运动需要一个原因（动力因）；然后，人们意识到动力无法解释事物的“何所为”或“善”（目的因），并且意味到变易的现象背后还有永恒的本体（形式因）。[①] 从这一进程中可以看出，当我们试图在同一个层面（例如，质料的层面）扩展知识时，往往会遭遇到难以调解的冲突，这其实是由事物的有限存在所决定的，并以辩证法的形式呈现出来。解决冲突的方法往往是要回溯到一个更深的层次，揭示出它们共同的根源。

当黄裕生把“哲学”或“爱智慧”描述为“在有—无之间摆渡”时[②]，他想要表达的似乎就是这个意思。在此，“有”特指有限事物的存在（Dasein），“无”（Nichts）则特指未被规定的、本原的存在（Sein）。正如黑格尔在《逻辑学》中指出的：未被规定的存在（unbestimmtes Sein）直接就是“无”，“存在和无的真理是两者的统一”[③]；只有在已经被规定的存在（bestimmtes Sein）即“定在”（Dasein）那里，“有”和“无”才是绝对对立的。因此，从“有”到“无”就是从有限存在回溯到本原存在，从“无”到“有”则是从本原的存在前进到有限存在。从历史的角度来看，哲学发展的契机就是当知识在有限存在领域的扩展遭遇困境时，适时地抽身退让到本原的存在，以求揭示出困境的根源，再重整旗鼓，向着有限存在进发。因此，黄裕生把哲学的摆渡描述为“返乡之旅”和“未来之旅”[④]，而不断引发摆渡之旅的“困境”或“契机”就呈现为“辩证法”（dialectics；διαλεκτική）的形式。在起初，辩证法不过就是辩论的技巧，教授辩证法的人被称作“智者”（Sophist；σοφιστής），他们培养自己的学生，使他们在城邦的公共辩论中赢得胜利。即便在今日，善辩之人也常被认为是有智慧的，人们甚至羡慕那些擅长以言辞混淆视听、颠倒黑白的精明人。然而，尽管同样推崇辩证法，但在那些自称“哲学家”或“爱智者”（φιλόσοφος；lover of wisdom）的人来说，辩证法提醒我们意识到自己的局限性，敦促我们通过怀疑和反思持续地趋近（而不是达到）真理。对此，柏拉图著作中的苏格拉底为我们提供了榜样。例如，当聪明的欧悌甫戎自以为确切地知道什么是“虔诚”（正题）时，苏格拉底以求教者的姿

---

① 亚里士多德（1993：32－57）。
② 黄裕生（2019：10）。
③ 黑格尔（2017：167）。
④ 黄裕生（2019：8－10）。

态提出一系列问题（反题），迫使欧悌甫戎不断地修正自己的看法（合论）。[①] 尽管这场对话最终也没有什么结果，但却让欧悌甫戎认识到了自己的无知，这至少为趋近真理扫清了障碍——在哲学的道路上，再没有什么东西是比自以为真理在握更大的障碍了。

在某种意义上，正是为了解决哲学领域各个层面上的辩证法，康德才提出了他的批判哲学。其中，有些是认识论层面的问题，有些是非常具体的问题；有些是哲学史上遗留下来的历史疑难，有些则是他本人发现并提出的问题。对于康德来说，辩证法不只是辩论的方法，也不只是检验真理的试金石，它还是理性活动自身的一种现象，即所谓“幻相的逻辑”（die Logik des Scheins）（A61 - 62/B85 - 86）[②]。一般来说，辩证法表现为观点的对立，正如前面欧悌甫戎的例子，正题是一个理性推理的结论，反题则意味着前者的推理存在漏洞。在普通的理性推理中，通过揭示出它在某个环节同知性与理性的普遍规则不一致就能揭示出幻相产生的原因，因为此类幻相“只是产生自对逻辑规则的缺乏重视”（A296/B353）[③]。但是，并非所有问题都能以这种方式得到解决——在康德看来，以往形而上学的纷争就是如此。形而上学的独断论者为了“灵魂是不是一个单纯的实体”“世界是否有一个开端”以及“上帝存在与否”等问题争论不休，各方似乎都有合乎理性的根据和论证，却找不到一个裁决的标准。康德把此类问题称作“先验的幻相”（der transzendentale Schein）（A295 - 296/B351 - 352）[④]，它们是从知性的先验应用（即把纯粹理性的概念当作客体来加以认识）中产生的。为此，形而上学的怀疑论用“同样明显的截然相反的主张与之对立”（B23）[⑤]，以彻底的怀疑摧毁知识的一切确定性，康德把它比作“憎恶地面的一切常设建筑”的游牧民族（A ix - x）[⑥]。这一对立在哲学史教科书上通常被称作“理性

① 柏拉图（2019：3 - 26）。
② 康德（2011a：81 - 82）。
③ 康德（2011a：246）。
④ 康德（2011a：245）。
⑤ 康德（2011a：43）。
⑥ 康德（2011a：4）。

主义与经验主义之争”，它既代表了那个时代哲学发展的盛况，也反映了的那个时代哲学发展的困境。如果我们把独断论看作正题，把怀疑论看作反题，那么，这一对立就是那个时代哲学领域最大的辩证法，而批判哲学的任务就是要解决这一辩证困境。

批判哲学（简单来说）就是经过对人类认识能力、欲求能力和判断力的批判，在明确了它们各自的合法应用范围与界限之后确立起来的形而上学体系。康德认为，要解决独断论与怀疑论的对立，让形而上学走上科学的道路，就必须抽身退回到它们共同的根源。独断论者未经批判地使用知性和理性的普遍规则，将其不合法地应用于那些超出可能经验范围以外的对象（灵魂、世界和上帝），殊不知它们在任何时候都只是可能的经验对象的思维规则；反之，怀疑论者未经批判地怀疑认识能力的一切合法应用，殊不知这种应用本身就是经验得以可能的条件。因此，康德的批判从对经验（经验性知识）的分析入手，通过抽掉其纯然经验性的部分（感官的印象），逐渐分离出直观的纯形式（时间与空间），知性的纯概念（范畴）以及统觉的综合统一（先验统觉），并由此确立起这些先天的东西的客观实在性（作为经验的可能性条件）及其合法应用范围（可能经验的领域），不仅使独断论与怀疑论的对立得到了解决，还将形而上学的内容限定在作为经验之条件的先验原理之上。这个问题的解决在哲学史上当然意义重大，但就本文的意图来说，我们可以把它看作哲学摆渡的“返乡之旅”和“未来之旅”的一个实例。然而，尽管这个例子是根本性的，但同样的例子（涉及更具体的问题）在康德著作中还有很多。在《道德形而上学的奠基》中是意志自由与自然必然性之间的矛盾（4：452－455）[①]；在《实践理性批判》中是德性完善的要求与感性脆弱性之间的矛盾（5：

① 康德（2013a：75－79）。这个矛盾是通过“定言命令式如何可能”这个问题揭示出来的，康德认为，定言命令式唯有通过“意志的自由”才是可能的，但意志的自由与自然的必然性（机械论的因果法则）似乎是不相容的。解决这一矛盾的办法，在根本上依赖于康德对显象（Erscheinung）和物自身（Ding an sich）的区分，根据这一区分，我们就可以把纯然作为理智实体的人看作属于知性世界（Verstandeswelt）的，把纯然作为动物的人看作属于感知世界（Sinnenwelt）的，从而把意志的自由看作一个超自然的原因，并由此避免了与自然必然性的冲突。

122－124）以及德性与幸福依据因果关系相结合的困难（5：124－132）[①]；在《判断力批判》中则是鉴赏判断的主观性与普遍性之间的矛盾（5：388－341），以及自然事物的机械论解释与目的论解释之间的矛盾（5：386－388）[②]。所有这些矛盾都不可能从任何某方的诡辩中得到解决，而是必须通过追溯其共同根源，并且最终依赖于对认识能力、欲求能力和判断力的批判与“划界”来解决。

但是，哲学的发展却并没有如康德所期待的那样被终结了。相反，批判哲学同样遭遇了它的对立面，先验观念论本身也在费希特、谢林和黑格尔那里发展出了更为丰富的形态。在黑格尔的《精神现象学》《哲学科学百科全书》与《哲学史讲演录》等著作中，哲学的发展更为清晰地被呈现为人类思想之辨证发展的整体进程，尽管黑格尔也未能如期所愿地终结这一进程。因此，真正来说，哲学本身毕竟表现为一个在“有”和“无”之间不断摆渡的过程，这也更加符合哲学作为“爱智慧”的本来面目。康德的批判哲学无疑包含许多重要的突破，但也有其种种局限性。接下来，我们将把注意力集中在“存在”和“自由”的问题上，它们也正是黄裕生格外关注的第一哲学问题。

---

① 康德（2010a：114－123）。此即为实践理性的两个二论背反，具体来说：首先，德性的完善要求“意向（Gesinnung）与道德法则的完全适合”（5，122），但这是人类这种特殊的（同时也是感性的）理性存在者在此生都无法达到的。为此，康德认为，达到德性的完善需要一种“无限进展的进步”（5，122），而这唯有通过“预设灵魂的不死才使可能的”（5，122）。其次，至善（das höchste Gut）要求德性上的完善或“至上的善”（das oberste Gut）与幸福按照因果关系的结合，即有德之人得享幸福，但自然之中没有这种因果关系的标志。为此，康德认为，“唯有假定自由的一个拥有与道德意向相符合的因果性的至上原因，尘世中的至善才是可能的”（5，125）。也就是说，需要一个上帝。

② 康德（2010b：159－163，205－207）首先，鉴赏的二论背反说的是：正题认为，鉴赏判断的规定根据“是纯然主观的（快乐或者痛苦）”（5，338），而不是“建立在概念之上的”（5，338）；反题认为，鉴赏判断可以提出普遍性要求，故而是建立在概念之上的。康德指出，鉴赏判断虽然是建立在概念之上的，但却不是建立在确定的概念之上的，而是建立在一个不确定的概念之上的，即“关于显象的超感性基底的概念”（5，340），所以此类判断虽然是主观的、但却不是个人的，而是具有普遍性的。其次，目的论的二论背反说的是：正题认为，一切事物都依据“纯然机械的法则”产生；反题认为，某些事物的产生无法仅仅依据机械论的法则得到解释，而是需要引入目的论的法则来解释（5，387）。康德认为，导致这一矛盾的根源在于混淆了“规定性判断力的原理”和“反思性判断力的原理”，后者“只是主观地对我们在特殊的经验法则上的理性应用有效”（5，389）。

## 二 康德的存在观念及其限度

一般来说，哲学是研究“存在”或“是”的科学。曾几何时，哲学几乎被等同于“Ontologie”（存在论/是论）。“存在”或“是”可以从两个方面来考察：一是任何可能事物的“是什么”，二是任何可能事物的“存在/是本身”。在汉语中。“存在”和“是”的关联不那么明显，但它们的同一性并不真的只是西方语言的独有特点。如果我们不仅仅在语法意义上使用“是”，而是把它看作一个实有所指的概念，那就不难发现，“是”在任何时候都指示“存在”或“有”。因为，“是什么”不仅表达了“什么”的存在，还表达了某个事物作为这个“什么”而存在；“某物是”则直接预设了这个“某物”存在着。

或许是由于海德格尔的影响，当代学界流行着一个说法：以往的哲学家们关心“存在者”而忽视了“存在本身”。这句话似乎也可以理解为：人们热衷于研究“是什么”而忽视了“存在/是本身”。然而，这个说法无论如何都有些偏颇。的确，康德没有像黑格尔或海德格尔那样去区分“Sein”（存在/是）和“Dasein”（定在/此在），或者（也可以说）说没有深入那个程度，但他依旧关心任何可能事物的“存在/是本身”。而且，对“存在/是本身”的关心并不真的能脱离对“是什么”的关心，从思想发展的角度来看，也必须首先从“是什么”切入。康德对于“是什么”的考察比较突出地体现在他的“范畴学说”中。在传统意义上，“范畴”（Kategorien）是谓词的类①，一切谓词均可以被归类在某个范畴之下。我们通过（图型化的）范畴来思维任何事物，说出它们“是什么”，并通过这种判断来把握事物作为什么而存在。从认识的时间顺序上来看，范畴是通过在

① “范畴”（Kategorie）一词源于古希腊文的“κατηγορία”（katēgoría），原本就是指谓词。亚里士多德在《范畴篇》中提出的十个范畴，其实就是十个最基本的谓词，它们是：“实体、数量、性质、关系、何地、何时、所处、所有、动作、承受”（1b）。参见亚里士多德（1990：5）。后来，中世纪的学者在沿用“categoria”（范畴）这个术语的同时，又使用了拉丁文的“praedicātum”（谓词），以便把范畴和一般的谓词区分开来，而德文中的“Kategorie”（范畴）和“Prädikat”（谓词）均直接来自拉丁文。

一切谓词中抽掉其经验性的差异获得的。但反过来说，这同时也表明，范畴本身并不直接来自经验。有经验论者曾认为，范畴来自于联想，但这个解释将威胁到范畴的普遍适用性。批判哲学告诉我们，甚至经验本身（作为经验性的知识）也必须以范畴为条件才得以可能，这也正是我们能够通过范畴来思维经验对象的根本原因，但同时也将其合法应用范围限定在了可能经验的领域之内。康德区分了四大类范畴：量（Quantität）、质（Qualität）、关系（Relation）和模态（Modalität）[①]。当我们把前三类范畴用于思维一个事物时，我们都是在思维事物（作为主词）及其特征（Merkmal）（作为谓词）的关系[②]。然而，第四类谓词却并非如此，我们通过它们只是在思维事物（作为主词）的存在模态（样态）：这个事物可不可能存在、现实存在着还是根本不存在、偶然地还是必然地存在着。其中，甚至"存在"（Dasein/Existenz）本身也是一个范畴（谓词），我们通过它来思维一个事物及其全部特征的现实性，这也正是事物之"是什么"的条件[③]。但是，"是什么"与"存在/是本身"并不是两个分离的与不同的东西，后者的基础性意义只是观念性的。

---

① 康德的范畴学说可以看作是对亚里士多德的范畴学说的修正，他曾指出："由于亚里士多德没有任何原则，所以他像偶然遇到它们那样把它们捡拾起来，最初找到了十个，他称之为范畴（陈述词）。"康德对亚里士多德的工作不满意，他认为其中一些根本不是范畴，必须剔除除去，还有一些则被忽略掉了。康德的四大类范畴之下还有12组范畴，它们是：单一性、复多性、全体性；实在性、否定性、限定性；依存性与自存性、因果性与隶属性、共联性；可能性－不可能性、存在－不存在、必然性－偶然性（A80/B106）。参见康德（2011a：93）。

② 甚至"实体"（substantia）也是如此。当我们把"实体"用于思维一个一般对象，说"某物是一个实体"，即表明我们认识到这个"某物"的自存性（Subsistenz），并且同时意识到还有一些东西作为"偶性"（accidens）依附于这个"某物"而存在，即作为它的"是什么"而存在，即便我们尚且不知道它到底是什么。因为，"实体"和"偶性"的概念总是同时作用的，正如我们在使用"原因"（Ursache）的概念时也（即便没有被明确地意识到）一并使用了"结果"（Wirkung）的概念。

③ 即便是关于那些并不现实存在的或者纯然虚构的事物的思维也是如此，除非它们在逻辑上就是不可能的，例如"四个角的三角形"。当然，像"飞马"或"鲁智深"这样的动物或人物，我们对它们的思维依旧是以其存在为基础的。只不过，我们只是在思维中假定它们存在，然后把它们当作一个存在着的动物或人物来思维，设想他们拥有何种特点或性格特征（其是什么）。而且，那种对"假定的存在"和"现实的存在"的区分其实是错误的，因为"存在"都是现实的，或者说"存在"即现实性（Wirklichkeit）。所以，"假定的存在"就是"假定的现实存在"或"假定的现实性"。

严格说来，“是什么”中的“是”（或“作为什么而存在”中的“存在”）与“存在/是本身”是一回事。抛开“是什么”来思维的“存在/是本身”只是一个抽象的概念，所以黑格尔说它是“绝对否定的东西”（das Absolut - Negative），并且直接就是“无”（Nichts）①。通过“是/存在”的抽象概念，我们并没有真正在思维什么；相反，现实中的“存在/是”只能通过“什么”展现出来。然而，“是什么”也易于限制我们对“存在/是本身”的理解，当我们总是把它们结合起来加以思维时，“Sein”（存在/是）就和“Dasein”（定在/此在）成了一回事，并因此成了一个与“Nichts”（无/否）绝对对立的概念。康德的问题大概就是如此，因为他总是依据“概念与其客体的关系”来考察“存在/是本身”。康德对“存在/是本身”的考察首先是从“Sein”的逻辑（语法）意义入手的，在这种意义上，“Sein”（是）表示“肯定”（Position）或“设定”（Setzung）。“Sein”（是）有两种用法：首先，在“S是P”（S ist P）的判断中，康德指出，“是”（ist）不是谓词P以外的另一个谓词，其功能是对S与P的关系的肯定，或者说是把P设定在与S的关系中。此类判断意味着：S作为P而存在、P作为S的P而存在。因此，“是”（ist）是对P的存在的表达，但同时也一并表达了S的存在。其次，在“S是/存在”（S ist）的判断中，“是”（ist）绝对地（即不在与他物的关系中）肯定或设定了S。此类判断意味着，S是一个现实的对象，相当于“有一个S”（es gibt ein S）或“S存在”（S existiert）。（B626 - 627）② 但是，存在判断的依据是什么？康德认为，鉴于人类认识能力的局限性，即知性唯有在感官对象那里才有其应用的标志，故存在判断的原理就是：“凡是与经验的质料条件（感觉）相

① 黑格尔（2017：165）。

② 康德（2011a：417）。康德在《证明上帝存在惟一可能的证据》中也提出了“Sein”（是）的两种用法，他首先指出：“存在（Dasein）是对一个事物的绝对肯定（die absolute Position），并由此同任何一个自身在任何时候都只与零一事物相关才被设定的谓词区别开来。”（2，73）然后，他区分“Sein”（是）的两种用法：首先，“某种东西可以是仅仅在关系中被设定的，或者更准确地说，仅仅被设想为某种东西的关系……这种东西是一个事物的标志（Merkmal）。这样一来，是（Sein），即这种关系的设定，不外乎就是一个判断的联结概念（Verbindungsbegriff）”（2，73）；其次，“倘若不仅仅是这种关系，而是自在自为的事物本身（die Sache an und für sich selbst）被看作被设定的，那么，这个是（Sein）也就无异于存在（Dasein）”（2，73）。康德（2003：80）。

关联的，就是现实的。”（B266）[①] 换句话说，就是事物能够与知觉（Wahrnehmung）发生关联，“无论是通过知觉直接地意识，还是通过把某物与知觉结合起来的推论来意识”（B629）。[②]

然而，康德毕竟不是一个贝克莱主义者。从批判哲学的立场出发，知觉固然是存在判断的标志，却还不是“存在/是本身”。关于对象的知觉以对象在感官中被给予为前提，所以“存在/是”毋宁是作为显象的对象（die Gegenstände als Erscheinungen）的“显现”（erscheinen）。但这也只是对于人类认识能力而言的，在康德看来，某种超感性的存在虽然在逻辑上并非不可能，却不是我们能够把握到的。然而，康德存在观念的局限性却并不在此。正如前文提到过的，康德始终在“概念与其客体的关系”中思维存在。也就是说，“存在/是本身”被理解为“任何确定的事物”的存在，而这个“确定的事物”即便尚未被说出“是什么”，也已经被预设为“是什么”。因此，“存在/是”就成了“任何某个是什么的事物的概念有一个现实的客体”，如果“没有”，这个事物就不存在。这其实符合我们一般人对“存在/是”或“有”的理解，但却没有道尽全部事实。即便从普通物理学的视角来看，我们也能注意到，单个的事物处于不断变化之中，它从别的事物中生成，并随着自身的毁灭而成为其他事物（或者其他事物的一部分），整个自然严格说来只是在不断改变其外在形态。因此，如果我们把自然世界看作一个整体进程，那么“存在/是”就是贯穿始终的，而确定事物的生灭——作为“存在”与“无”、“是”与“否”、“有”与“无”的转变——不过是作为整体“存在/是”的自身进程的诸环节。但是，在康德那里，由于他总是在概念与其客体的关系中思考“存在/是”，使得现实的事物成了某种静态的、彼此孤立的对象，“存在/是本身”也就被化约成了任何事物依据其概念与自身的“不存在/无”的对立。因此，对于康德来说，“Sein”（存在/是）和“Dasein”（定在/此在）是一回事，只有语法应用上的区别。正是因为意识到了这个问题，诸如黑格尔、海德格尔等学者才会试图超出“概念与其客体的关系”来思考“存在/是

① 康德（2011a：196）。
② 康德（2011a：419）。

本身”。

无论如何，“存在/是本身”作为一个抽象的概念什么也不是，但反过来说，作为通过谓词的思维（或思维偶性的方式），“是什么”并不适合被用于描述“存在/是”本身，因为后者甚至（在狭义的和较严格的意义上）根本就不是个谓词。相反，任何事物都必须通过“存在/是”才能是什么，就像黄裕生所说的：“‘是’是万物成为各种不同的什么东西的前提，它使一切事物成为某种相互有别的什么成为可能。”① 因此，基于确定概念的考察帮助我们从“是什么”走向“存在/是本身”，康德还从认识论的批判中揭示出了“存在/是”作为“显现”（erscheinen）的意义，但这不足以把我们送到终点，也不利于揭示出“存在/是”与“自由”之间直接的、而非间接的关联。

## 三 康德的自由观念及其限度

“存在”和“自由”可以说是哲学史上最重要的两大主题，黄裕生所说的“第一哲学问题”也就是“存在”和“自由”的问题。他以海德格尔的眼光指出，“存在/是本身”作为一种自我显现的敞开活动无非就是“此在的自由存在（Freisein）”②，“自由的本质（Wesen）就是让—存在（Sein－lassen）”③，并且通过把“自由”解释为一种退让，在“自由”和“存在”之间建立起了直接的关联④。这种作为“存在（是）的可能性”的自由观念与康德的作为“法则的必然性”的自由观念简直大相径庭，甚至是完全对立的。然而，从自由观念的发展历史来看，康德的自由观念虽然拥有种种局限性，但却构成了走向自由深处一个必不可少的关键环节。

自由意识扎根于普通人的意识之中，其最朴素的表达形式为“想干嘛

① 黄裕生（2019：46）。

② 黄裕生（2019：55）。

③ 黄裕生（2019：55）。

④ 黄裕生（2019：56）。黄裕生说：“自由不让是什么，却让是（存在）。让—是，就是让自身是，让……是自身。物就是在自由的这种退让中，才作为其自身存在，而不是作为对象或单纯的某物出现。换一个角度说，只是在自由的参与（einlassen）或协助下，物才作为自身存在。”

就干嘛”，故而与人的意志活动直接相关。因此，人的自由归根结底就是意志的自由，其实质在于意志活动不受外来因素的制约。古罗马人把自由公民称作“人格”（Persona），这原本是指古希腊—古罗马戏剧中的脸谱面具和人物①，后来被用作人类与神魔鬼怪的共名，因为他们都是能够自由思想和自由行动的理性存在者②。有理性的本性决定了人类存在者能够在认识活动与实践活动中充当主体，这也构成了自由的条件，使他们成为自己的思想与行动的原因，并且因此是道德上和法律上可归责的。③ 时至今日，世界各国的宪法和法律也都把公民视作“人格”，他们一方面因其自由而享有种种权利，另一方面也因其自由而要承担种种责任。然而，基于感性欲望的“想干嘛就干嘛”的自由似乎经不起最起码的反思，因为各种表象在人的心灵中引发愉快的情感似乎只是一种自然现象，而感性欲望就来自于这些情感对欲求能力（Begehrungsvermögen）或意愿能力（Willensvermögen）的影响。在感性欲望的影响下，理性又对欲求能力做出进一步的规定，才有了“我要如此行动”的意志。在这个过程中，规定欲求能力的理性（实践的理性）尽管表现出了一种自发性（Spontaneität），但却毕竟是被动的，并且由于那些先行的自然原因（感性欲望）而很难说是自由的。对此，古人已经有了较为清楚的认识。例如，奥古斯丁（在基督教的语境中）指出，“想干嘛就干嘛”的自由不过是一种“择恶的自

---

① 波爱修斯（2012：54）。波爱修斯指出：“personae（人格）这个词借自一个完全不同的来源，即借自喜剧和悲剧中用来表现不同角色的面具……希腊人也称这样的面具为πρόσωπα（prosopa），那是由于它们被戴在脸上……”，“那些演员戴上了面具，扮演悲剧和喜剧中的不同角色——赫卡柏、美狄亚、西蒙、克雷梅斯——而所有其他那些凭他们身上的若干特征就可以辨认的人，在拉丁文中就被称为persona（人格），而在希腊文中便称为πρόσωπα（prosopa）”。

② 波爱修斯（2012：53）。波爱修斯指出：“因此，如果位格（人格）只属于实质（实体，substantia），尤其是属于这些有理性的实质（实体），并且，如果凡是本性（本质，essentia）都是实质（实体），但并非存在于全体之中，而是存在于个体之中，那么，我们就找到了位格（人格）的定义了，即：‘具有理性本性的个别的实质’（具有理性本性的不可分的实体：Naturæ rationalis individua substantia）。”康德本人也明确指出：“理性存在者被称为人格（Personen）。”（4，428）康德（2013a：49）。

③ 康德曾在《道德形而上学》中说：“人格（Person）是其行为能够归责的主体。因此，道德上的人格性（die moralische Persönlichkeit）不是别的，就是一个理性存在者在道德法则之下的自由。”（6，223）康德（2013b：21）。

由”，因为它表现为人在“低等之善”中的任意选择，而不是使灵魂向上追求“高等之善”（上帝），并且使人最终难逃地狱的惩罚。[①] 但是，奥古斯丁对自由的思考不止于批判，而是提出了一个重要的观念：真正的自由是对自然之必然性的彻底超脱，但自由本身也是一种必然性——前者在基督教语境中被表述为：摆脱注定堕入地狱的命运，或享天国得救恩；后者则被表述为：服从上帝的诫命，遵从基督的教导。

康德实践哲学可以看作对奥古斯丁这一观念的世俗化发展，这首先表现为将自由与道德紧密结合在一起，其次表现为坚持道德性在来源上的独立性，即拥有完全不同于自然价值（自然善）的来源，并且正因为如此才是自由的。当然，作为“纯粹的理性主义者”（6：154－155）[②]，康德坚持：“道德为了自身起见，（无论是在客观上就意愿而言，还是在主观上就能够而言）绝对不需要宗教。”（6：3）[③] 尽管他也试图利用道德性来证明上帝（5：124－132）[④]，还想建立一种作为伦理共同体（die ethische Gemeinschaft）的道德宗教（6：96－100）[⑤]，但他自始至终都主张一种作为“世俗智慧”（Weltweisheit）的[⑥]、理性上自给自足的道德哲学。然而，世俗化并非康德的个人追求，而是那个时代的思想风尚。因此，在道德哲学

---

① 奥古斯丁（2010：135－136，173－174）。

② 康德（2011b：140－141）。康德在那里提出了两个重要的观点，第一个观点是关于道德义务和上帝诫命的观点。启示宗教首先把某个行动要求看作上帝的诫命，再据此将其视为道德义务，而这意味着道德性的根据是上帝的意志；相反，自然宗教（理性宗教）先把某个行动要求（通过理性）承认为道德义务，再据此将其视为上帝的诫命，而这意味着道德性的根据是理性本身。第二个观点是关于神圣启示，对于这种超自然的东西，康德既反对自然主义者的态度，即否定超自然启示的现实性，也反对超自然主义者的态度，即承认超自然启示是必需的。康德本人的态度与批判哲学的一贯态度是相符的，他既不肯定启示的现实性，也不否定其可能性，甚至承认它的历史性作用（作为引导真宗教的手段），并且将这种态度视作纯粹的理性主义者的态度。

③ 康德（2011b：1）。

④ 康德（2010a：116－123）。

⑤ 康德（2011b：84－88）。

⑥ 德语的“Weltweisheit”（世俗智慧）也可以译作“尘世的智慧”，它是一个与“神圣智慧”（heilige Weisheit）相对的概念。前者是指基于理性的知识，并且在康德那个时代经常被看作“哲学”的同义词；后者是指基于启示的知识，也就是狭义上的神学。“世俗智慧”这个词在古代基督教的语境中具有贬义，但在启蒙时代却被赋予了高度积极的意义，那个时代的哲学家和科学家也被称作“世俗智者”（Weltweisen）。

世俗化方面，康德面临来自幸福论、道德感学说和理性主义完善论的竞争。但是，无论我们是否以及在多大程度上认同他的思想，康德对其竞争对手提出的一个质疑都是十分重要的：所有这些学说都把道德原则建立在“质料的规定根据”（die materiellen Bestimmungsgründe）上，从而不仅使之缺乏道德性所要求的普遍性，还在事实上把道德行为化约成了物理现象①，以至于从根本上否定了自由的可能性。如果道德现象归根结底不过是一种特殊的自然现象，如果道德行为只是一系列（物理的和心理的）机械作用的结果，那么，我们就没有理由要求任何人为自己的行为负责。因此，在康德看来，这些学说败坏了道德。他认为，即便未经教化的寻常人也知道，道德行动是每个人都“应当”去做的事情，无论这是否会给自己和他人带来任何好处；道德的人是不图回报、不计后果要行道德之事的人，只有伪善者才仅仅把道德行动当作手段。因此，道德性就在于要出自（而不仅仅是按照）那些对每个人都普遍有效的实践法则行动，这些法则是实践理性的先天综合命题，是理性独立于任何内在的和外在的原因对欲求能力的规定②。

康德指出，道德性的最高原则就是：“要只按照你同时能够愿意它成为一个普遍法则的那个准则去行动。”（4：421）③ 其中，“准则”（Maxime）能够成为“普遍法则”（das allgemeine Gesetz）意味着“我”主观上有效的行动原则同时也能够成为对于每个人来说都在客观上有效的原则；“愿意”（wollen）则意味着“我”（以及其他每个人的）理性意愿（实践

---

① 心理现象也是一种特殊的物理现象。

② 理性对欲求能力的规定就叫作“理性的实践应用”或“实践的理性”（die praktische Vernunft），如果我们不仅把（广义的）“意志”（Wille）理解为任何一个特定的“我要如此行动”的意志，而是把它理解为理性存在者的一种能力，那么，意志作为理性的意愿活动（das vernünftige Wollen）就是实践理性。参见康德（2013a）。理性要么是依据一个先行的感性欲望（Begierde）或偏好（Neigung）来规定欲求能力，要么就是完全独立地规定它，后者就是所谓的“纯粹实践理性”（die reine praktische Vernunft）。对此，康德在《道德形而上学》的“导论”中解释得更加清楚，他还在那里区分了“任性”（Willkür）和（狭义的）“意志”（Wille）。根据他的区分：1. 如果欲求能力的规定根据是主体的“喜好”（Belieben），并且和“自己产生客体的行为能力的意识相结合”（6：213），就是“任性”（Willkür）；2. 如果“喜好”是在理性中发现的，而不是产生自情感，那么，“这种欲求能力就叫作意志（Wille）”（6：213）。康德（2013a：11－12）。

③ 康德（2013a：40）。

的理性）本身就是法则的规定根据，就是依据法则而行动的“责任”（Verbindlichkeit）的原因。[①] 同时，康德还援引了“自然法则”（Naturgesetz）“目的”（Zweck）和“立法”（Gesetgebung）的概念来强调这一原则的各个方面，并且把我们的道德判断类比为“一个可能的目的王国中的立法行为”[②]。康德认为，通过这一原则，我们能够认识到那种先天有效的实践法则，而这一事实本身又表明，理性“作为纯粹的理性而现实地是实践的”（5：3）[③]，进而“凭借这种能力……确立了先验的自由”（5：3）[④]。换句话说，既然纯粹理性（无须自身以外的任何原因）独自地就能规定意志，那么这一“理性的事实”（das Faktum der Vernunft）就已经表明，我们的意志（实践的理性）是自由的：它是它自己的原因。因此，道德法则就是自由的法则，道德行动就是自由的行动。但是，对于康德来说，自由表现为一种必然性。自由意味着，在道德行动中，我们的意志或实践理性作为一个原因开启了自然世界中的一个现象（行动），但它自身却不被自然的原因所规定。自由的必然性包括两个方面：1. 实践理性依据自身固有的必然原则行事；2. 道德法则是实践理性依据其固有原则的必然判断。在两个方面，意志或实践理性都仅仅就其独立于自然法则而言才是自由的。

---

① 康德在《道德形而上学》中指出：“通过一个法则下命令者（imperans）就是立法者（legislator）。他是根据法则的责任（Verbindlichkeit）的创作者（autor），但并不总是法则的创作者。”（6：227）康德（2013b：25）。康德的意思是说，唯有就“实证法”（die positiven Gesetze），理性存在者才是法则的创作者，但人不是自由法则的创作者，因为自由法则是理性依据其固有原则的必然判断。

② 当代许多学者把“目的王国”看作一个理想的伦理共同体，但正如前文中指出的，真正被康德称作“伦理共同体”的是他的道德宗教。其实，大可不必对“目的王国”作过度理解，它毋宁只是对道德性的最高原则的一个类比描述，通过同时使用“自然法则”“目的”和“立法”三个概念，使道德判断的整个过程以一种“更加接近直观，并且因此更加接近情感”的方式呈现出来。通过“目的王国”的理念，康德把道德判断描述为一个由理性存在者组成的民主城邦的立法活动，他们被设想为纯然理性的、而非感性的立法者，因此，在其共同的立法行动中，他们理性就是其意志的唯一规定根据（康德意义上的“目的”），他们制定的法则将如同自然法则一样实然有效，而不只是应然有效。这其实与“要只按照你同时能够愿意它成为一个普遍法则的那个准则去行动”的要求没有任何区别，除非我们与奥尼尔·奥诺拉（Onora O'Neill）和约翰·罗尔斯（John Rawls）一样，仅仅把普遍法则公式看作一个准则检验程序，忽视了“普遍法则”概念本身“去假言”的要求以及“愿意”在准则普遍化中的决定性作用。

③ 康德（2010a：1）。

④ 康德（2010a：1）。

谢林准确地把握住了康德的自由观念，并且指出："所谓'自由'，就是指某个东西仅仅遵循自己的本质的法则而行动……自在地看，它是自由，而从形式上看，它是必然性。"① 同时，在人的存在与自由的关系上，康德的态度无疑是本质主义（Essentialismus）的，即人的存在就是致力于通过自由的道德行动成为一个已然规定了的理想人格，这显然与当代人更为推崇那种"存在先于本质"的存在主义（Existentialismus）观念是格格不入的。

尽管如此，康德的努力依旧为存在主义的自由观开辟了道路。正如黄裕生指出的："康德限制知识不仅为信仰留下了位置，同时也为人的自在—自由留下了位置。"② 诚然，康德关于显象与物自身（Erscheinung und Ding an sich）、现象与本体（Phänomen und Noumenon）的区分一方面为知识（在可能经验范围内）的确定性和普遍性提供了保障；另一方面也避免了机械论（或者用现在的时髦说法叫"物理主义"）在一切领域的滥用，为自由腾出了地盘，为深入对自由的认识提供了广阔的空间。因此，尽管康德的作为必然性的自由观念在很多方面都并不令当代学者满意，但必须承认：除非经过它，不能走得更远。

## 余　论

最后，在康德的批判哲学中，存在与自由只能间接地关联起来。康德的认识论批判（正如刚才已经指出的）固然为自由腾出了地盘，但也把对存在的认识限制在经验领域。在经验领域中，任何事物的存在都依据机械论的法则被表象为有条件的，作为一个自由因（自身再没有原因的原因）的存在则成了一个无法被证实的先验理念，只能作为一个范导性的理念为知性在经验范围内的扩张划定界限。因此，存在与自由成了两个领域的东西。然后，通过对上帝的道德证明，康德才在"自然的一个拥有与道德意向相符合的因果性的之上原因"（5：125）③ 那里实现了存在与自由的统

① 谢林（2019：66）。
② 黄裕生（2019：224）。
③ 康德（2010a：117）。

一，但也仅仅是作为一种理性的必然信念被证明的。然而，正如黄裕生指出的，如果我们摆脱概念与客体的关系来看待“存在/是本身”，那么，“存在是”无非就是“物作为自身显现出来”，这意味着“它作为自身被敞（打）开，被公开（Öffnen）出来”①，而这种“自我敞开”或“自我显现”不是别的，正是“此在的自由存在（Freisein）”②。在这种意义上，存在与自由作为“让—存在”与“让—自由”直接地就是一回事，“自由与物自身在（显现）是同一件事（Ereignis），是同一性存在”③。从这个角度来看，自由也就不再呈现为必然性，而是存在的“自我敞开”或“自我显现”的无限可能性本身。

但是，这样一种存在与自由的观念也为某种“空洞的自我”提供了哲学基础。当代人倾向于把任何形式的理想人格当作一种陈旧的形而上学观念，进而把在各种关系中被定义的自我当作“相对的东西”，甚至当作自我的某种外来的负担，试图抽掉它们以寻求“绝对的自我”，但这种努力由于势必抵达一个空洞的、什么也不是的自我，从而要么使人陷入一种深重的自我迷茫，要么使人转过头来掉入一种纯然通过偏好来规定的自我，并最终使自由退回到随心所欲，使人格性被化约成情感主义的个性。同时，作为本原的可能性的自由观念在使人承担起价值创造的使命的同时，也极易导致价值上的虚无主义，最好也不过是价值上的多元主义。在过去的几十年间，价值上的多元主义获得了太多的赞颂，以至于很多人都忽视了隐藏在其脆弱的和谐稳定下的矛盾与冲突。霍布斯所说的“一切人反对一切人的战争”并不完全是危言耸听，当今世界的国际局势、社会生活也并不全是一片祥和。康德的思想反倒是提醒我们，曾几何时，人类对于自己的道德命运拥有确定的观念，对于世界与自身应当如何存在怀有确定的信念。因此，哲学的摆渡犹未终结，我们依旧远未成为“智慧的”，仍需在“爱智慧”的旅途中艰难前行。

---

① 黄裕生（2019：54）。
② 黄裕生（2019：55）。
③ 黄裕生（2019：55）。

**参考文献**

奥古斯丁，2010，《论自由意志：奥古斯丁对话录二篇》，成官泯译，上海人民出版社。

波爱修斯，2012，《神学论文集　哲学的慰藉》，荣震华译，商务印书馆。

柏拉图，2010，《理想国》，顾寿观译，吴天岳校注，岳麓书院。

黑格尔，2017，《哲学全书·第一部分·逻辑学》，梁志学译，人民出版社。

黄裕生，2019，《摆渡在有—无之间的哲学：第一哲学问题研究》，清华大学出版社。

康德，2003，《康德著作全集：第2卷》，李秋零主编，中国人民大学出版社。

——，2010a，《实践理性批判：注释本》，李秋零译注，中国人民大学出版社。

——，2010b，《判断力批判：注释本》，李秋零译注，中国人民大学出版社。

——，2011a，《纯粹理性批判：注释本》，李秋零译注，中国人民大学出版社。

——，2011b，《纯然理性界限内的宗教：注释本》，李秋零译注，中国人民大学出版社。

——，2013a，《道德形而上学的奠基：注释本》，李秋零译注，中国人民大学出版社。

——，2013b，《道德形而上学：注释本》，张荣、李秋零译注，中国人民大学出版社。

谢林，2019，《论人类自由的本质及其相关对象》，先刚译，商务印书馆。

亚里士多德，1990，《亚里士多德全集：第1卷》，苗力田主编，中国人民大学出版社。

——，1993，《亚里士多德全集：第7卷》，苗力田主编，中国人民大学出版社。